Vergleichende Politikwissenschaft

Die Schriftenreihe „Vergleichende Politikwissenschaft" wird im Auftrag der gleichnamigen Sektion der Deutschen Vereinigung für Politikwissenschaft durch Steffen Kailitz, Susanne Pickel und Claudia Wiesner herausgegeben. Ziel der Reihe ist es, Themen, Fragestellungen, Inhalte, Konzepte und Methoden politikwissenschaftlicher vergleichender Forschung und Lehre in ihrer ganzen Breite zu diskutieren. Die Reihe nimmt nach einem Begutachtungsverfahren hervorragende Arbeiten aus allen theoretischen und methodischen Richtungen der Vergleichenden Politikwissenschaft auf.

Die Sektion „Vergleichende Politikwissenschaft" ist eine der größten und ältesten Sektionen der Deutschen Vereinigung für Politikwissenschaft (DVPW). Der Bereich der Vergleichenden Politikwissenschaft (Comparative Politics) deckt von der Vergleichenden Regierungslehre bzw. dem Vergleich politischer Systeme über die Vergleichende Demokratie-, Autokratie-, Transformations- und Demokratisierungsforschung sowie die vergleichende Forschung zu Parteien und Interessenverbänden bis hin zur Vergleichenden Policy- und Wohlfahrtsstaatsforschung ein sehr breites Feld ab. Die Vergleichende Politikwissenschaft ist dabei in der inhaltlichen, geographischen und methodischen Ausrichtung (qualitative und quantitative Methoden) per se pluralistisch angelegt.

Die Schriftenreihe „Vergleichende Politikwissenschaft" bietet entsprechend der Ausrichtung und den Zielen der Sektion ein Forum für alle Wissenschaftlerinnen und Wissenschaftler, die sich in Forschung und Lehre mit Themen und Fragestellungen aller Teilbereiche der Vergleichenden Politikwissenschaft befassen. Die Reihe steht damit explizit Beiträgen aus allen theoretischen und methodischen Zugängen der Vergleichenden Politikwissenschaft offen, und es sind sowohl theoretisch und/oder konzeptionell, empirisch und auch methodisch ausgerichtete Schriften willkommen. Entsprechend der Internationalität der Vergleichenden Politikwissenschaft versteht sie sich auch als ein internationales Forum des wissenschaftlichen Diskurses. In der Reihe erscheinen deutsch- wie englischsprachige Bänder.

Die Qualität der Beiträge der Sektionsreihe sichert neben dem Herausgeberkreis ein wissenschaftlicher Beirat. Ihm dankt der Herausgeberkreis für seine engagierte Arbeit.

More information about this series at http://www.springer.com/series/13436

Fabian Klein

The Role of Scientific Expertise in Minimum Wage Policy Making

The Cases of Germany, the United Kingdom, and the United States

Springer VS

Fabian Klein
Berlin, Germany

ISSN 2569-8672 ISSN 2569-8702 (electronic)
Vergleichende Politikwissenschaft
ISBN 978-3-658-32745-3 ISBN 978-3-658-32746-0 (eBook)
https://doi.org/10.1007/978-3-658-32746-0

Responsible Editor: Stefanie Eggert
This Springer VS imprint is published by the registered company Springer Fachmedien Wiesbaden GmbH part of Springer Nature.
The registered company address is: Abraham-Lincoln-Str. 46, 65189 Wiesbaden, Germany

Acknowledgements

Writing this book—my doctoral dissertation—I have benefitted from the support of numerous people. Their help was essential for the success of this research project.

I would like to thank my first supervisor, Barbara Pfetsch, who supported me over the entire research process. Her ideas were crucial in helping me transform a crude dissertation proposal into a feasible research project. Her insistence on theoretical and methodological rigor was a beneficial influence throughout our numerous meetings.

Chris Weible, my second supervisor, generously invited me to and gave me a warm welcome on a three-months research stay at the University of Colorado, Denver. At a time when my research efforts had reached a dead end, he provided me with the criticism and the ideas necessary to overcome the barriers I was facing. Thank you.

Colleagues and fellow students have given me an enormous amount of feedback on my work. In particular, I would like to thank the participants of the Colloquium Empirische Kommunikationsforschung at Freie Universität Berlin, of the Berlin Graduate School for Transnational Studies' (BTS) research colloquia, of the Workshop on Policy Process Research at the University of Colorado, Denver, and of the panel on Public Policy, Politics, and Advocacy Coalitions at the ECPR general conference in Prague. I thank BTS faculty and staff for providing the intellectual (and physical) space in which my research could grow.

Vincent Dreher and Juniper Katz deserve my gratitude for investing a lot of time into helping me to ensure the reliability of the data sets used in this dissertation. I thank Justus Dreyling, Mathias Großklaus, and Peter Klein for proofreading the manuscript.

Writing this dissertation would have been a lonely endeavor without my friends and colleagues, in Berlin and in Denver. In particular, I would like to thank Kelley and Vicky Harp and the grad students at University of Colorado, Denver's School of Public Affairs who made me feel at home in Denver.

I want to thank Fritz-Thyssen-Stiftung and the German Academic Exchange Service for funding my research.

My partner Anne's love, support and interest in my work have given me the strength to overcome the manifold challenges and frustrations resulting from the smaller and bigger problems encountered during the research process. Thank you.

Abstract

The book examines the role of scientific expertise in minimum wage policy making in Germany, the United Kingdom, and the United States. It finds that scientific research is an important part of the public discourse on minimum wages. Newspapers frequently cite scholars and research institutions, providing their readers with a good sense of how research evaluates the effects of minimum wages. How often this happens depends on the context. Most importantly, newspapers from the United States cite researchers more frequently than newspapers from the two European countries. This is related to different cultural and institutional settings in the three countries, termed styles of using scientific expertise. The book also shows that scientific research influences the policy preferences of political actors such as trade unions, political parties, and government departments. The influence is based on policy-oriented learning. It is strong in Germany and the United Kingdom, and weaker in the United States. Again, this difference is related to different styles of using scientific expertise.

Contents

Introduction

1

When Germany introduced a general minimum wage on January 1, 2015, it joined a growing club including 26 of the 34 Organization of Economic Coordination and Development's (OECD) member countries (Organization for Economic Cooperation and Development, 2015). In Germany, the debate surrounding the introduction of the minimum wage focused on the socio-economic effects adversaries and proponents of the policy assumed it would have: Would the minimum wage alleviate poverty and foster social equality? Would it drive low-skilled or otherwise disadvantaged workers out of the labor market? Would the minimum wage lead to business failures and reduced economic growth? The debate in Germany mirrored the debates in other countries, where the minimum wage has been in existence for years, if not decades, but where the public discourse on the issue still centers on the presumed positive or negative effects.

The question of minimum wage effects on variables such as poverty, employment, and economic growth is an empirical one and should, given the existence of sufficient data, be amenable to scientific research. Indeed, over the course of the past 45 years, hundreds of scientific studies have been published in peer reviewed journals which, based on theoretical models or empirical analyses, evaluate the effects of minimum wages in many different countries. This knowledge finds its way to politicians, interest groups and other actors concerned with minimum wage policy. For example, in the United States, where a minimum wage has existed since 1938, a government-sponsored minimum wage study commission issued an in-depth survey of the academic literature on minimum wage effects already in the early 1980s (Minimum Wage Study Commission, 1981). Moreover, countless think tanks provide policy advice based on academic research. In the United Kingdom, the government's Low Pay Commission (LPC) has commissioned dozens of studies evaluating minimum wage effects since the introduction of the National

F. Klein, *The Role of Scientific Expertise in Minimum Wage Policy Making*, Vergleichende Politikwissenschaft,
https://doi.org/10.1007/978-3-658-32746-0_1

Minimum Wage in 1999 and summarizes the results in its annual reports. In Germany, the political discussion surrounding the introduction of the *Mindestlohn* was complemented by research about minimum wage effects commissioned by the Ministry of Labour and Social Affairs. In this context, many studies summarizing existing research on minimum wage effects were available for policy makers (see Chapter 7). In all three countries experts and their research played an important role in the public discourse about minimum wages taking place in newspapers (see Chapter 5).

Given the importance of minimum wage effects in the political debate, the large amount of scientific information available of the issue, and the vigor with which politicians set up scientific advisory bodies and commission studies, one might conclude that scientific expertise plays a major role in minimum wage policy making. Indeed, this is what many involved actors have claimed. In his 1995 State of the Union Address, President Bill Clinton supported a raise of the federal minimum wage: "I've studied the arguments and the evidence for and against a minimum wage increase. I believe the weight of the evidence is that a modest increase does not cost jobs and may even lure people back into the job market" (Clinton, 1995). Likewise, when the British government announced the first hike of the National Minimum Wage in 2000, it claimed that the decision had been based on information about the economic implications of a raise (Maguire and Elliott, 2000).

Such statements do not necessarily imply, however, that scientific expertise plays an important role in minimum wage policy making in the sense that it has the power to change an actor's policy preference. In the debate that followed President Clinton's 1995 drive for a minimum wage hike, it were mostly Democrats, the traditional supporters of the US minimum wage, who claimed that scientific evidence suggested that a minimum wage hike would not cost jobs. Many Republicans, by contrast, considered job losses to be an inevitable consequence of a minimum wage raise. Republican Senator Bob Dole claimed that there were strong economic arguments against a higher minimum wage (Clymer, 1996). In sum, positions on the minimum wage followed traditional party lines, and the scientific evidence cited by President Clinton might have been little more than support for a pre-held preference. Indeed, Levin-Waldman (1998) argues that minimum wage policy making in the US, while often perceived as a question about the economic effects of the minimum wage, really is a political question. Similarly, Waltman (2000) argues that, as there is research pointing to beneficial as well as research pointing to adverse minimum wage effects, its use in US minimum wage policy making is largely confined to serving as arguments for politicians who have made up their mind about the minimum wage already.

It is unclear, however, whether the fact that expertise is often used to support pre-existing positions means that it has no persuasive power. Beyond that, these results do not necessarily hold under different institutional and cultural circumstances. In the UK, for example, the Low Pay Commission not only provides research on minimum wage effects, but also issues influential recommendations regarding the size of the annual raises in the National Minimum wage, which are based on this research (Brown, 2009).

These examples from minimum wage policy making in Germany, the United Kingdom, and the United States illustrate questions that have been central in the academic literature dealing with the role that expertise plays in the policy process: How is expert knowledge used in policy making? Does expert knowledge have the capacity to influence political actors' policy preferences? And how does its use depend on the presence of specific institutional or other context variables? These are the questions that will guide us through this book, which deals with the use of scientific expertise in minimum wage policy making. Before specifying the exact research questions and the ways in which they will be answered, existing research on the of expertise in policy making is discussed.

1.1 Research about the Role of Expertise in the Policy Process

1.1.1 Using Expertise for What Purpose?

Starting in the 1960s, at a time when an increasing amount of money was being spent on the social scientific evaluation of government policies, social scientists began asking how governments used the knowledge thus gathered. Normatively, much of this research tried to supplant seemingly irrational decision-making by a more rational process based on science (Havelock *et al.*, 1971; Haveman, 1986). As Weiss and Heller (1986) note, however, initial enthusiasm about the opportunities for the scientization of politics soon turned into disappointment, as it became clear that evaluation results were often ignored in further decision making. Non-utilization of expertise in policy making thus became a topic. One reason for the non-use of research results identified in this literature is that social scientific research, occupied with general and often highly theoretical issues, often does not answer the knowledge needs of policy-makers who deal with questions concerning a specific policy in a specific situation—the two communities hypothesis (Caplan, 1979; Dunn, 1980). Moreover, research in science communication has argued that there are problems in communicating the results from research to a wider audience. The language of science is hard to understand for non-scientists, and its results often require translation to be useful for a wider audience (Weigold, 2001, pp. 172–173). Beyond that, it has been argued that scientific studies are not the only and not always the best source of information for policy makers, who would often learn more from their everyday experiences with the individuals and interest groups affected by their policies (Lindblom and Cohen, 1979; Lindblom, 1990). Scientific knowledge, in this view, is not privileged in its claim for veracity. Rather, it appears as an argument in the political debate, an argument which is based not only on impartial, systematic inquiry, but also on assumptions and normative judgements. Often, such views are connected to a normative stance directed against the enthusiasm for the scientization of politics. Accordingly, scientific expertise is not necessarily better than other forms of knowledge, and a too strong reliance on it might mean ignoring other valuable forms of knowledge, as well as undermine the democratic process (Habermas, 1968; Majone, 1989; Dunn, 1993; Fischer, 1993; Hoppe, 1999). Similarly, the literature on policy learning has identified many different ways in which politics can learn from the past or from other countries' experiences, with scientific research being only one of them (Dolowitz and Marsh, 1996).

In brief, in the scientific debate, expert knowledge was increasingly seen as uncertain and intermingled with normative questions. Science no longer appeared as a neutral arbiter that could supplant political arguments. Simultaneously, the view for how scientific expertise was used in the political debate broadened. Carol Weiss (1979) identified seven possible meanings of research utilization, which inspire much of the scholarship on the use of expertise in the policy process up to today: (1) a knowledge-driven model, in which basic research inspires applied research, which is then applied in policy making; (2) a problem-solving model, in which a political actor needs to take a decision between different policy alternatives and turns to research in order to find information about which alternative is best for solving the problem at hand; (3) an interactive model, in which political actors, seeking information about policy alternatives, draw on and interact with a wide range of sources including academic experts, but also practitioners, interest groups, and others; (4) a political model, in which research serves as an argument for political actors agreeing with its conclusions; (5) a tactical model, in which research is commissioned or used by political actors in order to demonstrate that their decisions are well-informed, and not so much because information is needed; (6) an enlightenment model, in which the results from single studies or research programs do not influence political actors' policy preferences, but in which the concepts and theories from this research may slowly make their way into the thinking of policy actors, influencing how they perceive social problems and the possible solutions to them; and (7) a model in which research, much like policy, is a dependent rather than an independent variable, reflecting the intellectual fads of their time.

In the early days of the research utilization literature, the influence of research on public policy had been thought of in terms of the knowledge-driven model or the problem-solving model. In contrast, Weiss and others argued that an influence was more likely to happen in terms of the interactive or the enlightenment model (Weiss, 1986). And, as Lindblom and Cohen (1979, p. 65) observe, even where the political model prevails and few policy actors are actually convinced by research that their pre-held beliefs about a policy are wrong, "in certain circumstances common especially in the bureaucracy, a tacit agreement comes into play according to which the victory goes to the superficial 'winner' of the debate." The influence of expert knowledge on public policy, the literature suggests, can take many forms.

1.1.2 Conditions of Expert Influence

Besides identifying different uses of scientific expertise, a good deal of the research utilization literature is occupied with the question under which conditions expert knowledge plays a larger or a smaller role in the policy process.

A *first* group of conditions refers to the nature of the available scientific knowledge. Proponents of the two-communities hypothesis have argued that, to become more influential, scientific research needs to change. For example, Frenk (1992) argues that there is a trade-off between scientific excellence and relevance of research for policy. Researchers, on the one hand, choose research questions according to the needs of the scientific discourse, need long time periods to arrive at results, and are specialized in specific sub-disciplines. Political actors, on the other hand, tend to require information on the problems they are currently dealing with, on a short time frame, and integrating results from different disciplines. Scholars in this vein have tried to move researchers towards incorporating those standards into their research projects and to create institutional mechanisms to ensure a closer communication between scholars and policy actors already during the early stages of the research process (for a critique of this approach, see Lindblom, 1990, chap. 15; Lomas, 2000; Nutley, Walter and Davies, 2007, pp. 136–141).

A *second* group of conditions considers the policy problem at hand. Based on a theoretical approach similar to Weiss's problem-solving model, the epistemic communities literature argues that, the more uncertain political actors faced with a choice between different policy options are about the consequences resulting from each option, the more likely they will turn to experts to find the best option. Complex and technical issues are, therefore, most likely to involve expert influence (Adler and Haas, 1992; Haas, 1992b). Conversely, experts need to be able to reduce political actors' uncertainty about the consequences resulting from different policy alternatives. The capacity to do so is related to the analytical tractability of an issue. The more an issue is structured in a way that it allows scientific research to come to clear and unambiguous messages about the effects of different policy options, the more influence experts have (Jenkins-Smith, 1990, pp. 189–194). Both the technical complexity of an issue as well as its analytical tractability seem be an issue of perception rather than an objective quality. As Haas (1992b, pp. 14–15) mentions, real-world crises or new information from research can remind political actors that an issue is less well understood than previously thought.

A *third* group of conditions addresses the wider institutional, cultural, and structural conditions that provide the framework for the relation between expertise and public policy. Institutions relevant in this context are, for example, knowledge brokers that facilitate the transfer of academic knowledge to political actors, such as think tanks and other policy advisory organizations (Weaver and Stares, 2001; Rich, 2004; Lomas, 2007; Meyer, 2010). Other institutions might facilitate fact-based discussion among political actors (Jenkins-Smith, 1990, p. 198). In terms of culture, for example, Boswell (2009, chap. 9), in a comparative study of the use of research in German and British bureaucracies, notes that the use of expertise in the UK seems to be higher because there is less of a dividing line between academia and the administration, allowing researchers to get directly involved in policy making. With regard to the structure of a political field, studies based on the Advocacy Coalition Framework (ACF; Jenkins-Smith *et al.*, 2014) have posited different uses of research depending on the coalition structure of a policy subsystem. In international comparison studies, context variables referring to these sorts of context variables present in a country have been clustered to form ideal types, such as Renn's (1995) styles of using scientific expertise, or Jasanoff's (2007) styles of knowledge-making (Richardson, Gustafsson and Jordan, 1982; Straßheim, 2013; Jung, Korinek and Straßheim, 2014).

Finally, a *fourth* condition refers to the users of scientific expertise. While an actor may use scientific expertise in many ways, policy-oriented learning from research results, which is implied by the problem-solving or the enlightenment model, involves belief change. Belief change, it has been argued, usually does not concern an actor's fundamental values and basic ideas about policy, that is, core beliefs. Rather, it mostly touches secondary aspects, that is, beliefs about policy instruments deemed to be plausible means to achieve these fundamental goals. As a result, political actors are only likely to learn from scientific expertise if the findings from research do not contradict their core beliefs (Jenkins-Smith, 1990, chap. 4.3).

1.1.3 Expertise and Theories of the Policy Process

A persistent challenge in much of the research dealing with the role of expertise in the making of public policy is its lacking embeddedness in theories of the policy process. Thus, much empirical research regarding how expertise is used in policy making either focuses on knowledge use in individual bureaucracies, or by individual policy makers. A recent example of the former is Biegelbauer (2013), who studies ministerial bureaucracies, asking based on what information they developed three different policy initiatives. Similarly, Boswell (2009) studies the use of scientific information in the UK Home Office, the German Federal Office for Migration and Refugees, and the European Commission with regard to immigration policy. An example of the latter is Oh (1997), who surveys officials in US state and federal bureaucracies involved in health policy about how important scientific information is in their decision-making (see also Hird, 2005).

Both types of study designs were dominant already in the early years of utilization research (Leviton and Hughes, 1981) and have been successful in uncovering the use and the conditions of use of scientific expertise by individual policy makers or individual bureaucracies. However, they only go halfway in explaining the use of research in the policy process. Thus, policy change does not come about through a single decision of an individual or an organization for or against a specific policy option. To understand how scientific expertise influences policy, it is necessary to embed the research results describing how individuals or individual organizations use expertise in a broader model of the policy process (Weiss, 1986; Cairney, 2017).

The number of publications doing so is relatively small and include Hall's (1989) model of the influence of economic theories on public policy and the epistemic communities literature (Adler, 1992; Adler and Haas, 1992; Haas, 1992b; Thomas, 1997; King, 2005; Becker and Hendriks, 2008; Mamudu, Gonzalez and Glantz, 2011; Cross, 2012, 2013). Both approaches, however, are focused on instances in which new scientific approaches lead to profound changes in policy, such as the adoption of Keynesianism, and are less suited to explain the role of expertise in the day-to-day policy process, where expert knowledge is one variable among many influencing policy.

The probably most advanced effort to do so is based on the Advocacy Coalition Framework (ACF; Jenkins-Smith *et al.*, 2014). The ACF is a theory of the policy process in which political actors' changing beliefs play a central role. Therefore, it allows a relatively smooth integration of many hypotheses from utilization and related research (Jenkins-Smith, 1990). Research based on the ACF has, for example, analyzed the way in which the structure of policy subsystems determines the use of expertise (Weible, Pattison and Sabatier, 2010). Given its arguable lead in integrating hypotheses on the use of expertise into a general model of the policy process, the theoretical model of this book, presented in Chapter 2, is based on the ACF.

1.1.4 Empirical Research Results

While all findings regarding the role of expertise in the policy process presented above are based on empirical research, some findings are better supported by empirical evidence than others. This subsection discusses the empirical support for different findings. The discussion concentrates on two issues on which existing research does not provide conclusive evidence, and on which the empirical analyses presented in this book focus. The *first* one is the problem of quantifying expert influence. The *second* one is the problem of identifying the conditions under which expertise is relevant.

1.1.4.1 Quantifying Expert Influence

As argued above, much research conducted since the 1970s has argued that scientific expertise does not necessarily have to be used in a way to influence an actor's policy preference. Still, a lot of empirical research has been preoccupied with exactly this question. It has asked to what extent the knowledge produced by scientific experts influences decisions over policy, or at least the policy preferences of actors involved in policy making. Depending on the research design used, these studies have come to quite different results.

On the one hand, a strong expert influence is found by research focusing on specific instances in which scientific expertise has influenced public policy. Examples include the research on epistemic communities cited above as well as research on the rise of Keynesianism in economic policy (Gourevitch, 1989; Rosanvallon, 1989; Salant, 1989; Weir, 1989). This research has demonstrated that scientific knowledge can, in some instances, have a strong influence on policy. A problem with this literature, however, is that the case selection is not done in a way to say much about a wider population of cases. For example, the seminal 1992 special issue of *International Organization* includes seven case studies of seven different policy fields. Six of these case studies find that an epistemic community—a group of experts connected by common beliefs and goals which are based on their professional knowledge—has had a substantial impact on the policy researched. (Adler, 1992; Drake and Nicolaïdis, 1992; Haas, 1992a; Hopkins, 1992; Ikenberry, 1992; Kapstein, 1992; Peterson, 1992). The special issue does not contain information on how these cases were chosen. One could assume, however that the cases were selected in a way that makes showing a strong expert influence likely, limiting the generalizability of the case studies.

On the other hand, studies looking at the utilization of scientific expertise in single bureaucracies tend to find a more modest influence of scientific research. In two reviews of utilization research from the 1970s, Leviton and Hughes (1981) and Weiss (1977) find strong evidence for a use of research according to the enlightenment model in a number of different bureaucracies in the US and Germany, although, based on these studies, it is hard to quantify the impact of such a research use on actual decisions. More recently, Boswell, (2009) studying the UK Home Office, the German Federal Office for Migration and Refugees and the European Commission, finds that in-house research is mostly used to signal competence in an issue area, but is sometimes also used as information based on which decisions are made. Hird (2005), surveying legislators in US state legislations, finds that research by nonpartisan think tanks is valued as a means to broaden one's information base, but ascribed little influence in directly affecting decisions. As these studies do not pick their cases according to whether an expert influence can be assumed, their results are probably more representative than those from epistemic communities research. Besides from the observation that scientific expertise does not have a strong direct impact on policy decisions, however, they have a problem at quantifying expert influence, or at comparing the strength of expert influence to other influences on policy. The reason for this is methodological: As Weiss (1977, p. 535) notes, the diffuse impact associated with the enlightenment model is difficult to track. Therefore, it is difficult for interviewees such as Hird's state legislators to reconstruct where the information on which their decision was based originated.

A third source of empirical knowledge on the degree of influence that scientific expertise has on policy are ACF studies on policy-oriented learning (for an overview, see Jenkins-Smith *et al.*, 2014, pp. 198–201). In some of these, the source of policy-oriented learning is not scientific expertise, but practitioner's knowledge (Elliott and Schlaepfer, 2001). Scientific expertise might even be explicitly discarded as non-relevant for learning (Larsen, Vrangbæk and Traulsen, 2006). In others, learning from experts is deemed to be more important, helping political actors or coalitions of actors to better understand and justify their own policy preference (learning within coalitions), but also leading to a convergence between the preferences of different actors or coalitions (Weyant, 1988; Meijerink, 2005; Bukowski, 2007). These works equally have a problem with quantifying the influence of scientific expertise: How much new change in the scientific evaluation of an issue is needed to effectuate what change in actors' policy preferences?

There is little research that solves this problem. An exception is Farrow (1991), who analyzes how decisions by the US Department of the Interior over the number of offshore leases for oil and gas resources sold by the government are affected by the department's in-house cost-benefit analyses. Instead of asking decision-makers within the department about how they use this expertise, Farrow codes the evaluation of costs and benefits in the department's analyses and uses them as independent variables in a regression with the number of offshore leases sold as a dependent variable. Like this, he can make a statement about how strong a change in the assessment of costs and benefits would be necessary to effectuate changes in the number of leases sold. The effect Farrow finds is relatively weak, with major changes in the in-house analyses effectuating only small changes in policy.

1.1.4.2 Conditions of the Use of Scientific Expertise

While there is a sizeable amount of work analyzing *whether* scientific research is used by political actors or influences their decisions over policy, empirical analyses of the conditions under which this happens is rarer. While some conditions are comparatively well researched, knowledge on others is dear. *First*, among the conditions relatively well studied are those regarding which kind of research is valued among political actors. Thus, there are a number of empirical results indicating that research using quantitative methodologies or formal theories are most likely to be taken serious by policy makers (Weyant, 1988; Landry, Amara and Lamari, 2001; Hird, 2005, chap. 5). Moreover, Oh (1997) finds that the amount of scientific information available is positively correlated with the impact of scientific research on policy.

Second, a few publications empirically test the link between the level of conflict between the political actors engaged in a policy subsystem and the amount of learning taking place. For example, in a long-term analysis of the Dutch coastal flooding policy, Meijerink (2005) finds that ecological research was mostly relevant for a pro-environmental coalition of actors during a time in which conflict in the subsystem was high. For the opposing coalition, this research only became relevant once another issue strongly dividing the two coalitions was resolved. Similarly, in an analysis of environmental policy at Lake Tahoe, United States, Weible et al. (2010) find that scientists are more likely to be seen as allies supporting an actor's policy preference in adversarial subsystems with high levels of conflict, with opportunities for learning from research whose conclusions contradict an actor's policy preference being higher in collaborative subsystems.

Third, there are some results regarding the effect of uncertainty. Epistemic communities research has been built on the argument that uncertainty about the effects of a policy is what makes political actors turn to epistemic communities for advice (Haas, 1992b). There are a few studies corroborating this argument, showing that governments' interest in research increased when they became more uncertain about the effects of a given policy (King, 2005), or decreased when they became more certain (Drake and Nicolaïdis, 1992). Others, however, have argued that some degree of uncertainty is inherent in most policy fields, and more uncertainty will not necessarily lead to more expert influence (Cross, 2012).

Fourth, there is very little knowledge about how different styles of using scientific expertise in different political systems that have found much attention in the literature (Renn, 1995; Weaver and Stares, 2001; Jasanoff, 2007; Straßheim, 2013) impact the role that scientific expertise plays in the policy process. Thus, related research mostly describes *how* those styles differ from one another but does not ask how those styles mediate the influence that expertise has on policy.

Finally, there is mixed evidence regarding the notion that policy-oriented learning from scientific expertise can only affect an actor's peripheral beliefs, and that expertise in conflict with existing core beliefs will necessarily be rejected (Jenkins-Smith *et al.*, 2014, p. 200). On the one hand, such an effect is documented in several experimental studies, in which respondents are confronted with scientific information, and react differently based on their pre-existing beliefs and their political partisanship (Corbett and Durfee, 2004; Hart and Nisbet, 2012). On the other hand, of the ACF studies analyzing policy-oriented learning, several have found that learning also included changes of core beliefs (Elliott and Schlaepfer, 2001; Larsen, Vrangbæk and Traulsen, 2006). While in these cases actors did not learn from scientific expertise, the studies cast doubt on the notion that policy-oriented learning from scientific expertise will only happen if the political actor's core beliefs do not contradict the research results.

1.1.5 Two Research Gaps and How to Address Them

In sum, after more than four decades of utilization research, there is now a solid understanding of the varied roles scientific expertise plays in the policy process.

We also understand that the fact that decision makers frequently discard evaluation results does not mean that expertise is not used. Indeed, many studies have documented instances in which scientific research has had an impact on policy. However, a *first* gap remains regarding the quantification of expert influence. If expert knowledge is relevant for the preference formation of political actors, how much research arguing that a given policy is desirable does it need to convert a critic into a supporter?

Second, the growing body of literature on the background conditions that influence the role scientific expertise plays in the policy process has improved our understanding of what kind of knowledge political actors are most likely to use. Yet, there is a general dearth of empirical research comparing the role expertise plays in different institutional, cultural, and structural settings. In particular, the effect of different styles of using expertise in different political systems on the degree to which scientific research influences public policy is largely untested. A reason for this seems to be the low number of comparative, especially cross-national comparative studies, which would be able to systematically vary the circumstances of expert influence across the different cases. Moreover, the question of who is most likely to learn from scientific expertise is still open.

An analysis trying to address both of these gaps needs to have a research design with two features: The *first* one is to conduct a *comparative* study of the role of scientific expertise in the policy process. As was argued in the previous section, there is not enough research comparing the role of scientific expertise under different circumstances, in particular when these circumstances refer to broad institutional and cultural constellations that characterize different styles of using expertise prevalent in different countries. Additional variation regarding variables thought to mediate expert influence can be brought into the analysis by choosing a long period of analysis. *Second*, the methodology used to analyze the influence of expertise on political actors' policy preferences should be compatible with the goal of quantifying expert influence. As was argued above, the two methodologies prevalent in the literature—tracing the over-time development of policy subsystems or single bureaucracies using document analysis or qualitative interviews, or conducting surveys asking political actors about their use of expertise—are of limited use in this respect. The methodology used by Farrow (1991)—coding the content of scientific expertise presumably used by political actors and correlating it with policy output or the preference of a political actor—seems to be most adequate.

1.2 Research Questions and Research Design

1.2.1 Research Questions

With these goals in mind, it is now possible to specify the research questions guiding the analysis in this book. Analyzing minimum wage policy making in Germany, the United Kingdom, and the United States between 1970 and 2015, we will *first* ask to what degree scientific expertise is present in the media discourse on minimum wages, and how this presence is affected by different context variables. *Second*, the analysis concentrates on the influence of scientific expertise on the policy preferences of political actors dealing with minimum wages, asking to what degree this influence happens, and how it is affected by different circumstances.

Answering these questions does not amount to a comprehensive picture of the role of scientific expertise in the policy process. For example, looking at media discourses and the political actors involved in minimum-wage policy tells us nothing about how minimum wages get on the political agenda, what minimum wage laws are adopted, and how they are implemented. It does, however, give us an insight into who are the actors that shape these processes and what these actors publicly say about minimum wages. In other words, instead of researching the role scientific knowledge plays in the different stages of the minimum wage policy process (Jann and Wegrich, 2007), this book analyzes minimum wage policy subsystems, the public communication about what's happening within them, and the role scientific expertise plays for this (Sabatier, 1988).

The two research questions address different aspects of this role. On the one hand, looking at the presence of researchers and research in the media discourse on minimum wages tells us whether scientific information about the effects of minimum wages reaches and is discussed in front of the general public. Chapter 2 argues that such public discussion of scientific expertise, besides giving voters a means to evaluate claims made about the effects of a proposed minimum wage legislation, is often linked to a political use of scientific research. On the other hand, looking at the influence of scientific expertise on the policy preferences of political actors is a way to analyze the use of scientific expertise for policy-oriented learning in which political actors' beliefs are influenced by scientific information about the effects of minimum wages.

1.2.2 Analyzing Minimum Wage Policy

We answer the two research questions with regard to minimum wage policy. Minimum wage policy is a typical issue in the realm of social and economic policy, which is expected to be somewhat influenced, but not dominated by scientific expertise. In part, minimum wage policy making is driven by the kind of concerns usually connected to a strong expert influence. Thus, it combines widely accepted goals (such as low unemployment and higher incomes for workers) with an uncertainty among political actors regarding the way in which minimum wages contribute to these goals. However, minimum wage policy making also involves normative questions. For politicians, demanding a minimum wage can be a signal to their voters that they care about the poor, and that they do not accept the injustice of wages too low for workers to make ends meet (Levin-Waldman, 1998). Minimum wages are, in other words, widely representative of a large class of policies which are neither purely technical, nor completely dominated by normative concerns. While this book is exclusively concerned with minimum wage policy, it is plausible to hope that the main conclusions from this research travel to other issues that are similarly structured.

Analyzing the role of scientific expertise in the policy process is only possible if such expertise exists. This is clearly the case for minimum wages. Hundreds of theoretical and empirical studies, mostly conducted by economists, are available to political actors seeking to find information regarding the effects of the minimum wage. While much of this work studies the impact of minimum wages in the US, there is a substantial number of studies dealing with minimum wages in other countries, notably the UK and Germany. As will be shown in Chapter 4, this body of scientific knowledge has evolved over time, with research from the 1970s and 1980s, on average, delivering far more pessimistic conclusions regarding minimum wage effects than today's scholarship. There is also cross-country variation, with British researchers being more favorable in their evaluation of the minimum wage than their US and German counterparts. As we will see, this variation makes it possible to study to what extent changes in the scientific evaluation of a policy are related to changes in the policy preferences of political actors.

Finally, the minimum wage is an issue which lends itself to international, long-time comparisons. Minimum wages have existed for many years in some countries (such as the United States) and have more recently been introduced in others (for example in Germany and the United Kingdom). Moreover, as the impressionistic account given at the beginning of this chapter has suggested, the political questions associated with the minimum wage are similar in different countries. Usually, they involve a blend of principled and normative concerns on the one hand (How much government interference into labor markets do we want? Are we willing to accept very low wages?), and of concerns regarding their effects, on the other hand (Are minimum wages an adequate means to fight inequality? Do they hurt employment and the economy?). This makes it possible to compare minimum wage policy making across different countries. Lastly, minimum wages are an issue which, once a statutory minimum wage has been introduced, does not disappear from the political agenda. Even in the US, where the federal minimum wage was introduced already in 1938, the necessity of adjusting the minimum wage to inflation and earnings ensures that the issue prominently appears on the political agenda every couple of years, making it possible to track over-time changes in the minimum wage policy preferences of important actors.

1.2.3 Comparisons Across Countries and Time

As detailed in Chapter 3, the role of scientific expertise in minimum wage policy making will be analyzed in three different countries: Germany, the United Kingdom, and the United States. The three countries were chosen because they are similar enough to allow a sensible comparison. *First*, the three countries are established democracies with similar levels of economic development. *Second*, by the end of the period of analysis, in 2015, all three countries had introduced a nation-wide, statutory minimum wage. *Third*, in the three countries, the minimum wage issue divides economically progressive from economically conservative actors, with organizations such as trade unions and left-wing political parties being mostly supporters of the minimum wage, and employer organizations and right-wing political parties typically opposing large minimum wage hikes. *Fourth*, in all three countries, the minimum wage has been appearing frequently on the political agenda over the course of many years. *Finally*, in all three countries, there has been enough research on the issue to potentially influence this discussion.

Yet, the three countries differ in ways to provide variation on variables thought to mediate the role that scientific expertise plays in the policy process. While the federal minimum wage is old in the US, the National Minimum Wage was introduced in 1999 in the UK, and, in Germany, a general statutory minimum wage only came into effect in 2015, opening up the possibility to compare long-established modes of minimum wage policy making with policy making in situations in which the minimum wage was new and uncertainty about its effects was supposedly high. Differences also exist in the institutional settings and political cultures of the three countries, and in the structures of the minimum wage policy subsystems there.

Finally, in this book, minimum wage policy making is analyzed over long time periods. In the United States, the analysis follows the policy process on the issue from 1970 to 2015; in the UK and Germany, the analysis starts a few years before the introduction of a general minimum wage enters the political agenda for the first time: 1990 and 1992, respectively. The long period of analysis makes it possible to follow the development of different actors' positions on the minimum wage, in the light of a changing evaluation of minimum wage effects by experts.

1.2.4 Combining Quantitative and Qualitative Methods

Both the scope of the analysis—minimum wage policy in three countries over 45 years—as well as the goal of quantifying expert influence on the political actors' policy preferences require the use of quantitative methods. Most of the analyses presented in this book rely on the quantitative analysis of two original data sets. The first one describes how scientific research evaluates minimum wages. It was constructed by coding several hundreds of articles drawn from a broad range of scientific journals between 1970 and 2014, which evaluate minimum wage effects on employment, poverty, the economy or on other variables. The second one describes the political actors involved in minimum wage policy making, and the statements that these actors publicly make concerning the minimum wage. It was constructed by coding several hundreds of newspaper articles which were published in quality papers in Germany, the United Kingdom and the United States during the period of analysis, using a methodology developed by Heikkila et al. (2016).

These data sets are analyzed individually and combinedly to address the two broad questions guiding the research presented in this book. They will be used to identify the actors which are occupied with minimum wage policy in the three countries. The analyses will also show how often researchers, think tanks, and other research-related actors are cited in newspaper articles on minimum wages, and whether the scientific expertise that finds its way into newspaper articles is an adequate representation of the research that is published in scientific journals. Moreover, the data is used to analyze whether and under what circumstances the beliefs of political actors regarding the effects of minimum wages are in line with the results from the research published in scientific journals. Finally, we analyze whether and under which circumstances the minimum wage policy preference of political actors depends on how scientific journal articles evaluate minimum wage effects.

To avoid making judgements which are based on spurious correlations or questionable interpretations of the data, these quantitative analyses are followed by three brief case studies. These investigate how three different actors involved in minimum wage policy making in Germany formed their preference towards the minimum wage, and to what extent this was influenced by scientific expertise.

1.3 Structure of the Book and Main Findings

Before the results of the empirical analyses are presented, *Chapter 2* develops a theoretical model of the influence of scientific expertise on minimum wage policy making based on the ACF. It specifies and advances testable hypotheses about the circumstances under which scientific expertise and research-related actors become an important part of the political debate on minimum wages taking place in the mass media, and are able to influence the policy preferences of different actors involved in minimum wage policy.

Chapter 3 discusses methodological questions that will be relevant throughout the remainder of this book. It specifies the comparative design of the empirical analyses conducted in this book, indicating how Germany, the UK and the United States provide variance on those variables thought to mediate the role scientific expertise plays in the policy process. It also provides details on how the two data sets central to this book—the one describing scientific expertise on minimum wages and the one describing statements political actors involved in minimum wage policy make in newspaper articles—were constructed.

Chapter 4 is an empirical analysis of the actors involved in minimum wage policy in the three countries, and of the positions they have towards the minimum wage. Using data gathered from newspaper articles, it shows that the actors and coalitions involved in minimum wage policy are relatively similar in all three countries. Trade unions and left-wing political parties are the main supporters of the minimum wage, while right-wing political parties and employer organizations are its main critics. There are, however, also differences between the three countries. In the US, the minimum wage policy subsystem is characterized by a comparatively strong polarization between minimum wage supporters on the one hand, and its critics on the other hand, a pattern that has not changed much since the 1970s. Germany and the United Kingdom, in contrast, started out with a strong polarization between supporters and critics, but experienced a rapprochement of both sides prior to or shortly after the introduction of the minimum wage.

Chapter 5 focuses on the role scientific expertise and actors promoting this expertise play in the public discussion about minimum wages taking place in the mass media. It analyzes how often and with what positions newspapers in the three countries cite researchers working on minimum wages, or refer to their publications. It shows that scientific expertise is an important part of the media discourse on minimum wages in all three countries, but finds differences between the United States on the one hand, and the two European countries on the other, with minimum-wage related research being less visible in the UK and Germany. Another variable influencing the visibility of scientific research in newspaper articles is the number of scientific articles on minimum wages published, which is positively correlated with the public visibility of scientific expertise. Chapter 5 also analyzes the degree to which the research results that are being discussed in newspapers reflect the results published in scientific journals, and find a relatively close match between research and its representation in the mass media.

Chapter 6 continues by analyzing whether scientific expertise influences how political actors think about minimum wage effects, and how they position themselves towards the minimum wage. It compares the statements political actors make about how the minimum wage impacts employment, poverty and the economy with the research results published in scientific journals. Doing so, it finds a surprisingly strong match between what science says about minimum wage effects on the one hand, and what political actors says on the other hand. A regression analysis shows that this match also exists for minimum wage policy preferences. If most research published in scientific journals points to desirable minimum wage effects, then political actors are more likely to support the minimum wage. As changes in experts' evaluation of the minimum wage are correlated with future changes in political actors' minimum wage preferences, but not vice versa, the correlation is interpreted as a causal connection, with changes in scientific expertise leading to changes in political actors' policy preference. Different circumstances mediate this influence: In the US, expert influence is significantly weaker than in the two European countries. Moreover, scientific expertise seems to be less influential in election years. In contrast, some other variables discussed in the literature review above have no effect on the degree of influence which scientific expertise has on the minimum wage policy preferences of political actors. These include the number of scientific studies published, the agreement among these studies, and political actors' uncertainty over the effects of minimum wages. Moreover, contrary to expectations, actors who have moderate views towards the minimum wage (and are thus expected to have no core policy beliefs strongly contradicting the implications from scientific research on the minimum wage) are not more likely to be influenced by experts.

Chapter 7 tests the validity of the core result from Chapter 6, that is, that scientific expertise influences the policy preferences of some political actors. It is designed to rule out the possibility that this result is based on spurious correlation or on variables that don't measure what they are supposed to measure. To this end, the role of scientific expertise in the preference formation of three political actors in Germany—a trade union and two political parties—is analyzed. The results show that the main variables used in the quantitative analyses measure the concepts they are supposed to measure and that the observable implications of a causal link between scientific expertise and the preferences of political actors can be observed.

Chapter 8 brings together the results from the previous analyses. It paints a picture in which the results from scientific research play an important role in minimum wage policy making, as arguments in the public discussion on minimum wages, but also as an influence that can eventually lead political actors to change their position on the minimum wage. The exact role that is played depends on the circumstances, most importantly on styles of policy making that differ from country to country. The chapter discusses the implications of these results for the literature.

Theoretical Model 2

To make sure that the results from the empirical research presented in this book can be integrated into the existing literature, it is necessary to root the analysis in a coherent theoretical model. This chapter develops such a model which is based on the Advocacy Coalition Framework and integrates results from the wider literature on research utilization, science communication, and other fields. The model specifies the kind of expertise which is in the center of the analyses in this book, that is, minimum wage related research published in scientific journals; it describes the ways in which this expertise reaches political actors involved in minimum wage policy, and the different uses to which these actors can put the expertise.

The model has three main components: scientific expertise, that is, the expert discourse on minimum wages; the media discourse, in which scientific expertise on minimum wages may or may not play a role; and the political actors involved in minimum wage policy, that is, the minimum wage policy subsystem. The chapter starts by describing these core concepts, and then goes on to specify hypotheses about how expert discourses influence the media discourse on minimum wages and minimum wage policy subsystems.

2.1 Scientific Expertise and the Expert Discourse

The idea underlying research on the role of expertise in the policy process is that there is something distinct about expert knowledge which sets it apart from other kinds of knowledge—for example the knowledge of civil society groups—and which makes the use of expert knowledge in policy making a distinct field of study. Boswell (2009, pp. 23–25) argues that expert knowledge is associated

F. Klein, *The Role of Scientific Expertise in Minimum Wage Policy Making*, Vergleichende Politikwissenschaft,
https://doi.org/10.1007/978-3-658-32746-0_2

with two features. *First*, it is held by people who, as a function of their educational training and institutional position, are considered to be experts (see also Hird, 2005, pp. 35–39). *Second*, it must satisfy certain procedural and substantive requirements, such as having theoretical and conceptual coherence, and employing a methodology regarded as sound by significant parts of the expert community. This definition, of course, stays uninformative if it is not stated what the relevant educational training, the relevant institutional positions, and the procedural and substantive requirements are. Boswell chooses them in a way that expert knowledge equates to the results of academic research. This definition thus narrows down the notion of expert knowledge to being the professional knowledge of academic researchers. It contrasts with broader notions of expert knowledge being produced by a broad variety of actors, many of them from outside of academia. For example, epistemic communities—expert groups with a shared knowledge base and a common political project—have been defined in ways to encompass a variety of members, some of them working in academia, and others in government agencies, civil society organizations, or the private sector (Mamudu, Gonzalez and Glantz, 2011). More fundamentally, it has been argued that academic knowledge does not necessarily have a greater truth claim on statements about social phenomena than the knowledge held by professionals outside of academia (Majone, 1989; Fischer and Forester, 1993), making the restriction of the term expert knowledge to academic knowledge unwarranted.

This book, in contrast, is preoccupied with a narrowly defined kind of expertise, that is, scientific expertise. It deals with the results of academic research which are published in outlets directed at a scientific readership, such as scientific journals. This is not because there are reasons to believe that the wider community of experts including practitioners is of less relevance in the policy process. Rather, the limitation on scientific expertise reflects the presumption that scientific expertise is one form of expertise which plays an important role in the policy process, and the practical concern that it is not possible to study all forms of expertise at the same time. Moreover, scientific expertise, in contrast to the expertise provided by professionals such as those working inside government bureaucracies, is publicly available, making it easier to study it.

Scientific expertise is produced through a communicative process leading to the emergence of a more or less coherent body of knowledge on the effects of minimum wages. In this process, scholars—mostly researchers at universities or other research institutions—publish research on minimum wage effects. Doing so, they develop or criticize existing theories, add empirical knowledge to what was known before, and thus reinforce or contradict existing knowledge. While the plethora of research on minimum wages is published in a variety of outlets including journals, books and conference papers, and does not deliver homogeneous results, it is bound together by the existence of a scholarly community which takes note of and engages with minimum wage research. In the following, the body of knowledge emanating from this communicative process will be called the *scientific discourse* or the *expert discourse on minimum wages.*

The expert discourse on minimum wages does not produce homogenous conclusions. Still, it is possible for researchers and others to review the existing scientific publications in order to draw general conclusions about the effects of minimum wages. For example, a literature review of over 100 studies of minimum wage effects on employment finds that a majority of studies "give a relatively consistent (although not always statistically significant) indication of negative employment effects of minimum wages" (Neumark and W. L. Wascher, 2006, p. 1). Such conclusions can change over time. Thus, a study by Bosch et al. (2009, p. 33) notes that, while the view that minimum wages have strong negative effects on employment used to be near-consensual up to the 1990s, it has now been called into question by newer research results.

The fact that the main conclusions to be drawn from the expert discourse on minimum wages vary over time provokes the question whether there also is geographical variation. In other words, is there a single global expert discourse on minimum wages? Or are there different regional or national expert discourses that come to different conclusions about the effects of minimum wages? In part, geographical variation can result from different objects of study and does not contradict the idea of a global expert discourse. A British researcher studying the British National Minimum Wage might find that it has effects different from those that an American scholar found studying the US federal minimum wage. Geographical variation, however, might also result from different theoretical or methodological approaches used in different countries or regions. In this case, British researchers would come to systematically different conclusions about minimum wage effects in general. While it is an empirical question whether the expert discourse on minimum wages is better described as an international or a domestic one, the literature at least suggests that the notion of national expert discourses on minimum wages is not unrealistic. A number of studies point to researchers preferably citing publications by scholars working in the same country as they do, to collaborate more often domestically than internationally, and to adhere to different theories and methodologies in different countries (Waever, 1998; Cronin, 2008; Frenken, Hardeman and Hoekman, 2009; Hennemann, Rybski and Liefner, 2012). Such expert discourses, which exhibit strong variation between countries, would be adequately described as being domestic rather than global, even if there is a lot of cross-border communication in science.

2.2 The Media Discourse on Minimum Wages

The debate around minimum wages does not only take place between researchers. In addition to a scientific discourse among researchers, there is a public discourse on minimum wages in which arguments relating to minimum wage policy are exchanged, and which involves a wider audience including political actors, but also the general public. The public discussion of minimum wage policy may take place in different venues such as panel discussions, publications, speeches delivered in parliament, or newspaper articles. Instead of analyzing the public discourse as a whole, this book will only be concerned with a subset of it, the *media discourse*. It is defined here as comprising all minimum-wage related publications in general-audience media (Gamson and Modigliani, 1989, pp. 2–3). While the preceding section conceptualized an international scientific discourse next to domestic ones, the media discourse will be treated as exclusively domestic, meaning that there are separate media discourses in the three countries analyzed in this book.

The analyses of the following chapters will not be concerned with the media discourse as such. Rather, they focus on spillovers from the expert discourse into the media discourse, that is, on instances in which the mass media reports on scientific research on minimum wages. Such reporting may happen as part of the science coverage on a newspaper's science pages (Weigold, 2001, pp. 166–169), but is more likely to be part of the usual coverage of minimum wage politics, for example when studies are cited in a discussion of how a planned minimum wage rise would affect employment.

2.3 Minimum Wage Policy Subsystems

The third main concept in the theoretical model is the minimum wage policy subsystem. Policy subsystems are a concept from the Advocacy Coalition Framework. They have their intellectual roots in Heclo's (1978) conceptualization of issue networks, which expanded the perception of actors involved in a given policy beyond the iron triangle of interest groups, government agencies and legislative (sub-) committee to encompass a broader range of actors (Jenkins-Smith *et al.*, 2014, p. 190). Policy subsystems, accordingly, comprise the "set of actors who are involved in dealing with a policy problem" (Sabatier, 1987, p. 659), including government actors, interest groups, civil society organizations, academic experts, journalists, and others. Given that policy subsystems are bound to a specific policy problem, their geographical scope tends to be linked to that problem. Local policy problems will be connected to local policy subsystems, national policy problems to national policy subsystems, and so on.

The actors in policy subsystems can be grouped into different advocacy coalitions who coordinate their actions to advocate a common policy project (Jenkins-Smith *et al.*, 2014, pp. 191–192). Advocacy coalitions are held together by shared beliefs. Within the ACF, beliefs are usually divided into a deep core, which contains fundamental normative and ontological axioms which are not specific to an issue; a policy core, which contains issue-specific values and beliefs concerning the fundamental strategies for achieving these values; and secondary aspects, which contain beliefs about the specific instruments necessary to implement the policy core and are more open to change than the stable core beliefs (Sabatier, 1987). Scientific and technical information plays a major role within these belief systems, as it helps to specify the perceived relation between normative goals and the contribution of different policies to these goals (Jenkins-Smith *et al.*, 2014, p. 192).

Public policy usually reflects the beliefs of one or several coalitions (Sabatier, 1993). Which coalitions manage to leave their mark on a policy crucially depends on the resources that the actors within each coalition have at their disposal to influence government's decisions. Such resources are influenced by factors external to the policy subsystems, such as socio-economic conditions, public opinion, the systemic governing coalition, and events in other policy subsystems. The use that coalitions make of such resources is, moreover, shaped by coalition opportunity structures, such as the degree of consensus that is needed to achieve policy change (Jenkins-Smith *et al.*, 2014, p. 194). Policy change, in this framework, happens as a result of perturbations inside or outside of a policy subsystems which may change the coalitions' resources, through a negotiated agreement between opposing coalitions in a subsystem. Another road to policy change is policy-oriented learning—belief change by actors who have made new experiences or have been confronted with new information (Sabatier, 1987; Jenkins-Smith *et al.*, 2014, pp. 202–203).

2.4 Scientific Expertise: From Expert Discourse to Media Discourse and Political Actors

The notion that scientific expertise plays any role either in the media discourse or in the interactions taking place within minimum wage policy subsystems obviously requires that there is some link between the expert discourse and a wider set of actors involved in minimum wage policy making. Political actors can only use scientific research on minimum wage effects if they know about it. Given that the literature from research utilization and science communication has pointed at a gap between scientists and policy-makers as well as the wider public (Caplan, 1979; Dunn, 1980; Weigold, 2001), this link should not be taken for granted. The connection running from the expert discourse to the media discourse and to policy subsystems can take different forms, and its nature is dependent on the cultural and institutional context.

On a general level, there are three basic mechanisms by which scientific expertise from the expert discourse spills into the media discourse and the policy subsystem. The *first* one is driven by researchers themselves, who can actively try to communicate their research results to a wider audience by formulating press releases, writing articles directed at a general audience, or reaching out to political actors by organizing talks and conferences. Scholars, in this sense, could be 'pushing' their professional knowledge into the media discourse and the political sphere. Surveys among scientists have shown that the degree to which this happens varies between individual researchers, disciplines, and countries (Bauer and Jensen, 2011; Peters, 2013). Likewise, studies of advocacy coalitions have found scientists play an active role in some policy subsystems (e.g. Meijerink, 2005; Bukowski, 2007; Nedergaard, 2008), but not in others (e.g. Larsen, Vrangbæk and Traulsen, 2006).

Second, in addition to this 'push' mechanism, journalists and political actors interested in minimum wages policy can take the initiative and 'pull' scientific expertise out of the expert discourse. They can do so, for example, by reading publications from the expert discourse (or by letting their staff do so), by arranging meetings with researchers, or by participating in workshops bringing together researchers and political actors (Biegelbauer, 2013).

Third, actors and organizations other than researchers themselves might act as brokers, transferring knowledge from the expert discourse to political actors and translating it into a language comprehensible for non-experts (Lomas, 2007; Meyer, 2010). Relevant organizations in this category are what Weaver and Stares (2001) call policy advisory organizations, a category encompassing publicly and privately funded think tanks, blue-ribbon commission, government advisory bodies, and similar organizations. When reporting about minimum-wage related research, the mass media can also serve as a brokers, taking a middle position between the expert discourse and a wider public (Weigold, 2001).

The different channels through which scientific knowledge from expert discourses reaches political actors are no neutral transmitters. Given the vast amount of research on the effects of minimum wages, actors involved in the transfer of knowledge from the expert discourse to the minimum wage policy subsystem must make decisions regarding which elements of the discourse are important, and which are not. They may privilege those contributions to the expert discourse that conform to the highest methodological standards, those that they deem to be most relevant for the policy problem that actors in their country are currently facing, or those that are closest to their own political views. For example, advocacy-oriented think tanks frequently choose to convey those parts of expert discourses into the political system that conform to their basic political orientation (Rich, 2004).

Knowing who takes the initiative in communicating scientific expertise is thus important for knowing what kind of expert knowledge reaches political actors and is communicated to the general public via the mass media. Partly, this should depend on the individual actors, who may choose to contact a given researcher or to read a policy paper written by a think tank. It also depends, however, on features of the policy subsystem and the political system an actor is embedded in. For example, in the US, in addition to research-oriented, non-partisan think tanks, there are many advocacy-oriented think tanks dealing with economic and social policy that are committed to specific political goals (Rich, 2004). In contrast, in Germany, the most important economic and social policy think tanks tend to be government-funded, research-oriented, and less strongly attached to particular political positions (Thunert, 2001). While both type of institutions can be important in bringing research results from the expert discourse to journalists and political actors, they will likely do so in different ways.

Such cross-country differences are not limited to the presence or absence of specific institutions such as think tanks but extend to the political culture more broadly. They have been described as different styles of using scientific expertise (Renn, 1995), as styles of knowledge-making (Jasanoff, 2007, chap. 10), or as modes of embedding epistemic authority (Straßheim, 2013). While the precise ways in which these styles are characterized and the number of different styles identified varies, there is a distinction between two different ways of bringing expertise into the policy process present in all three accounts. The first of these styles of using scientific expertise has been termed pluralistic (Jasanoff, 2007), adversarial (Renn, 1995), or advocatory (Straßheim, 2013). This institutional and cultural configuration is often connected with the US. It involves expertise being mainly brought into policy subsystems by interested actors such as lobby groups or advocacy think tanks, which seek to substantiate their policy preferences with scientific evidence. The result of this process is not a consensus or a synthesis reflecting all different approaches, but rather a situation in which each group has enhanced its capability to argue for its own policy preference (Straßheim, 2013, p. 16). This contrasts with a second group of styles, which includes Jasanoff's (2007) corporatist and embodied styles of knowledge-making, Renn's

(1995) corporatist and consensual styles, and Straßheim's (2013) rationalistic discourse. Here, the state plays a larger role in bringing scientific expertise into policy subsystems, for example by funding applied research and policy analysis, and by establishing institutions delivering science-based policy advice. This is more likely to lead to a synthesis which is, at least to some degree, accepted by most political actors. With regard to the countries analyzed in this book, these styles of using expertise have been associated with Germany and the UK (Renn, 1995; Jasanoff, 2007).

2.5 Using Scientific Expertise

Where scientific expertise is transferred to a wider group of actors, it possibly becomes relevant in the policy process. Subsequent chapters will analyze two different aspects of the role scientific expertise plays for minimum wage policy making.

2.5.1 Scientific Expertise in the Media Discourse

The *first* aspect is the presence of scientific expertise in the media discourse on minimum wages. This means that the mass media, when reporting about minimum wages, do not only cite politicians and interest groups, but also scholars and their research results. The presence of scientific expertise in the mass media tells us several things about the role scientific expertise plays in the minimum wage policy process. At the most basic level, the inclusion of research results in media reporting on minimum wages means that research results on minimum wages become known to a large audience: to the actors in minimum wage policy subsystems, but also the general public not usually involved in minimum wage policy. While the former group, as argued above, has many means to access knowledge from the expert discourse, the mass media are arguably the only source from which most people can learn about research regarding the effects of minimum wages. Consequently, when scientific expertise is present in media reporting on minimum wages, the public will have better chances to evaluate the claims political actors make about what effects proposed changes in minimum wage legislation will have.

When the results of scientific research on minimum wages become known to the general public, this also means that political actors will have to justify their claims regarding the effects of minimum wages in the light of this research. Scientific expertise thus becomes an argument in the political debate. Other arguments referring to the effects of minimum wages, whether they are based on science or not, have to engage with these scientific arguments (Majone, 1989). In practice, this means that political actors whose policy preference is in line with the study's conclusions are incentivized to use it as argumentative ammunition for their cause. Actors whose policy preference is contradicted by the study's conclusion, by contrast, will have to mobilize additional arguments—possibly different studies—to strengthen their cause (Pellizzoni, 2011). The presence of scientific expertise in the media discourse can, therefore, spark an additional use of research, which is in line with Weiss's (1979) political model of research utilization.

This link between political research utilization and media coverage of scientific expertise can also be seen from the other end: The presence of scientific expertise in the media discourse can be the result of political actors' efforts to publicize research results in line with their policy preference. Thus, while journalists might include research into their coverage of minimum wage politics because its results meet some standard of newsworthiness (Eilders, 2006), the probability with which research results are included in a piece on minimum wages can be increased by public relations activities of scholars or knowledge brokers (Turk, 1986; Cameron, Sallot and Curtin, 1997). To the extent that these scholars and brokers leave the realm of pure science and become advocates of a particular policy, these activities conform to the model of political research utilization (Pielke, 2007, chap. 2). Chapters 4 and 7 present examples of such activities: Political parties and interest groups commission and publicize surveys of the scientific literature on minimum wages to support their political arguments, thus increasing the presence of scientific expertise in the media discourse.

2.5.2 Influence on Political Actors' Policy Preferences

The *second* aspect of the role of scientific expertise in the policy process considered in this book is the influence of the expert discourse on the expressed beliefs and policy preferences of the actors in minimum wage policy subsystems. This means that political actors are less likely to make statements about the effect of minimum wages when these statements contradict research results from the expert discourse, and are more likely to support higher minimum wages when the expert discourse comes to generally favorable conclusions regarding minimum wage effects.

The mechanism which is presumed to underlie this influence is policy-oriented learning from the expert discourse, meaning that political actors adjust their beliefs according to the content of scientific expertise (Sabatier, 1987; Weible, Pattison and Sabatier, 2010). In Weiss's (1979) terms, such learning results from utilization in the forms specified by the knowledge-driven model, the problem-solving model, and the enlightenment model. Policy-oriented learning may take place within belief systems, meaning that political actors only learn from those parts of the expert discourse that are compatible with their core policy beliefs. In contrast, an influence of the expert discourse on actors' policy preferences presupposes learning across belief systems, that is, from those parts of the expert discourse which are not compatible with existing core beliefs. While the original formulation of the Advocacy Coalition Framework regarded core beliefs as largely stable and policy-oriented learning across belief systems as unlikely (Sabatier, 1987), empirical studies have documented instances of such learning (Elliott and Schlaepfer, 2001; Larsen, Vrangbæk and Traulsen, 2006).

The remainder of this chapter formulates hypotheses regarding the extent to and the conditions under which both aspects of the role of scientific expertise in minimum wage policy making, the discussion of scientific expertise in the media discourse on minimum wages and its use for policy-oriented learning across belief systems, are likely to be observed. The most general hypotheses refer to whether these uses of expertise take place with regard to the domestic and the international expert discourse:

H1.1: *Scientific expertise from the domestic expert discourse is present in the media discourse on minimum wages.*

H1.2: *The domestic expert discourse influences the beliefs and preferences of actors in minimum wage policy subsystems.*

H1.3: *Scientific expertise from the international expert discourse is present in the media discourse on minimum wages.*

H1.4: *The international expert discourse influences the beliefs and preferences of actors in minimum wage policy subsystems.*

Given that many newspaper articles including information on many actors were analyzed for this research project, it is likely that some form of public discussion of scientific expertise, or of influence on actor preferences, is found. The more important question, therefore, will be, how common both phenomena are, and how their prevalence depends on the circumstances under which policy making takes place. These are systematized in the next subsection.

2.5.3 Variables Mediating the Use of Scientific Expertise

The literature review from Chapter 1 has grouped the variables usually discussed as mediating the use of scientific expertise into four groups: properties of the expert discourse, issue properties, institutional and cultural circumstances, and user attributes. This classification also guides the discussion in this section.

2.5.3.1 Properties of the Expert Discourse

The condition for scientific research to enter the media discourse or influence political actors at all is that there is a minimum amount of scientific knowledge about minimum wages that journalists and political actors can use in one way or another. To be of use in public discussions over minimum wages and for policy-oriented learning, this scientific knowledge must, moreover, address at least some of those problems connected to an issue that are perceived to be relevant by the actors in a policy subsystem or the wider public. In other words, the gap between the expert discourse and political actors' needs must not be too big (Caplan, 1979). For the countries and time periods analyzed in this book, this is unproblematic. As will be shown in later chapters, the amount of research on minimum wage effects is large, and these effects are an important part of the political debate around minimum wages in all three countries. Scientific knowledge on minimum wage effects has, however, increased over time, as has the number of studies published each year. With the amount of useable knowledge increasing, one could expect the public discussion of research and its use for policy-oriented learning to increase as well, as more researchers try to spread their research results ('push mechanism'), and the number of studies which might potentially convince political actors increases (Oh, 1997).

H2.1: *The more studies of minimum wage effects are published, the more scientific expertise is part of the media discourse on minimum wages.*

H2.2: *The more studies of minimum wage effects are published, the higher the influence of scientific expertise on the beliefs and preferences of political actors in minimum wage policy subsystems.*

A factor that plays into the influence of scientific expertise on political actors is the degree of agreement among scientists. Thus, a major motivation for political actors to engage in policy-oriented learning across belief systems is to get clarity over the likely effects of different policy alternatives, which allows them to better pursue their political goals (Haas, 1992b). Experts, however, have been hypothesized to be able to provide an authoritative answer to such problems only if there is some basic agreement among themselves (Jenkins-Smith, 1990, pp. 189–194). The influence of expert discourses is therefore expected to be stronger when there is a strong coherence among the research results that form the expert discourse.

H2.3: *The influence of scientific expertise on the beliefs and preferences of political actors in minimum wage policy subsystems is higher when coherence in the expert discourse is high.*

Moreover, the argument has been made that studies using formal theories or quantitative methodologies are most likely to convince political actors (Weyant, 1988; Landry, Amara and Lamari, 2001; Hird, 2005, chap. 5). The publications in the expert discourse on minimum wages mostly come from the economics discipline and generally adhere to these standards. As there is very little variation on this variable, no hypotheses are formulated. Given that the scientific expertise on minimum wages takes this form, however, this is another reason to expect some form of research utilization throughout the later analyses.

2.5.3.2 Issue Properties

In addition to properties of the expert discourse, issue properties may mediate the role scientific expertise plays in the policy process. Thus, those issues that are most likely to involve a strong demand for and an important role of scientific expertise are the ones that are connected with enough technical complexity so that political actors are uncertain about the implication of different policy alternatives (Adler and Haas, 1992; Haas, 1992b). As was argued in the previous chapter, political debates about the minimum wage are often about its effects, the determination of which is technically complex. Such complexity can be expected to generally increase the probability that scientific expertise is part of the media discourse on minimum wages, or influences the beliefs and preferences of political actors. The issue under investigation, minimum wages, is constant over all empirical analyses presented in this book. One can therefore expect some form of research utilization throughout the later analysis.

Complexity and the related uncertainty, however, is subjective rather than objective (Haas, 1992b, pp. 14–15). When subjective uncertainty rises, so does the expected demand for scientific expertise ('pull mechanism'). The research design of this book (see Chapter 3) does not allow to measure how uncertain an individual actor is about the effects of minimum wages. However, it is possible to identify situations in which uncertainty among political actors can be expected to be generally higher. Haas (1992b, pp. 14–15) argues that this can happen when new information from research reminds political actors that an issue is less well understood than commonly thought. In our case, this is expected to happen when new studies on minimum wages strongly contradict traded knowledge on minimum wage effects. Moreover, the uncertainty surrounding minimum wage policy is expected to be higher when the minimum wage is a new policy. In this situation, political actors cannot draw on their own practical experience to assess minimum wage effects and are more likely to turn to research instead.

H3.1: *More scientific expertise is present in the media discourse on minimum wages when the minimum wage is a new policy.*
H3.2: *The influence of scientific expertise on the beliefs and preferences of political actors in minimum wage policy subsystems is higher when the minimum wage is a new policy.*
H3.3: *More scientific expertise is present in the public discourse on minimum wages when new research results strongly contradict traded knowledge about minimum wage effects.*
H3.4: *The influence of scientific expertise on the beliefs and preferences of political actors in minimum wage policy subsystems is higher when new research results strongly contradict traded knowledge about minimum wage effects.*

2.5.3.3 Culture, Institutions, and Coalition Structure

A third group of variables that mediate the role that scientific expertise plays in minimum wage policy making refers to the broader context of the policy process. A first set of conditions are the different styles of using scientific expertise discussed above. These styles are usually thought of as transgressing the limits of a single policy subsystem. Instead, they apply to the systemic level, to countries as a whole. The theoretical model differentiates between two broad styles. On the one hand, a pluralistic style is connected with scientific expertise being brought into the policy process by interested actors seeking to substantiate their policy preferences. As discussed above, such political uses are often connected to the presence of scientific expertise in the media discourse. Actors seeking to substantiate their policy preferences with scientific arguments often do so publicly, drawing, for example, media attention to studies they commissioned. One can, therefore, expect scientific knowledge to be particularly present in the media discourse of countries with a pluralistic style of using expertise. In contrast, a consensual, corporatist, or embodied style is connected with scientific expertise being provided to political actors by nonpartisan, often government-sponsored actors. Political actors can be expected to have more trust in this kind of nonpartisan expertise than in the expertise wielded by interested actors. This makes policy-oriented learning from scientific expertise across belief systems more likely. Conversely, the availability of universally accepted expertise should make it harder for political actors to pick out and promote only those studies that support their preferred policy. With the political use of scientific expertise being hampered, political actors have less incentives to make research a matter of the public discussion on minimum wages.

H4.1: *Under the conditions of a pluralistic style of using expertise, scientific expertise is more present in the media discourse on minimum wages than under the conditions of a consensual or corporatist style.*

H4.2: *Under the conditions of a pluralistic style of using expertise, the influence of scientific expertise on the beliefs and preferences of political actors in minimum wage policy subsystems is weaker than under the conditions of a consensual or corporatist style.*

Besides these system-wide differences, the coalition structure of policy subsystems may mediate the role scientific expertise plays in the policy process. Thus, existing research has provided evidence that policy-oriented learning across belief systems is more likely in collaborative policy subsystems with medium levels of conflict between the coalitions (Meijerink, 2005). Conversely, the political use of scientific expertise has been argued to be highest in adversarial policy subsystems (Weible, Pattison and Sabatier, 2010). Again, such political use should be linked to a high visibility of scientific expertise in the public discussion around minimum wages.

H4.3: *Scientific expertise is more present in the media discourse when the policy subsystem has an adversarial coalition structure, and less present in the media discourse when the policy subsystem has a collaborative coalition structure.*

H4.4: *The influence of scientific expertise on the beliefs and preferences of political actors is higher in collaborative policy subsystems and lower in adversarial policy subsystems.*

2.5.3.4 Actors Properties

A final variable potentially mediating the role of scientific expertise relates to the potential user of expertise. Thus, as mentioned before, there is a tendency among political actors to reject expertise that is strongly at odds with their core beliefs (Jenkins-Smith, 1990, chap. 4.3). Based on this, one can expect actors who do not have strong positive or negative prior beliefs regarding the desirability of minimum wages to be most likely to engage in policy-oriented learning across belief systems. This makes expert influence on these actors' beliefs and preferences more likely.

H5.1: *The beliefs and preferences of actors without strong positive or negative prior beliefs regarding the desirability of minimum wages are more likely to be influenced by the expert discourse.*

2.6 The Expert Discourse as a Dependent Variable

Finally, a complete model of the role of scientific expertise in minimum wage policy making should not only specify how research becomes relevant in the media discourse and influences the beliefs and preferences of political actors. It should also pay attention to how the expert discourse itself is influenced by the media discourse and by developments in the policy subsystem. This comes close to Weiss's (1979) sevenths mode of research utilization. Research not only influences society, it is also influenced itself by the intellectual fashion of its time.

Specifically, two types of influences are considered. *First*, in terms of (first-level) agenda-setting (McCombs and Shaw, 1993), the fact that minimum wages are on the media or on the political agenda could get researchers interested in the effects of minimum wages, leading to more scientific publications on the issue in the future. As discussed in Chapter 3, the research presented in this book only uses data on the media agenda, that is, on how often newspapers write on minimum wages, but no data on the political agenda. Given that there potentially is a high correlation between the media and the political agenda (Kleinnijenhuis and Rietberg, 1995), the hypothesis formulated here does not discriminate between the two. In other words, the analyses presented in this book allow us to assess whether the political or the media agenda influence the research agenda, but not which one of the two.

H6.1: *Increased political or mass media attention to the subject of minimum wages leads to an increased number of scientific studies on minimum wages.*

Second, the ways in which political actors think about the minimum wage could shape the way in which scholars research the minimum wage, and thus influence the results of that research. This could happen in analogy to a second-level agenda setting effect (McCombs *et al.*, 1997): The fact that the political discussion of minimum wages focuses on a particular aspect of minimum wages—such as their effects on employment—could lead researchers interested in minimum wages to focus on their employment effects as well. Given that most research finds that minimum wages (slightly) reduce employment (see Chapter 5), a focus on such effects would invoke a more negative overall picture of minimum wages in the expert discourse. Conversely, if most scientific studies focused on minimum wage effects on poverty, which are mostly thought to be beneficial, the overall picture of minimum wages in the expert discourse would be more favorable. More directly, political actors could influence the scientific evaluation of minimum wages by commissioning research in a way to deliver convenient results.

H6.2: A more positive evaluation of minimum wages by political actors leads to a more positive evaluation of minimum wages in the expert discourse.

2.7 Summary

This chapter has developed a theoretical model of the use of scientific expertise for minimum-wage policy making. The model is built around three major concepts: the expert discourse on minimum wages, the media discourse, and minimum wage policy subsystems. Figure 2.1 shows a graphical representation of the model.

The expert discourse on minimum wages, at the top of Figure 2.1, is the sum of scientific publications evaluating the effects of minimum wages on variables such as employment, social inequality or economic growth. The expert discourse on minimum wages can be conceptualized as an international or as a domestic expert discourse, with the first concept emphasizing science as a global process, and the second concept pointing to cultural and other divisions that might make domestic research more significant in the domestic policy process. To what extent domestic scientific expertise is more likely to be used in the policy process than international scientific expertise is an empirical question which will be explored in the following chapters.

The media discourse on the left includes all mass media reporting on minimum wages. In contrast to the expert discourse, it is only conceptualized as a domestic discourse. The analyses presented in later chapters are not so much focused on the media discourse on minimum wages as such, but mainly in the frequency and the ways in which scientific research from the expert discourse is cited in the mass media.

Finally, minimum wage policy subsystems, in the bottom right corner, include all actors and organizations regularly trying to influence minimum wage policy making, such as political parties, interest groups, civil society actors, journalists, and others. While not all scholars contributing to the expert discourse on minimum wages are automatically actors in minimum wage policy subsystems, some, who are not only researchers, but also political activists, are. The actors in a policy subsystem can be organized into advocacy coalitions, bound together by common beliefs. The geographical scope of policy subsystems is determined by the scope of the policy. This book, which deals with nation-wide minimum wages, analyzes three nation-wide minimum wage policy subsystems: in the United States, in the United Kingdom, and in Germany.

The arrows in Figure 2.1 represent the relations between the expert discourse, the media discourse, and the minimum wage policy subsystem. *First*, the number of studies in the expert discourse on minimum wages was hypothesized to depend on the attention paid to minimum wages in the media discourse. How the expert discourse evaluates minimum wages was, moreover, hypothesized to depend on the evaluation of minimum wages by the actors in the minimum wage policy subsystem.

Second, the presence of scientific expertise in the media discourse was expected to be influenced by the expert discourse. Thus, the more scientific studies evaluating minimum wage effects are published, the more research is expected to be present in the mass media. Moreover, the presence of scientific expertise in the media discourse was hypothesized to be affected by the coalition structure of the policy subsystem. Other variables hypothesized to influence how often the mass media reports on research on minimum wage effects are uncertainty and the style of using scientific expertise.

Third, the beliefs and preferences of the actors in minimum wage policy subsystems are expected to be influenced by the expert discourse. This influence was hypothesized to be stronger when more scientific studies are published, agreement in the expert discourse is high, uncertainty is high, the policy style is consensual/corporatist, and when the coalition structure of the policy subsystem is collaborative.

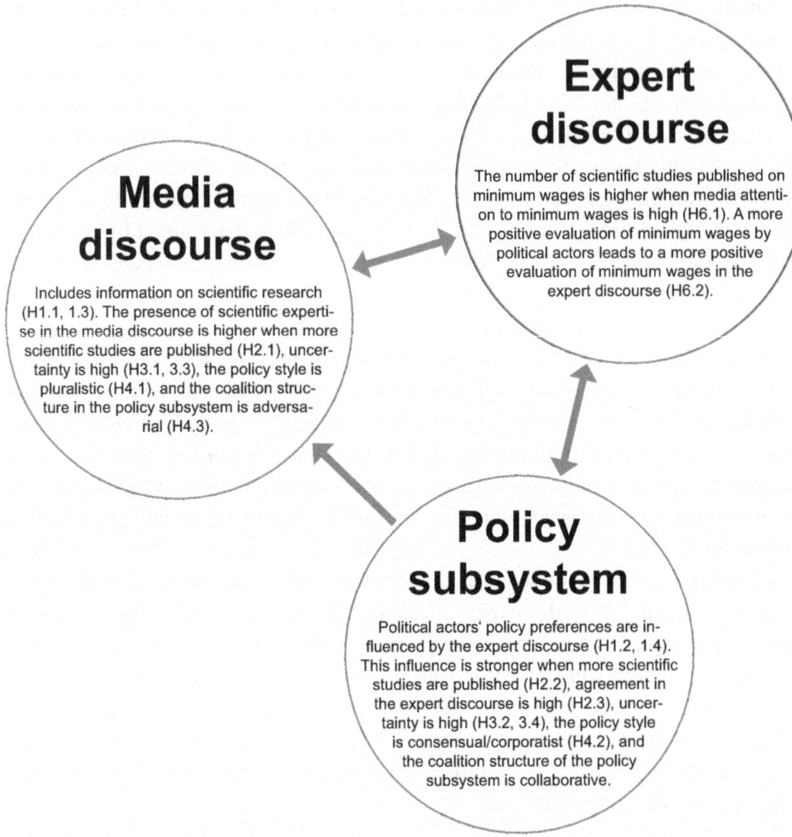

Figure 2.1 The theoretical model

Methods and Research Design

3

This chapter presents the methodological design of the research presented this book, which is geared towards testing the hypotheses formulated in the previous chapter. The theoretical model has three main components, on which empirical data is needed: the expert discourse on minimum wages, the (presence of scientific expertise in the) public discourse on minimum wages, and the minimum wage policy subsystem. The connections between those three concepts, moreover, were hypothesized to be dependent on context variables referring to properties of the expert discourse, issue properties (uncertainty), the institutional and cultural context, and actor properties. To maximize variation on those context variables, the empirical analyses compare minimum wage policy making in three countries—Germany, the UK, and the US—over a long time period. This chapter outlines the rationale behind the selection of the three countries, describes the process of gathering the data used in subsequent analyses, and gives an overview of how this data is used to analyze the role of scientific expertise in the three countries.

3.1 Case Selection: Minimum Wages in Germany, the United Kingdom, and the United States

The selection of countries to analyze follows a logic of similarities and differences. On the one hand, the three countries were chosen in a way to be similar enough to allow sensible comparisons. Thus, with Germany, the United Kingdom,

---

Electronic supplementary material The online version of this chapter (https://doi.org/10.1007/978-3-658-32746-0_3) contains supplementary material, which is available to authorized users.

F. Klein, *The Role of Scientific Expertise in Minimum Wage Policy Making*, Vergleichende Politikwissenschaft,
https://doi.org/10.1007/978-3-658-32746-0_3

and the United States, three liberal democracies with similar levels of economic development were chosen. All three countries have a country-wide minimum wage and, as will be detailed in Chapter 4, the minimum-wage policy subsystems of all three countries are populated by a similar set of actors and organizations. These can be grouped into advocacy coalitions along similar lines of conflict. On the other hand, the three countries differ in ways that provide variation for the explanatory variables of the theoretical model, such as the styles of using scientific expertise, the point in time when the minimum wage was first introduced, the degree of conflict within national minimum wage policy subsystems, and features of the expert discourse. Additional variance is generated through the over-time analysis. This section gives a short overview of minimum wage policy in the three countries and then summarizes the similarities and differences between them.

3.1.1 Minimum-Wage Policy Making in the United States

The United States first introduced a federal minimum wage with the Fair Labor Standards Act (FLSA) of 1938. Since then, the FLSA has been amended several times, with five amendments taking place within the period of analysis from 1970 to 2015. Besides increases in the nominal minimum wage, amendments often include changes in minimum wage coverage for specific worker groups, such as tipped employees or young people. The amendments do not follow a regular time table, but take place when political support from Congress and the President is strong enough. The political initiative for past minimum wage hikes has sometimes come from Congress and sometimes from the President. The time periods between minimum wage hikes have varied substantially, and there has been a considerable volatility in the real minimum wage. Besides the federal minimum wage, many States have additional minimum-wage laws setting higher wages than the federal minimum (Waltman, 2000).

Regarding national styles of using scientific expertise, the US is generally thought to be the archetype of the pluralistic (Renn, 1995), adversarial (Jasanoff, 2007) or advocatory (Straßheim, 2013) style. In this style, scientific expertise is mainly brought into the policy process by interested actors seeking arguments to bolster their policy preferences. While such broad generalizations do not necessarily apply to all issue areas to the same extent, there are two observations that suggest that this characterization also applies to the field of minimum wage policy. *First*, it has been suggested in the literature that there is an extraordinary high number of think tanks, often advocacy-oriented, active in the fields of social and economic policy in the US (Rich, 2001, 2004). This is echoed by the findings from Chapter 4, where it is shown that advocacy-oriented think tanks and research funded by interest groups plays an important role in the US minimum wage policy subsystem. *Second*, the non-partisan, often state-sponsored institutions which commission, conduct and summarize research for policy makers, and which are characteristic of consensual or corporatist styles, are less pronounced in the US minimum wage policy subsystem. Thus, while think tanks performing such roles, such as the American Enterprise Institute or the Brookings Institution (Rich, 2001), do exist in the US, they play a comparatively small role in the minimum wage policy process (see Chapter 4). With the Federal Minimum Wage Study Commission, a government body producing scientific advice on minimum wages briefly existed in the late 1970s and early 1980s, yet produced only one single report (Minimum Wage Study Commission, 1981). Another difference between the US and the two European countries is the level of conflict between the advocacy coalitions. The political divide between actors favoring and actors opposing higher minimum wages is sharper in the US (for a substantiation of this claim, see Chapter 4).

The fact that the minimum wage is an old policy in the US provides the opportunity of studying policy making over a long time, that is, from 1970 to 2015. The start date of 1970 was chosen because only a small number of scientific articles evaluating the effects of minimum wages was published before 1970. Thus, the analysis sets in at a time in which minimum wages started to receive increased scientific attention, making the use of minimum-wage related research by political actors more plausible. Moreover, the period of analysis from 1970 to 2015 is long enough to cover an important over-time development in the US expert discourse. While the evaluation of minimum wages in scientific research had long been unfavorable, a marked change occurred throughout the 1990s, with research providing a much more positive picture of minimum wages thereafter (see Chapter 5). This over-time change provides variation on a major explanatory variable. It might also have increased uncertainty among political actors, with new research results challenging long-held beliefs.

3.1.2 Minimum-Wage Policy Making in the United Kingdom

Britain introduced its first general minimum wage with the National Minimum Wage Act of 1998, continuing an older tradition of statutory wage regulation in some trades under the Wages Council system that existed between 1909 and 1993 (Metcalf, 1999). In contrast to the irregular amendments to the FLSA in the United States, adjustments of minimum-wage rates in the UK take place annually.

A central role in determining the magnitude of the yearly uprating is played by the Low Pay Commission (LPC). Established in 1997, this body consists of nine individuals, three of them with a background in trade unionism, three with a business background, two from academia, and a chair (Brown, 2009, p. 430). The commissioners enter the LPC as individuals rather than representatives, supposed to find a consensus rather than to negotiate for 'their' group. To do so, the LPC commissions research—over 70 studies had been financed by 2009 (Brown, 2009, p. 432)—and extensively consults individuals and organizations affected by the minimum wage (Metcalf, 1999; Brown, 2009). Based on the research and the consultations, the LPC regularly formulates recommendations to the government for the annual minimum wage increase. The government then sets the minimum wage rate. While it is not obliged to follow the LPC's recommendations, it has largely done so in the past (Brown, 2009).

In terms of the explanatory variables specified in the theoretical model from Chapter 2, minimum-wage policy making in the United Kingdom differs from the US in several ways. Thus, the style of using scientific expertise in the UK can be described as corporatist/consensual (Renn, 1995; Jasanoff, 2007). In countries thus characterized, the state plays a much larger role in providing scientific expertise in policy making, setting up institutions that commission, conduct or summarize research. In contrast to research by interested actors such as advocacy-oriented think tanks, this expertise is more suited to produce consensus about how to evaluate different policy alternatives. The central role of the Low Pay Commission in the process of setting the British National Minimum Wage is clear evidence that this characterization not only holds for the United Kingdom as a country, but also for the field of minimum wage policy.

Given that the National Minimum Wage was introduced only in 1998, the British case provides an opportunity to study the influence of the uncertainty of political actors about the effects of a minimum wage. Thus, this uncertainty was hypothesized to be higher in the years surrounding the first introduction of a minimum wage. The British case also differs from the US with respect to the coalition structure in the minimum wage policy subsystem. In the UK, there is less polarization between the coalitions in the minimum wage policy subsystem, with opposition to the minimum wage being less fundamental (a detailed presentation of the coalitions in the British minimum wage policy subsystem is provided in Chapter 4). Finally, as will be discussed in Chapter 5, the British expert discourse provides a much more favorable evaluation of different minimum wage effects than its US counterpart. Also, it does not exhibit the stark shift in the evaluation of minimum wage effects that is visible in the US expert discourse. Given that a general minimum wage did not exist in the UK up to the late 1990s, the period of analysis is shorter than for the US. It starts in 1990, shortly before the political debate about the introduction of a general minimum wage sets in, and ends in 2015.

3.1.3 Minimum-Wage Policy Making in Germany

Germany, which has had a relatively high percentage of workers covered by collective agreements for a long time (Ellguth and Kohaut, 2005), was the last of the three countries studies in this book to introduce a general minimum wage in 2015. Given the consent of both trade unions and employer organizations, the government has held the power to make collective agreements binding for all employers in (West) Germany since after World War II. However, this was and still is a tool relatively rarely used *(Allgemeinverbindlich-Erklärung*; see Bispinck and Schäfer, 2006, p. 276). In 1996, under the impression of the German construction industry being undercut by foreign competition, government's capacity to set a minimum wage was strengthened by the *Arbeitnehmer-Entsendegesetz*. The law allowed the federal government to make a minimum wage set by a collective agreement binding for all employees (Schulten and Bispinck, 2013, p. 762). While the *Arbeitnehmer-Entsendegesetz* was initially confined to the construction sector, it was extended to more sectors in subsequent years. In the early 2000s, trade unions and left-wing political party *Die Linke* began campaigning for a general minimum wage. Their cause was taken up by the Social Democrats in their federal election campaign of 2009, and the minimum wage became law in 2015 (Nowak, 2015). While the initial wage level of 8,50 Euros was set in a purely political manner, further increases are determined under the participation of the *Mindestlohnkommission*, a body consisting of three trade union and three employer representatives, a chair, and two researchers in advisory capacity but without voting rights. Every other year, the *Mindestlohnkommission* makes a proposal for the adjustment of the minimum wage, which the federal government may either accept or reject, but not alter. Moreover, the commission evaluates the effects of the minimum wage on the protection of workers, on unemployment and on the conditions of economic competition (Ring, 2015).

In terms of the context in which minimum wage policy making takes place, Germany is more similar to the British case than to the US. Germany is usually also considered to be a country with a consensual/corporatist style of using scientific expertise (Renn, 1995; Jasanoff, 2007). This characterization also extends to the field of minimum wage policy. With the *Mindestlohnkommission*, a body similar to the British Low Pay Commission was created in Germany, publishing its first evaluation of the effects of the German minimum wage in 2016 (Mindestlohnkommission, 2016). Even prior to the existence of the Mindestlohnkommission, state-sponsored, nonpartisan, and research-oriented think tanks and related institutions such as the Deutsches Institut für Wirtschaftsforschung, the Institut für Arbeitsmarkt- und Berufsforschung, or the German Council of Economic Experts played a major role in providing expertise to the actors in the German minimum wage policy subsystem (Thunert, 2001; see Chapters 4, 7).

Similar to the case of the UK, the period of analysis in Germany was chosen to cover the entire discussion leading to the introduction of a general minimum wage in Germany. Thus, it starts in 1992, shortly before the discussion about the introduction of a minimum wage in construction starts, and ends in 2015. Among others, this allows to study the effects of uncertainty connected to the introduction of a general minimum wage. The coalition structure in the German minimum wage policy subsystem resembles it British counterparts, the divide between supporters and critics of the minimum wage being less stark than in the US (see Chapter 4). The German expert discourse, which generally negatively evaluates minimum wages, exhibits strong over-time variance in its evaluation of minimum wage effects (see Chapter 5).

In sum, the countries selected for the analysis are similar enough to allow sensible comparisons. All three are economically advanced democracies in which minimum wages have been a political issue for at least 20 years. The periods of analysis were chosen in a way to cover this entire discussion, except for the US. Here, the analysis only starts in 1970, at a time in which minimum wage effects became a more important object of scientific research. In all three countries, the discussion about introducing or raising the minimum wage is linked to questions about minimum wage effects on employment and other variables. Finally, in all three countries, there is scientific research that potentially helps to assess those effects.

There are differences between the three countries that provide the necessary variance for the explanatory variables specified in the theoretical model. These differences concern the evaluation of minimum wages in the expert discourse, which is relatively positive in the UK and relatively negative in the US and Germany. There is also variation regarding the style of using scientific expertise, which is consensual/corporatist in the United Kingdom and Germany, and pluralistic in the US. While the US federal minimum wage was already introduced in 1938, the German and British national minimum wages are younger, thus allowing us to study the role that uncertainty related to a lack of experience with minimum wages plays for research utilization. Such uncertainty is also expected in times in which rapid changes in the scientific evaluation of minimum wages challenge established knowledge about minimum wage effects. Such shifts can be observed in Germany and the United States. Finally, there is variance in the coalition structure. The polarization between minimum wage supporters and critics is relatively high in the US and lower in Germany and the UK. Table 3.1 summarizes the comparative design of the study.

Table 3.1 Variables significant for case selection

	Germany	UK	US
Evaluation of minimum wages in the expert discourse	Mostly negative	Mostly positive	Mostly negative
Style of using scientific expertise	Consensual/corporatist	Consensual/corporatist	Pluralistic
Uncertainty I: minimum wage introduced in	1998	2014	1938
Uncertainty II: rapid shift in the expert discourse	Yes, early 2000s	No	Yes, 1990s
Coalition structure in the minimum wage policy subsystem	Unstable; mostly low polarization	Unstable; mostly low polarization	Stable; high polarization
Period of analysis	1992–2015	1990–2015	1970–2015

3.2 Two Data Sets

The main goal of the research presented in this book is to test the hypotheses specified in the theoretical model from Chapter 2. In the quantitative analyses in Chapters 4 to 6, this is done by combining two different data sets. The first one describes the expert discourse on minimum wages. This data was gathered by coding scientific articles evaluating minimum wage effects on employment, the economy, poverty, and other variables. The second data set describes the presence of scientific expertise in the media discourse, as well as the actors in the minimum wage policy subsystems of the three countries. It was created by coding newspaper articles about minimum wages that have appeared in the three countries. This section describes how the two data sets were created. Then, the ways in which the analyses from later chapters contribute to testing the hypotheses from the theoretical model are outlined.

3.2.1 First Data Set: The Expert Discourse on Minimum Wage Effects

3.2.1.1 Operationalization

In Chapter 2, the expert discourse on minimum wages was defined as the body of knowledge on minimum wages emanating from a communication process among scholars. The most important form of communication in this process is the publication of scientific studies in books, scientific journals, and conference articles. While a complete picture of the expert discourse would encompass analyzing all publication types, questions of availability had to be taken into account. Papers presented at conferences are usually not archived, and books—especially old ones—can be hard to obtain. The research presented in this book therefore concentrates on articles evaluating the effects of minimum wages that were published in scholarly journals.

Practical considerations aside, this restriction to scientific journal articles is based on the assumption that the articles published in scientific journals are a good representation of the entirety of research in the expert discourse. Scientific journals are among the most prestigious and most-read outlets for research, and it can be assumed that the most important research results discussed on scientific conferences will ultimately be published in scientific journals. Similarly, research results contained in monographs and edited volumes are often also—at least partly—published in scientific journals. Evidence underpinning these assumptions is provided later in this book. Chapter 5 shows that the expert discourse on minimum wages, as it is described by our data, is in line with accounts found in literature reviews on minimum wage effects. Chapter 7 shows that it is also in line with how political actors in Germany perceive the scientific evaluation of minimum wages.

Defining what a scholarly journal is can be tricky. Using definitions of (social) science like the one provided by King et al. (King, Keohane and Verba, 1994, pp. 7–8), one might come up with an ideal-type definition of a scholarly publication. It could be defined as a publication directed at making descriptive or explanatory inferences based on empirical information, which uses explicit and therefore reproducible methods of gathering and analyzing data to come to uncertain conclusions. The problem with such a definition remains that it necessarily rests fuzzy at its margins, making it hard to determine where exactly science begins. To avoid the problem of having to define for a large number of publications whether they are scientific or not, the search for scientific articles was carried out in Scopus and Web of Science, databases of scientific publications which are widely used in bibliographic research summarizing the scientific output on a given issue (Norris and Oppenheim, 2007; Almeida, Pais and Formosinho, 2009). Any article thus found was assumed to satisfy the standards of science.

Moreover, it had to be ensured that the expert discourse on minimum wage is operationalized in a way to include only research results that are potentially relevant for political actors willing to use scientific expertise. As minimum wage effects have been argued to depend on the level of economic development (Lustig and McLeod, 1996, pp. 63–66), only those scientific journal articles analyzing the effects of minimum wages in OECD countries were considered. Furthermore, as the theoretical model argues that the role of the domestic and the international expert discourse might differ, both concepts had to be operationalized. The *international* expert discourse contains all scientific articles researching minimum wage effects in at least one OECD country. The *domestic* expert discourse, for example of Germany, only includes those articles that are either authored by scholars affiliated with a German research institution, or that explicitly analyze minimum wage effects in Germany. This operationalization is intended to mirror the idea behind the concept of a domestic expert discourse. For those actors engaged in bringing scientific knowledge to actors into the minimum wage policy subsystem, research conducted in Germany or explicitly referring to Germany might be more visible, or more relevant.

3.2.1.2 Gathering Data

To find the articles, Scopus and Web of Science were searched for the terms "minimum wage*", "Mindestl*", and the word for minimum wage in several other European languages in article titles and abstracts. As individual journals in both databases are often covered for less than the entire period during which they were published, a second step was taken to complete the data. For all those journals from which articles on minimum wage effects were found in the first step, a separate search in other available online archives of these journals was conducted.

Of the articles thus found, only those published between 1965 and 2015 were retained, meaning that the time period for which scientific article data was gathered is a little longer than the period of analysis for the United States. This is because the variables describing the scientific evaluation of minimum wages used in the analyses of the following chapters are partly constructed using time lags and multi-year moving averages. For example, in Chapter 6, an actors' minimum wage preference in 1970 will be explained using scientific journal data from the years 1965 to 1969. Moreover, of the articles found, not all address minimum-wage effects. After sorting out those dealing with other subjects, the search yielded 376 articles which either had authors from a US research institution or analyzed data from the US, 112 articles which either had authors from a research institution in the UK or analyzed data from Britain, and 56 articles which either had authors from a research institution in Germany or analyzed data from there. For the international expert discourse, encompassing articles from those three and other countries, 730 articles were found. The number of articles in the sample increases over time. Only 46 of the articles were published between 1970 and 1980, comparing to 309 articles published between 2000 and 2010.

As the sample most probably does not include all relevant scientific journal articles on minimum wages, the question of potential biases arises. These relate to the concern that by searching journals listed in the Scopus and Web of Science databases, one does not draw a representative sample of all research on minimum wage effects published in scholarly journals. Two types of biases are relevant here. *First*, new publications might be more readily available in online archives than old ones. Given that the period of analysis for Germany and the UK only starts in the 1990s—a time period usually well covered in electronic archives—this problem mainly concerns research connected to minimum wages in the United States. To assess its gravity, one can look at how many journals in the sample were publishing articles before 1965 (the start of the analysis in the US), but electronically available only from 1966 or later. Thus, from the originally 888 journals in the sample, 216 were obviously not related to evaluating minimum wages in OECD countries, and therefore excluded from the analysis. Of the remaining 672 journals, the year in which the journal was first published could be determined for all but 40 journals. Of these 632 journals, 491 (78%) were available from 1965 or from the first year of publication. This suggests that, while parts of the over-time growth can be expected to originate from a biased sample, this effect should be relatively small and can by no means account for the strong rise in the number of articles published on minimum wage effects that occurred between the 1960s and the 2000s.

A *second* possible bias arises from uneven coverage of the three countries in the Scopus and Web of Science databases. Indeed, both databases have been noted to be more complete in their coverage of English-language journals from the United States and Britain than in their coverage of non-English journals from other countries (Norris and Oppenheim, 2007). To assess the gravity of this problem for Germany, the list of scientific journals from Germany from which articles were found in Scopus and Web of Science was compared to the more encompassing list of scientific journals in the economics discipline in Ulrich's Periodicals Directory (ProQuest, 2014). The comparison indicated that the relevant journals from Germany were well covered.

3.2.1.3 Coding

After the data had been gathered, the articles were coded. The text corpus for coding was the article abstract. The article itself was not regarded, except if the abstract indicated that the article contains results regarding minimum wage effects but did not specify these results. In this case, coding was done based on the article introduction and conclusion. The motivation behind restricting the text corpus to the abstract was to allow a single person to code several hundreds of scientific journal articles. This assumes that an article's most important results are contained in the abstract.

The restriction to an article's most central findings is also reflected in the way the abstracts were coded. Rather than capturing every nuance of an article's findings, the codebook aimed at grasping the basic message a political actor could take out of the research. For example, a seminal paper by Card and Krueger (Card and Alan B Krueger, 1993) compares employment in fast food restaurants in New Jersey and Pennsylvania before and after the minimum wage was raised in New Jersey from 4.25$ to 5.05$ in 1992. It finds that employment did not decline in New Jersey after the raise. The codebook does not capture the specifics of this research design: what regions and what professions were analyzed, by how much the minimum wage was raised, and so on. Instead, it grasps a more general message that could be taken from the article: A minimum wage hike in the US does not harm low-wage employment. This presupposes that experts and political actors perceive such results to be generalizable to a certain extent. This is not self-evident: The results from Card and Krueger do not eliminate the possibility that a much higher raise had led to job losses, or that other worker groups were harmed by the raise. The decision to treat the results as generalizable is based on two arguments. *First*, researchers themselves tend to engage in such generalizations. Thus, in the abstract of the paper, the authors claim that the results "challenge the prediction that a rise reduces employment" (Card and Alan B Krueger, 1993, p. 1). Similarly, a review of the literature on minimum wage effects on employment comes to the general conclusion that existing research supports "the conventional view that minimum wages reduce employment among low-skilled workers" (Neumark and W. Wascher, 2006, p. 122). *Second*, varying minimum wage effects under different circumstances might not be a problem in practice. Thus, even though it makes sense to assume that minimum wage raises of different sizes have different effects, the minimum wage raises that happen in the three countries, and on which the research results are typically based, are moderate in size. The question what effects minimum wage hikes to an extremely high level would have is therefore of little relevance, in research as well as in policy making. Circumstances varying between countries might be more relevant, in the sense that minimum wage effects might not be generalizable across countries. This problem, however, is alleviated by the fact that the analyses presented in this book divide the scientific research on minimum wages into national expert discourses, with empirical research in a domestic expert discourse mostly using data from the respective country.

Research results in the expert discourse are, therefore, treated as general statements about minimum wage effects. To capture those effects, the codebook records an article's evaluation of minimum-wage effects in 13 different categories, most of which have further subcategories: (1) minimum-wage effect on employment; (2) minimum-wage effect on unemployment; (3) minimum-wage effect on the hours worked by individual workers; (4) minimum-wage effect on wages; (5) minimum-wage effect on household incomes; (6) effect of minimum wages on prices and inflation; (7) minimum-wage effect on economic inequality; (8) minimum-wage effect on poverty; (8) minimum wage effect on economic efficiency or growth; (9) effect on economic welfare; (10) other, specified effects; (11) normative evaluation of minimum wages; (12) efficiency or effectiveness of minimum wages in reaching a specified goal compared to another policy. Moreover, bibliographical data such as publication years, author affiliation, and the name of the journal in which the article was published was recorded.

For each subcategory in categories 1 through 9, it was coded whether the article evaluated the relation between minimum wages and the respective variable. If it did, it was coded whether the relation was evaluated to be positive, nonexistent, or negative, and if it was explicitly stated to be strong or weak. For category 10, it was coded whether the other, specified effect was deemed to be desirable, nonexistent, or undesirable, and if it was deemed to be strong or weak. For category 11, it was coded whether minimum wages were judged to be normatively desirable, neutral, or undesirable, and if this was explicitly judged to be a strong or a weak normative argument. For category 12, it was coded whether minimum wages were superior, of equal value, or inferior to a specified alternative with regard to reaching a specified goal, and of the superiority or inferiority was explicitly judged to be weak or strong.

For the use in the empirical analyses of the following chapters, these categories were aggregated into broader categories describing minimum wage effects on employment and unemployment, poverty and inequality, economic growth and well-being, and other effects. The reason is that the presence of a very large number of categories and sub-categories makes it hard to characterize the overall evaluations and trends in the expert discourse. Moreover, a major part of the analyses of the subsequent chapters links the evaluation of minimum wage effects in the expert discourse to the evaluation of minimum wages and their effects by political actors, who express their beliefs in newspaper articles. The expression of these beliefs in newspaper articles is often rather broad, and is not well matched by the very detailed categories outlined above. The categories were therefore aggregated into the following variables.

The variable *employment* was created to capture minimum wage effects on employment and unemployment. To determine its value, the variables in the categories minimum wage effects on employment (category 1) and minimum wage effects on unemployment (category 2) were considered. If more desirable than undesirable minimum wage effects on employment and unemployment were found, employment was coded 1. If no effect was found, or if the number of desirable and undesirable effects equaled out, employment was coded 0. If more undesirable than desirable effects were found, the variable was coded −1. Doing so, effects evaluated to be strong were given double, effects evaluated as weak half weight. The same procedure was applied to form the other aggregate variables. The variable *poverty* was created to capture minimum wage effects on poverty and inequality, considering minimum wage effects on the income of poor workers (a subcategory of category 5), minimum wage effects on inequality (category 7), and minimum wage effects on poverty (category 8). The variable *economy* was created to capture minimum wage effects on the economy and economic welfare, considering the variables indicating minimum wage effect on inflation (category 6), economic efficiency or growth (category 8), and on economic welfare (category 9). Next, a category called *other effects*, collecting other minimum-wage effects which can be clearly determined to be desirable or undesirable, was created. For this variable, the codes for minimum wage effects on the incomes of groups other than poor people (a subcategory of category 5), other minimum wage effects (category 10), and the codes for the variable indicating whether the minimum wage is a better or worse alternative to reach a given goal (category 12) were considered. Finally, a fifth variable, *total effect*, was created to capture the overall evaluation of minimum wage effects in a scientific article. Therefore, the other four variables, employment, poverty, economy, and other effects, were added up. If the sum was larger than 0, total effect was coded 1, indicating that more desirable than undesirable effects were found; if it was 0, total effect was coded 0. If it was smaller than 0, total effect was coded −1.

3.2.1.4 Reliability Test

To test the reliability of the coding procedure, ten percent—76 randomly selected articles—of the original sample of scientific journal articles were re-coded several months after the original coding, and the results were compared. The idea behind this test was that to ensure that the coding instructions from the codebook were precise enough to allow one person to code an article in the same way if coded twice.[1]

The first way in which intra-coder reliability was tested was in terms of percentage agreement. The results from the two coding procedures were compared, and percentage agreements were computed by dividing the number of agreements by the total number of articles. This was done for all variables used in the analyses of the subsequent chapters, i.e. the variables describing the year in which the article was published and the national expert discourse to which it belongs, as well as the five aggregate variables described above. Except for the variable other effects, for which there is a percentage agreement of 86.7 percent, the percentage agreements range from 92 percent to 100 percent, indicating a high reliability of the coding procedure.

Percentage agreements, however, have been argued to be misleading (Krippendorff, 2004). For example, most scientific articles do not research minimum wage effects on the economy. An ignorant coder who, without reading any article at all, would code most articles in a way to indicate that it does not contain information about minimum wage effects on the economy, would therefore have a relatively high percentage agreement with a faithful coder. Therefore, values for Krippendorff's (2004) Alpha were computed, a reliability measure avoiding this problem by comparing the number of agreements between the two coders with the number of agreements expected from ignorant coders. Alpha ranges between −1 and 1, with 1 signifying perfect agreement, 0 signifying the amount of agreement between ignorant coders, and -1 signifying perfect disagreement. Alpha is a statistical measure: its precision is higher if many observations are used to conduct the intercoder reliability test, and if the variance of the variable being tested is high. Krippendorff suggests that the lower bound of the confidence interval of Alpha be at least .67 (Krippendorff, 2004).

[1] In contrast to an inter-coder reliability test, an intra-coder reliability does not allow inference on whether different people can understand the codebook in the same way. Therefore, it would have been desirable to also conduct an inter-coder reliability test. This was impossible due to the limited resources available for this project. The coding of the scientific articles requires significant knowledge in the economic literature on minimum wages, and the training of a third person to do the coding would have taken too much time.

The values for Krippendorff's Alpha are reported in Table 3.2. All point estimates are above the minimum required value of .67, although two variables—poverty and economy—are close to this limit. The confidence intervals, which were computed using a bootstrap procedure by Gruszczynski (2013), reach below .66 for four variables: poverty, economy, other effects, and the variable indicating whether an article is part of the German expert discourse or not. For the latter variable, this clearly seems to be related to the fact that only very few articles from the German expert discourse were in the sample for the intra coder reliability test, leading to a very wide confidence interval. Given that the alpha values for the United Kingdom and the United States are satisfactory, and that the coding procedure is the same for Germany, a valid coding procedure can be assumed with respect to this variable. For the other three variables, the too low lower bounds of the confidence intervals for Alpha seem to be a combination of a relatively low point estimate and a wide confidence interval.

As there is doubt regarding the reliability of the coding for the three variables poverty, economy and other effects, no important conclusions should be based on an analysis of these three variables. To avoid doing so, causal analyses of later chapters will either be based on the employment or on the total effect variables, for which coding reliability is high.[2]

3.2.1.5 Scale of Measurement

The measurement of the evaluation of minimum wages in a single scientific article from the expert discourse as described above is ordinal in scale. This means that the three values which were used to code an article's overall evaluation of the minimum wage can be brought into an order (−1: mostly undesirable effects are found; 0: desirable and undesirable effects are found, or no effect is found; 1: mostly desirable effects are found). The three values, however, cannot be interpreted in the sense that the distance between −1 and 0 equals the distance between 0 and 1.

This has consequences for how to deal with the data. Statistics textbooks often advocate an argument made by Stevens (1946), linking different measurement scales to different methods with which a particular type of data can be analyzed (Velleman and Wilkinson, 1993). Hence, when describing ordinal data, one should not use parametric statistical methods that assume equidistance between the values of a variable, such as means or regression analyses. Thus, in our case, if you do

[2]The three 'problematic' variables are used in some descriptive analyses designed to give a broad overview of the domestic and international expert discourses, where a slightly biased representation of the expert discourse due to inaccurate coding would not change the overall picture.

Table 3.2 Krippendorff's Alpha: results from the intracoder reliability test from coding scientific journal articles

Variable	Alpha (point estimate)	Upper Bound (95% CI)	Lower bound (95% CI)
year	1	n.d.[a]	n.d.
employment	.93	1	.85
poverty	.75	.91	.56
economy	.69	.90	.41
other effects	.68	.84	.49
totaleffect	.94	1	.86
Germany	.83	1	0
United Kingdom	.93	1	.75
United States	.95	1	.86

[a]The computation of bootstrapped confidence intervals for Alpha is not possible if the agreement between the two coding runs is 100 percent.

not know whether the distance between an evaluation of the minimum wage coded −1 and an evaluation coded 0 is the same as the distance between an evaluation coded 0 and an evaluation coded 1, you cannot claim that the "average" of two evaluations in scientific journal articles, one coded with −1 and one coded with 1, equals 0.

Even though it is prominent in textbooks, this argument is often refuted. In practice, ordinal data is frequently described using means and standard deviations, and often enters regression analyses as a variable. Common examples are data derived from questionnaires using Likert scales (Norman, 2010), or levels of democratization (e.g. Barro, 1996). Theoretically, this approach is underpinned by the argument that, while using parametric methods on ordinal data is wrong strictly speaking, measures such as means, correlations and regression coefficients are usually pretty robust to the violation of the assumption that the data needs to be at least interval in scale (Norman, 2010). Discarding such measures for ordinal data, from this perspective, potentially means ignoring parts of the available information, thus leading to a less efficient estimation (Borgatta and Bohrnstedt, 1980).

Instead of taking sides in this debate, the statistical analyses presented in later chapters accommodate both sides of the argument. Thus, where statistical measures are used to describe the expert discourse, this will usually be done by describing the whole distribution of the data (that is, the percentages of −1's, 0's and 1's). Where this is not possible, for example when variables describing the average evaluation of minimum wages in the expert discourse enter regression analyses, this average evaluation is computed in two different ways. On the one hand, it is computed by taking the mean evaluation of minimum wages in the expert discourse. On the other hand, and in line with Stevens' reasoning, the average is computed as the fraction of scientific journal articles in the expert discourse that do not find undesirable minimum wage effects. As will be seen, both types of analyses deliver very similar results (see Chapters 5, 6).

3.2.2 Second Data Set: Media Discourse and Minimum Wage Policy Subsystems

The second data set used in the empirical analyses throughout this book describes the media discourse on minimum wages and gives insights into the minimum wage policy subsystems in the three countries. This data was collected by coding newspaper articles on minimum wages.

3.2.2.1 Selecting Articles

To collect those articles, a search was conducted in six newspapers, selected in a way to include two quality papers—one center left, the other center-right—for each country: *Frankfurter Allgemeine Zeitung* and *Süddeutsche Zeitung* for Germany; *The Guardian* and *The Times* for the UK; and *The New York Times* and *The Wall Street Journal* for the United States. Digital archives of those newspapers were searched for the words "minimum wage" and "minimum wages" (for the newspapers from the United States and the United Kingdom) or "Mindestlohn" and "Mindestlöhne" (for the German newspapers) in the article headlines. For the US newspapers, the search was conducted for the time period between 1970 and 2015. For the newspapers from Germany, the search was conducted for the time period between 1992 and 2015; for the UK, the search was conducted for the years from 1990 to 2015.

This search delivered a total of 2825 articles, which is a wealth of empirical material, but too much to code with the available resources. Instead of reducing the number of years to be analyzed (and thus reducing the possibilities of a long-term analysis of the role of expert discourses in minimum-wage policy making), the strategy chosen to reduce the number of articles to code was to draw a random sample from the population of articles. The articles that were coded were randomly selected so that four articles from each year and each newspaper are in the sample. If the population of articles from a given newspaper in a year was less than four, all of the available articles were coded. This gave a total of 635 articles in the sample.

3.2.2.2 Coding

For the coding, a coding scheme from Heikkila et al. (2016) was adapted in a way to fit the purposes of this book. The basic principle of the coding scheme is to code each political actor mentioned in an article, together with the actor's position and expressed beliefs on minimum wages. For example, the topic of a newspaper article might be a party congress of Germany's Social Democratic Party (SPD). In the article, several politicians from that party may be cited with statements including information about their position towards minimum wages. For example, politician A, member of the SPD, may be cited with the words: "I support the introduction of a minimum wage". Another politician, B, of the same party, might be reported to have criticized A, claiming that a minimum wage would be a bad idea because it would increase unemployment. In this case, two actors would be coded: A, member of the SPD, supports the minimum wage; B, member of the SPD, opposes the minimum wage, believes a minimum wage increases unemployment. As can be seen, each actor is assigned an organizational affiliation. If an actor is reported to have several affiliations—for example a member of the SPD and Minister of Labour and Social Affairs—he or she is coded twice, once as a party representative, and once as a representative of the Labour ministry. Actors without organizational affiliation and actors only vaguely referred to (e.g. "most Social Democrats think…", in contrast to "the Social Democratic Party thinks…") were not coded. An exception to this rule were vague references to scientific research and researchers ("economists generally believe…"), which were coded as being a statement referring to the (fictional) organization *Research*. In addition to the organizational association of an actor, the type of organization, such as trade union, national government, or political party was coded. The number of actors coded varies strongly between articles. In the 635 articles coded, a total of 2945 non-unique actors were identified.

For each actor, several variables describing his or her position towards minimum wages were coded. A first group of variables describes overall approval of minimum wages, ranging from *pro-minimum wage* if an actor supports the introduction of a minimum wage or, if a minimum wage already exists, raising the minimum wage; *middle/neutral towards minimum wage*, if an actor supports introducing or raising a minimum wage, but wants a lower minimum wage than another actor mentioned in the same article; and *anti-minimum wage*, if an actor opposes introducing or raising the minimum wage, or wants to abolish or lower an existing minimum wage. The reason that opposition to a higher minimum wage is put into the same category as the more radical positions of lowering or abolishing the minimum wage is that, given inflation, sustained opposition to raising the minimum wage over longer time periods is equivalent to lowering and, finally, to abolishing the minimum wage. A second group of variables describes statements of an actor regarding the effect of a minimum wage on employment: *employment risk*, which was coded 1 if an actor stated that minimum wage reduced employment or increased unemployment and 0 otherwise, *employment benefit*, which was coded 1 if an actor stated that minimum wage increased employment or decreased unemployment; *employment risk min*, which was coded 1 if an actor stated that a minimum wage poses no or only a small risk for employment; and *employment benefit min*, if an actor stated that a minimum wage has little or no benefits with regard to employment. The same logic of (minimal) risks and (minimal) benefits was also applied to four further groups of variables describing what an actor stated regarding minimum wage effects on the economy, effects on poverty and economic inequality, and on the normative implications of minimum wages.

The analyses in later chapters will rarely refer to the variables in the codebook as such. Rather than looking at three variables specifying whether an actor supports minimum wages, opposes them or takes a middle position, most analyses use a single, aggregate variable telling us an actor's stance towards minimum wages. This new variable, *minimum wage stance*, takes the value 1 if an actor supports the minimum wage, 0, if the actor takes a neutral stance, and −1 if he or she opposes the minimum wage. In a similar procedure, variables describing an actor's expressed beliefs regarding the normative desirability of minimum wages and their effects on employment, the economy, and poverty were constructed. These aggregate the four variables on each of the subjects (e.g. Employment Benefit, Employment Risk, Employment Risk Min, Employment Benefit Min) into a single variable ranging from 1 (desirable effect on employment) to −1 (undesirable effect on employment).

3.2.2.3 Reliability Tests

3.2.2.3.1 Intercoder Reliability

The coding of the newspaper articles was done by the author of this book. To test the reliability of the coding, a double strategy was chosen. First, at the beginning of the coding, an intercoder reliability test was conducted. To this end, 14 articles from different newspapers and different time periods were drawn from the sample and coded independently by the author and another coder, giving data on 110 (coder A) and 106 (coder B) actors and their expressed beliefs regarding minimum wages. As some actors identified by A were not coded by B and vice versa, the total number of actors coded is 118. Coder A identified 94.9 percent of these 118 actors, coder B 89.7 percent, which were taken to be satisfactorily values. For those actors who were identified by both coders, another set of analyses was conducted. These test to what degree the coding of those variables describing an actor's overall support of minimum wages and his or her beliefs regarding the effects of minimum wages on poverty, the economy, and employment, as well as their normative desirability, overlapped between the two coders. Percentage agreements for each variable range from 91 percent to 100 percent, signifying a high degree of agreement between the two coders.

Table 3.3 Alpha values of aggregate variables

Variable	Alpha (point estimate)	Upper Bound (95% CI)	Lower Bound (95% CI)
Minimum wage stance	0.94	0.99	0.88
employment Effect	0.98	1	0.93
economic Effect	0.94	1	0.67
poverty Effect	0.60	1	−0.13

Similar to the procedure for the intra-coder reliability test of the scientific article data, values for Krippendorff's (2004) Alpha were computed for the aggregated variables. As can be seen in Table 3.3, the point estimates are above .90 for the variables minimum wage stance, employment effect, and economic effect, and the lower bounds of the confidence intervals are at .67 or above for all three variables. In contrast, for the variable poverty effect, the point estimate is lower and the confidence interval is very large, indicating that the test sample did not include enough statements by political actors regarding the effects of minimum wages on poverty to make a claim about the reliability of the coding procedure.

3.2.2.3.2 Drift

In addition to analyzing whether the coding instructions were precise enough to allow two different coders to come to similar results when coding the same articles, a second test was conducted to ensure the consistency of the coding process over the whole period of coding, which took about one month. To that end, the same articles used to conduct the intercoder reliability test described above were coded a second time at the end of the coding period. Thus, they were coded by the same person—the author of this book—twice.

In general, the results suggest a high consistency of coding over time. Regarding the identification of actors, in the first run, 89 percent of all actors coded in the two runs combined were identified; in the second run, 98 percent of all actors coded in the two runs combined were found. While indicating a relatively high level of consistency, this suggests that a slight drift might have happened in the sense that coding an actor became more likely over time. With regard to those variables describing an actor's beliefs regarding minimum wage effects and the desirability of minimum wages, over-time percentage agreements are very high, ranging from 95.9 percent to 100 percent. Again, the Alpha values for the aggregate variables were computed (see Table 3.4). All values are very high and suggest very little drift over the period of coding.

Table 3.4 Alpha values for the drift test, aggregate variables

Variable	Alpha (point estimate)	Upper Bound (95% CI)	Lower Bound (95% CI)
Minimum wage stance	0.96	1	0.92
employment Effect	0.96	1	0.86
economic effect	1	n.d.[a]	n.d.
poverty effect	1	n.d.	n.d.

[a]The confidence intervals cannot be computed via bootstrapping when the agreement between the two coding runs is 100 percent.

3.2.2.3.3 Reliability Tests of Newspaper Data: Summary

Overall, the reliability tests presented above suggest that the data gathered in the newspaper analysis can be used for further analyses. Regarding intercoder reliability, percentage agreements are high to very high. Regarding Krippendorff's Alpha, the results also point to a generally high level of intercoder reliability. For the variable describing an actor's beliefs regarding the effects of minimum wages on poverty, no clear assessment of the intercoder reliability was possible, as this variable was not coded often enough in the test sample. Moreover, the results for the drift analysis suggest that coding over time was largely consistent. All in all, the results of the reliability tests suggest that the newspaper data set can be used for further analyses, with the possible exception of the poverty effect variable.

3.2.2.4 Actor Preferences: Scale of Measurement

Describing the evaluation of minimum wages by actors in minimum wage policy subsystems involves challenges similar to the ones encountered when describing the evaluation of minimum wages in the expert discourse. As the expert discourse data, the data on political actors' evaluation of the minimum wage is ordinal in nature. In dealing with this problem, the same approach as the one described above for the expert discourse data is used.

First, to describe the data, the full distribution of views towards the minimum is used where possible. *Second*, the average evaluation of the minimum wage by political actors will enter one regression analysis in Chapter 6, testing whether the preferences of political actors shape expert opinion. Similar to what was discussed above, both the mean and an alternative measure based on the percentage of actors supporting the minimum wage are used. *Third*, the evaluation of the minimum wage by political actors is the dependent variable in several analyses. Here, regression methods designed for ordinal dependent variables are appropriate.

3.2.2.5 One Data Set, Two Uses

In the following analyses, the data gathered from the newspaper articles is used in two different ways: to describe the media discourse on minimum wages and to describe minimum wage policy subsystems. The former use of the data amounts to analyzing *how* newspapers report on minimum wages, the latter use is about analyzing the *actors* that newspapers write about.

3.2.2.5.1 Using the Newspaper Data to Analyze the Media Discourse

The theoretical model developed in the previous chapter specified hypotheses relating to two different features of the media discourse: The *first* one is how frequently the mass media reports on minimum wages, that is, how high minimum wages are on the media agenda. In Chapter 6, this variable will be operationalized by counting the number of articles found for a given year when searching the archives of the abovementioned newspapers. The *second* feature is to what degree the media discourse includes scientific information on the effects of minimum wages. In Chapter 5, this variable is operationalized by counting the number of times newspaper articles cite minimum wage scholars or their research. In both cases, therefore, the focus is on *how* newspapers report on minimum wages.

An obvious problem with this approach is that it equates the media discourse with quality newspaper reporting, ignoring other channels such as tabloids or television. These other channels' coverage of minimum wage policy making is likely to systematically differ from quality newspapers, for example in being less detailed and giving less room to scientific expertise. While the limitation to newspapers was necessary given the limited amount of resources available for this research, it is important to keep in mind that only a part of the media discourse was analyzed when interpreting the results of subsequent analyses. Thus, the fact that quality newspapers frequently write about minimum wage research tells us something about how much information about scientific research reaches these newspapers' readers. It does not necessarily tell us something about people relying on television to get information about minimum wage politics and policy.

3.2.2.5.2 Using the Newspaper Data to Analyze Minimum Wage Policy Subsystems

The second use of the data gathered from newspaper articles is to analyze the actors newspapers write about. For this, two kinds of information from newspaper articles are used: *First*, by counting which actors are mentioned how often in newspaper articles, newspaper reporting is used to identify the most important actors in the minimum wage policy subsystem. *Second*, the newspaper data is used to identify the different beliefs and preferences political actors hold regarding the minimum wage.

This method of mapping minimum wage subsystems by analyzing the content of newspaper articles has strengths as well as it has weaknesses. The main strength is that the method allows a look into the past, making it possible to identify actors in a policy subsystem as well as their policy-oriented beliefs for past years and over long time periods. While surveys among political actors, which have been used in other research (e.g. Weible and Sabatier, 2009) arguably allow a more detailed look into policy subsystems, they are costlier and can only capture the present, not the past. On the other hand, analyzing minimum-wage policy subsystems through a content analysis of newspaper articles brings about two problems worth discussing here.

The *first* problem is that newspapers are no perfect mirror of reality, thus making it difficult to identify the most important actors in minimum wage policy subsystems by simply counting how often they appear in newspaper articles. This problem is related to the gate-keeping function of the media. Unable to report everything about every issue there is, newspapers each day have to select a relatively small number of news to report, and can only cover certain aspects of each news item (Shoemaker and Riccio, 2015). As this selection happens according to criteria such as those determining the news value of an event, the representation of minimum wage policy subsystems in the news media can be supposed to systematically differ from the original subsystems. Some actors could be selected not because they play a particularly important role in the minimum wage policy subsystem, but based on their positions towards minimum wages. For example, a typical statement in an article from a US newspaper on congressional votes on a minimum-wage related law is that, while most Democrats voted for a proposed minimum wage hikes, Democratic Representatives A and B voted against it. This kind of reporting makes sense from a news-value perspective. However, it results in a biased representation of the position of the Democratic party when coding it according to the coding scheme presented above. Thus, while the actual situation is that most Democrats support the minimum wage, coding the statement leaves us with the information that two Democracts—A and B—oppose the increase. Whereas it is necessary to keep in mind that there are likely differences between the policy subsystem and its representation in newspaper articles, this problem does not gravely distort the picture of minimum wage policy subsystems painted in this book. Thus, the qualitative analysis from Chapter 7 as well as the comparison of coalition structures identified in Chapter 4 with available knowledge about minimum wage minimum wage policy making in the three countries suggest a match between the data gathered from newspaper articles and the actual minimum wage policy subsystems.

The *second* problem is rooted in the fact that the actors making statements about minimum wages in a newspaper article may not be sincere. For example, when an employer organization rejects a minimum wage hike saying that this would increase unemployment, the true reason for the organization to oppose a rising minimum wage might be to avoid higher costs for its members. In other words, the statement that minimum wages threaten employment might be instrumental and not reflect the actor's true beliefs. When dealing with information from newspaper articles, one should therefore keep in mind that one is dealing with expressed beliefs, which are not necessarily an actor's true beliefs. Again, however, the qualitative interviews conducted with political actors in Germany which are presented in Chapter 7 suggest that the data gathered from newspaper articles generally convey an accurate picture of an actor's beliefs and preferences regarding the minimum wage.

3.3 Conclusion

In this chapter, the comparative design of this study and two main data sets on which the analysis of the role of scientific expertise in minimum wage policy making is based were presented. In the following chapters, the two data sets will be analyzed and combined in different ways to test the hypotheses specified in the theoretical model. Analyses of the frequency with and the ways in which scientific expertise is present in the media discourse are presented in Chapter 5. Given that the theoretical model specifies connections between the expert discourse and the presence of scientific expertise in the media discourse—for example, expertise is supposed to be more visible in newspapers when more scientific studies on minimum wages are published—these analyses partly connect both data sets. Chapter 6 mostly presents analyses of the influence of the expert discourse on the beliefs and preferences of actors in minimum wage policy subsystems. Again, this requires connecting data on the expert discourse with data gathered from newspaper articles.

Throughout this chapter a number of claims were made on which the methodological design of this research project hinges. *On the one hand*, these concern the way minimum wage policy is made in the three countries: Are the arguments relevant in the three countries for supporting or opposing higher minimum wages comparable? Do Germany, the United Kingdom and the US vary as claimed regarding the coalition structure in minimum wage policy subsystems and the style of using scientific expertise? *On the other hand*, the claims concern the validity of the two main data sets used in this book: Is the data gathered from newspaper articles a valid measure for describing minimum-wage policy subsystems, and is the data gathered from scientific journal articles a valid measure for describing the expert discourse on minimum wages?

Information substantiating the first set of claims, concerning the way minimum wage policy is made in the three countries, is provided in Chapter 4. Analyzing data from newspaper articles, this chapter provides background knowledge on the minimum wage policy subsystems of the three countries, arguing that the minimum-wage policy making in Germany, the United Kingdom and the United States is characterized by the set of differences and similarities on which the comparative design presented in this chapter is based.

The second set of claims, relating to the validity of the two data sets, is tested in Chapter 7, which presents a qualitative analysis of the German minimum wage policy subsystem between 2003 and 2012. Chapter 7 demonstrates that the two datasets measure what they are intended to measure, and provide an opportunity to test whether implications of the causal pathways presumed to be behind the correlations found in Chapter 6 can be observed. The design of the qualitative analysis is discussed in Chapter 7.

4 Minimum wage policy subsystems in Germany, the United Kingdom, and the United States

Before multivariate analyses linking expert discourses to actors in the minimum-wage subsystems can be conducted, it is important to get a deeper understanding of the minimum-wage policy subsystems each of the three countries. To do so, this Chapter analyzes the data gathered from newspaper articles.

4.1 The US Minimum-Wage Policy Subsystem

Of the three countries in the sample, the United States were the first to introduce a general, national minimum wage. In 1970, the start date of the empirical analysis, the introduction of the federal minimum wage lies already more than 30 years in the past. As will be shown below, this translates in a stable coalition structure within the US minimum wage policy subsystem. The polarization between the two main coalitions is strong, and advocacy-oriented think tanks stand out among the actors providing scientific expertise to the other actors in the minimum-wage policy subsystem.

4.1.1 Actors

The literature usually describes minimum-wage policy in the US as a partisan issue with two advocacy coalitions. Accordingly, on the one hand, there is a coalition pressing for higher minimum wages, consisting of trade unions and Democratic politicians. On the other hand, there is a coalition with business organizations and Republican politicians at its core, trying to prevent minimum wage

F. Klein, *The Role of Scientific Expertise in Minimum Wage Policy Making*, Vergleichende Politikwissenschaft,
https://doi.org/10.1007/978-3-658-32746-0_4

raises. When it comes to Congressional voting, the lines between the two coalitions tend to be blurred, with Democratic Representatives and Senators from the South sometimes voting against minimum wage raises. Likewise, their Republican counterparts from regions with strong trade unions sometimes vote with the majority of Democrats (Levin-Waldman, 1998).

The results of the empirical analysis tally with this general picture. In the whole sample of articles, a total of 451 unique organizations—like the Democratic Party or the Chamber of Commerce—were coded to be a part of the US minimum wage policy subsystem. Most of these actors, however, appear only once or twice in the data set, suggesting that they do not play a significant role in the subsystem. Focusing on those organizations that were coded at least five times, one is left with 40 organizations, which are listed in Table 4.1. While, as discussed in the previous chapter, the number of appearances in newspaper articles should not be taken as an exact measure of an actor's importance in the US minimum wage policy subsystem, the table can provide us with a rough overview of who are the relevant actors.

The actors can be grouped into a small number of categories. The by far most important organizations are the two major political parties, reflecting the fact that it is common for newspaper articles on minimum wages to report how Republican and Democratic politicians position themselves towards the issue. The second largest group are government agencies, such as the Department of Labor, the Federal Reserve Board, and the Bureau of Labor Statistics. These often enter the debate by providing background information, such as a statistic on how many people get the minimum wage, without explicitly taking sides, but, at other times, advocate raising or not raising the minimum wage. A third group comprises most presidents in office during the period of analysis. The fourth group are Congress members from both parties, often sponsors or prominent opponents of minimum-wage legislation. Fifth, interest groups are prominently featured in the subsystem, such as the American Federation of Labor—Congress of Industrial Organizations (AFL-CIO), or the Chamber of Commerce of the United States.

A sixth group of actors are what will be called research-related actors from here on. These are actors providing scientific expertise on minimum wages, such as researchers working at universities and other research institutions, or actors related to think tanks and other bodies engaged in providing research-based policy advice. With regard to the US minimum wage policy subsystem, the most important research-related actors are think tanks Employment Policies Institute, Economic Policy Institute, and Fiscal Policy Institute, individual researchers Alan Krueger, David Card, David Neumark, Lawrence Katz and Sar A. Levitan, and government-related advisory bodies Federal Minimum Wage Study Commission,

Table 4.1 Actors in the US minimum wage policy subsystem

Actor (Abbreviation)	Times counted	Actor (Abbreviation)	Times counted	Actor (Abbreviation)	Times counted
Democratic Party (DEM)	164	Federal Minimum Wage Study Commission (FMWSC)	12	Representative Dick Armey (RDA)	7
Republican Party (REP)	152	President George Bush Senior (PGBS)	12	Bureau of Labor Statistics (BLS)	6
Department of Labor (DOL)	61	David Neumark (DNE; Researcher)	11	National Federation of Independent Businesses (NFIB)	6
President Bill Clinton (PBC)	43	Representative Augustus F. Hawkins (RAH)	11	New York Governor Andrew M. Cuomo (NYGAC)	6
AFL-CIO (AFL)	31	New York Times (NYT)	10	Senator Bob Dole (SBD)	6
Senator Edward M. Kennedy (SEK)	30	President Jimmy Carter (PJC)	10	Wal-Mart (WAMA)	6
President Ronald Reagan (PRR)	24	President George Bush Junior (PGBJ)	9	Council of Economic Advisors (COA)	5
Chamber of Commerce of the United States (COC)	23	Representative John H. Dent (RJD)	9	Fiscal Policy Institute (FPI)	5
Federal Reserve Board (FED)	20	Senator Orrin Hatch (SOH)	9	New York Assemblyman Sheldon Silver (NYASS)	5

(continued)

Bureau of Labor Statistics, and Council of Economic Advisors. Some of these research-related actors are related to interest groups. The Employment Policies

Table 4.1 (continued)

Actor (Abbreviation)	Times counted	Actor (Abbreviation)	Times counted	Actor (Abbreviation)	Times counted
President Richard Nixon (PRN)	18	Lawrence Katz (LKA; Researcher)	8	Representative Dennis Hastert (RDH)	5
Employment Policies Institute (EPI)	17	National Restaurant Association (NRA)	8	Senator Harrison A. Williams (SAW)	5
Alan Krueger (AKR; Researcher)	14	Sar A. Levitan (SAL; Researcher)	8	Senator Trent Lott (STL)	5
David Card (DCA; Researcher)	14	Department of the Treasury (DOT)	7		
President Barack Obama (PBO)	14	Economic Policy Institute (ECONPI)	7		

Institute has ties to the restaurant industry, while the Economic Policy Institute and the Fiscal Policy Institute are linked to the labor movement (Lipton, 2014). David Neumark, an economist at University of California, Irvine, has received support for several of his papers from the Employment Policies Institute (Neumark and Wascher, 1995, 2007; Neumark, Salas and Wascher, 2013). Alan Krueger has co-edited a book published by the Economic Policy Institute (Mishel *et al.*, 2002). The high visibility of these actors is in line with a pluralistic/adversarial style of using scientific expertise in the US minimum wage policy subsystem. At the same time, the three government-related organizations are more in line with what would be expected under a consensual/corporatist style. However, the most visible among them, the Federal Minimum Wage Study Commission, only existed from 1977 to 1981 (Neumark and W. L. Wascher, 2006, p. 2). The Bureau of Labor Statistics is cited with background data (such as the number of workers directly affected by a minimum wage hike) in the newspaper articles, but not with statements evaluating the effects of minimum wages.

4.1.2 Coalition Structure

The actors in the minimum wage policy subsystem can be clustered into coalitions connected by common beliefs about the desirability and effects of minimum wages. To get a first impression of the coalition structure, it is instructive to look at support for the minimum wage by each actor in the policy subsystem.

Table 4.2 lists those actors and organizations in the US minimum wage policy subsystem for whom at least five statements regarding their support for the minimum wage were coded, using the abbreviations from Table 4.1.[1] For most actors, a clear tendency for or against higher minimum wages is visible. Among those actors strongly opposing higher minimum wages are interest groups such as the Chamber of Commerce, the National Federation of Independent Businesses, and the National Restaurant Association, as well as the Federal Reserve Bank and some individual Republican Members of Congress. Among those actors most strongly supporting the minimum wage are the trade union federation American Federation of Labor—Congress of Industrial Organizations and individual Democratic Members of Congress. There are few actors and organizations that have opposed the minimum wage in some instances and supported in others, among them being actors connected to the Republican Party, President George Bush Junior and actors connected to the Democratic Party. In general, the executive branch of Government—presidents and labor departments—populates the more moderate regions in the middle of the table. As can be seen, only one of the researchers from Table 4.1 is included, reflecting the fact that scholars are often quoted in newspapers with statements about minimum wage effects, but rarely explicitly take sides in the minimum wage debate.

Besides the overall stance of an actor towards the minimum wage, the actors' assessments of minimum wage effects on poverty, employment, the economy, as well as their normative evaluation of the minimum wage were coded. This data provides an overview of which arguments are of most concern when it comes to raising the minimum wage. Not every time an actor is mentioned in a newspaper article, information regarding the actor's beliefs regarding the minimum wage effects is given. Out of the 1428 times an actor from the US was mentioned in the newspaper articles in the sample, information about the actor's expressed beliefs regarding minimum wage effects was given in 564 cases. Out of all expressions

[1] In this table, the observations regarding the Department of Labor were split up according to the President at the time at which their statement regarding their support for minimum wages was made. It appears twice, once under President Ronald Reagan (DOL PRR), and once under President Bill Clinton (DOL PBC).

Table 4.2 Support for the minimum wage by the most important actors in the US minimum wage policy subsystem. For the meaning of actor abbreviations, see Table 4.1

Actor	Oppose higher minimum wage (%)	Mixed Position (%)	support higher minimum wage (%)
COC	100	0	0
FED	100	0	0
NFIB	100	0	0
NRA	100	0	0
RDA	100	0	0
SOH	89	11	0
EPI	89	11	0
DOL PRR	86	14	0
SBD	80	20	0
PRR	78	22	0
PJC	67	33	0
PRN	60	40	0
REP	57	25	19
PGBS	33	67	0
NYT	30	0	70
NYASS	20	20	60
PGBJ	17	67	17
DEM	7	10	83
DOL PBC	0	36	64
PBC	0	33	67
RJD	0	11	89
PBO	0	8	92
AFL	0	0	100
SAL	0	0	100
SEK	0	0	100
SHW	0	0	100

of beliefs regarding minimum wage effects, assessments of effects on employment are most common, and were voiced in 380 cases. Effects on the economy were discussed 179 times and effects on poverty 133 times. Explicit normative evaluations of the minimum wage were rare and only happened 30 times. Moreover, a closer look at the data suggests that some actors are more likely to express beliefs regarding minimum-wage effects than others. Researchers are less likely to take explicit positions regarding the overall desirability of minimum wages but are very likely to make statements about their effects, especially on employment. Actors from political parties, on the other hand, are much less likely to do so.

To identify the coalition structure of the US minimum wage policy subsystem, a hierarchical cluster analysis is performed (Jain, Murty and Flynn, 1999). The clustering, visualized in the dendogram in Figure 4.1, is based on all statements regarding the desirability or effects of minimum wages captured by the coding scheme. It includes those actors from Table 4.1 for which at least five such statement were coded. As can be seen, the results are similar to the ones depicted in Table 4.1, which is based on the support for minimum wages only. Thus, cutting the dendogram (somewhat arbitrarily) at a height of .06 (Everitt *et al.*, 2010), one is left with three belief coalitions.[2] The pro-minimum wage coalition on the left-hand side of the plot largely corresponds to the actors supporting the minimum wage in the lower half of Table 4.1, while the anti-minimum wage coalition on the right-hand side of the dendogram corresponds to the actors opposing the minimum wage in the upper part of Table 4.1. The Presidents Carter, Bush Senior, Clinton and Bush Junior, who were identified as having moderate positions towards the minimum wage above, form a moderate group of their own. Given that they were President at different points in time, it does not make sense to designate this group as a coalition; we will treat them as an unconnected group of actors instead. Two actors, the FED and SAL, do not fit into this coalition structure.

4.1.3 Coalition Beliefs

To get a better idea of what beliefs are constitutive for each of these three groups, Table 4.3 shows how often actors from the two coalitions and the presidential group were coded with different statements about minimum wages. The table reports only those variables which were coded often enough to make some contribution to the coalition structure. As can be seen, the overall stance towards minimum wages coincides with the evaluation of minimum wage effects. When

[2] As discussed in Chapter 2, the term advocacy coalition presupposes some form of collaboration between the actors in one coalition, trying to further common policy goals. As this collaboration cannot be analyzed here, we use the term belief coalition instead, indicating that these actors are bound together by common beliefs, but that we do not have information on whether they cooperate to further their common goals (Weible and Sabatier, 2009).

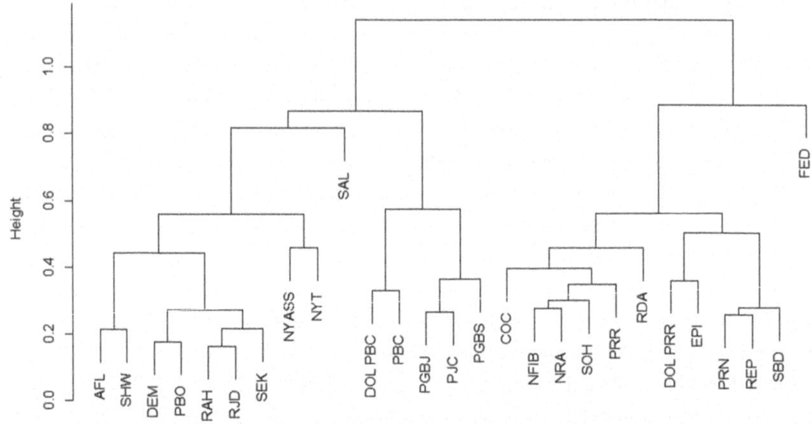

Figure 4.1 Dendogram of the coalition structure in the US minimum-wage policy subsystem, taking into account all coded variables and all actors included in Figure 4.1; distance measure: average Euclidean distance between clusters. For abbreviations, see Table 4.1

compared to actors in the Anti Coalition, the average actor in the Pro Coalition is more likely to take a positive overall stance towards minimum wage raises and to underline the poverty benefits of such raises. Actors in this coalition also frequently minimize negative employment effects of the minimum wage and claim that the minimum wage is normatively desirable and has little economic risks or even has economic benefits. The beneficial impact on poverty is the most common argument made actors in this coalition to support minimum-wage raises. On the other side, the average member of the Anti Coalition takes a negative stance towards minimum wage raises, and is more likely to underline the undesirable side effects of minimum wages. These relate to poverty, employment, and the economy. Moreover, actors in this coalition do not see the minimum wage as normatively desirable. The most important argument for actors in this group brought forth against minimum wage hikes are the employment risks of minimum wages, followed by negative side effects on the economy. Finally, the members of the third group find themselves between the other two coalitions. They are relatively rarely in outright opposition against minimum wage hikes, but often take a neutral position or no position at all. Compared to the Pro Coalition, arguments regarding the beneficial effect of the minimum wage on poverty are made much less frequently in this group. Compared to the Anti Coalition, the negative effect of the minimum wage on employment is judged to be much less important.

Table 4.3 Coalition beliefs in the US minimum-wage policy subsystem. Pro Coalition: AFL, SHW, DEM, PBO, RAH, RJD, SEK, NYASS, NYT; Middle Group: DOL PBC, PBC, PGBJ, PJC, PGBS; Anti Coalition: COC, NFIB, NRA, SOH, PRR, RDA, DOL PRR, EPI, PRN, SBD, REP. Reading example: "In 14 percent of the times in which an actor from the Pro Coalition was coded from a newspaper article, this actor made the statement that minimum wages alleviate poverty."

	Variable	Pro Coalition	Middle Group	Anti Coalition
Overall stance	Pro	77%	32%	9%
	Anti	5%	5%	57%
	Neutral or Mixed	6%	33%	16%
	Not Specified	12%	32%	18%
Poverty	Poverty Risk	0%	1%	3%
	Poverty Benefit	14%	3%	1%
	Poverty Benefit Min	0%	0%	3%
Employment	Employment Risk	1%	5%	32%
	Employment Benefit	3%	3%	0%
	Employment Risk Min	6%	5%	1%
Norms	Normative Benefit	5%	0%	0%
Economy	Economic Risk	1%	8%	11%
	Economic Risk Min	4%	3%	1%
	Economic Benefit	2%	0%	0%

4.1.4 Change Over Time

In the discussion above, the US minimum-wage policy subsystem was treated as being constant over time. To see to what extent the coalition structure in the subsystem has changed during the period of analysis, the hierarchical clustering visualized in Figure 4.1 was repeated on two subsets of the data. The first subset spans the first half of the period of analysis from 1970 to 1992, and the second one spans the second half from 1993 to 2015. The results are displayed in Figure 4.2

The coalition structure is similar in both periods. As before, the Pro Coalition mostly consists of trade unions, the Democratic Party, and some prominent politicians linked to the Democratic Party. In the Anti Coalition, employer organizations and some prominent politicians linked to the Republican Party dominate. The moderate cluster consists of Presidents Nixon and Bush Senior, as well as the Republican Party and Senator Bob Dole in the former half of the period of analysis. In the latter half of the period of analysis, it is composed of Presidents

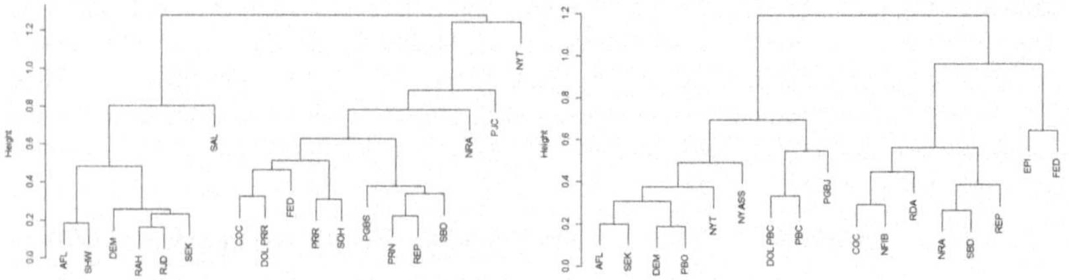

Figure 4.2 Dendogram of the coalition structure in the US minimum-wage policy subsystem in the first half (1970–1992; left) and the second half (1993–2015; right) of the period of analysis; distance measure: average Euclidean distance between clusters. For abbreviations, see Table 4.1.

Clinton and Bush Junior, as well as the Department of Labor under President Clinton. While some actors leave or enter the policy subsystem over time, cases of actors changing coalitions are rare. Moreover, the distance between the two coalitions stays roughly the same over time.

4.1.5 Summary: The US Minimum Wage Policy Subsystem

Analyzing data from the newspaper analysis described in Chapter 3, this section has mapped the minimum-wage policy subsystem in the United States. While hundreds of actors were mentioned in connection with minimum wages in the data set, only a relatively small number show up repeatedly, indicating their continuing presence in the policy subsystem. Those actors fall into several categories, the most important being political parties, interest groups, Presidents and government agencies, Members of Congress, and Researchers. Except for researchers, who rarely make explicit statements in support of or opposition to the minimum wage, these actors can be grouped by their overall stance towards minimum wage hikes. This grouping suggests the presence of a Pro and an Anti Coalition, and of a small number of moderate actors between them. This picture is confirmed when taking other variables describing an actor's beliefs regarding the effects of minimum wages and their normative desirability into account. Thus, there is a Pro Coalition supporting higher minimum wages, which argues that they are a way to alleviate poverty, and downplays potential negative employment effects. The Anti Coalition opposes higher minimum wages, mainly based on the notion that the minimum wage threatens employment. The Moderate Group takes a neutral to positive stance towards minimum wages, putting less emphasis on their potential benefits regarding the alleviation of poverty as well as on their potential risks regarding employment. While there has been some fluctuation over time regarding the actors in the subsystem, the subsystem's coalition structure has stayed largely the same between 1970 and 2015.

4.2 The UK Minimum-Wage Policy Subsystem

The minimum wage policy subsystem in the UK is much younger than its US counterpart. As discussed in Chapter 3, the UK's National Minimum Wage was only introduced in 1997. As will be shown, this translates into an instable coalition structure with important changes happening around the introduction of the NMW. The polarization of the policy subsystem is lower than in the US, and government-related actors and organizations play a more important role in bringing scientific expertise into the policy subsystem.

4.2.1 Actors

The existing literature on the introduction and subsequent evolution of the NMW provides an overview of what to expect regarding actors and advocacy coalition in the UK minimum wage policy subsystem. As in the US, the most important actors seem to be the major political parties, trade unions, employer organizations, and government agencies. Moreover, the Low Pay Commission is likely to play an important role in the policy subsystem. Regarding the coalition structure, the literature suggests that the UK subsystem is more volatile than its US counterpart. Thus, both the Labour Party and the trade union movement, who were the central actors behind the introduction of the NMW in 1997, were initially skeptical of a statutory minimum wage, preferring collective bargaining to guarantee adequate wage levels. Likewise, employer organizations like the Confederation of British Industry shifted from steadfastly opposing a minimum wage to a general acceptance of the NMW shortly after its introduction (Metcalf, 1999).

The empirical analysis of the data gathered from the *Times* and the *Guardian* supports and adds details to this overall picture. Simple counting of how often different actors were coded from the newspaper data provides a first impression of who the most important actors in the subsystem are. Since the time span of the analysis is shorter for the UK than for the US, the minimum requirement for an organization to appear in Table 4.4 is that it was coded at least 3 times. This leaves us with a subset of 38 actors from a population of 211 organizations coded. These which can be grouped into a small number of categories. *First*, the three major political parties—Labour, the Conservatives, and the Liberal Democrats—play an important role, with Labour being the most visible of all actors in the subsystem. The *second* large group are interest groups. On the one side, there is the Trades Union Congress, Britain's largest federation of trade unions, as well as several of its larger member unions such as the Transport and General Workers' Union and GMB. On the other side, there are the employer organizations Confederation of British Industry and British Chamber of Commerce. *Third*, the government or government departments form an important group of actors, with the Treasury and the Department of Trade and Industry being the most important ones. The Prime Ministers Tony Blair and John Major appear as individual actors, while Prime Ministers Gordon Brown and David Cameron only appear once in the data set and are thus not included in Table 4.4.

Table 4.4 Actors in the UK minimum-wage policy subsystem

Actor (abbreviation)	Times counted	Actor (abbreviation)	Times counted	Actor (abbreviation)	Times counted
Labour Party (LAB)	92	Department of Business, Innovation and Skills (DOB)	10	National Institute for Economic and Social Research (think tank) (NIESR)	4
Low Pay Commission (LPC)	46	GMB (trade union) (GMB)	9	Unite (trade union) (UNITE)	4
Trades Union Congress (TUC)	45	Low Pay Unit (think tank) (LPU)	8	Electrical, Electronic, Telecommunications and Plumbing Union (EETPU)	3
Conservative Party (TOR)	42	Prime Minister Tony Blair (PMB)	8	Employment Appeal Tribunal (EAT)	3
Government of the United Kingdom (GOV)	39	The Times (TIM)	8	Federation of Small Businesses (FSB)	3

(continued)

Table 4.4 (continued)

Actor (abbreviation)	Times counted	Actor (abbreviation)	Times counted	Actor (abbreviation)	Times counted
Confederation of British Industry (CBI)	32	HM Revenue and Customs (HMRC)	7	Institute of Directors (IOD)	3
HM Treasury (HMT)	30	Bank of England (BOE)	6	Patrick Minford (researcher) (PMI)	3
Department of Trade and Industry (DOT)	28	National Union of Public Employees (NUPE)	6	Policy Exchange (think tank) (POLEX)	3
Unison (trade union) (UNI)	19	Chartered Institute of Personnel and Development (think tank) (IPD)	5	Prime Minister John Major (PMJM)	3
Transport and General Workers' Union (TGWU)	14	George Bain (researcher) (GBA)	5	Resolution Foundation (think tank) (REF)	3
British Chamber of Commerce (COC)	13	Organisation for Economic Cooperation and Development (OECD)	5		
Department of Employment (DOE)	12	Amalgamated Engineering Union (AEU)	4		
Liberal Democrats (LIB)	12	Amicus (trade union) (AMICUS)	4		
The Guardian (GUA)	11	Inland Revenue	4		

The most important research-related actor is the Low Pay Commission, which is the second-most visible organization in the policy subsystem. The only individual researcher, George Bain, is also connected to the LPC, having served as Chairman of the Low Pay Commission between 1997 and 2002. Moreover, several think tanks are present. Some of them, for example the Low Pay Unit and the Chartered Institute for Personnel and Development have an explicit political mission. Others, such as the National Institute for Economic and Social Research, are more oriented towards nonpartisan analysis (Stone, 2001). Moreover, with the Organisation for Economic Cooperation and Development, an international organization providing scientific expertise on minimum wages, is present. The dominance of a government-related actor providing scientific analysis on minimum wages is what would be expected under a consensual/corporatist style of using expertise. Apparently, this does not exclude the parallel presence of advocacy-oriented think tanks.

There are some other ways in which the British minimum wage policy subsystem differs from its US counterpart. Thus, individual parliamentary representatives seem to get much less attention (and are rather quoted as representatives of their party), while government departments are more prominent. Individual researchers are more visible in the US, while think tanks are cited more often in the British newspapers. Trade union organizations are much more prominent in the UK, representing 9 of the 39 most important actors. Political parties are important in both policy subsystems, but while there is a balance between the representation of Republicans and Democrats in the US, the minimum wage appears first and foremost as a Labour issue in the UK sample of newspaper articles.

4.2.2 Coalition Structure

To get an overview of the coalition structure of the UK minimum-wage policy subsystem, this section starts by analyzing the support for the minimum wage by the most important actors in the policy subsystem. Table 4.5 shows the support for the minimum wage of all organizations for which this variable has been coded at least three times.[3] As shown, the number of organizations in fundamental opposition to the minimum wage is lower than in the US, encompassing the John Major government and AEU, a trade union which opposed the introduction of a minimum wage in the early 1990s, trying to keep wage setting in

[3] In this and the next table, ministries such as the Department of Employment were split up according to the head of government at the time at which their statement regarding their support for minimum wages was made. For example, Table 4.5 includes information on Her Majesty's Treaury under Prime Minister Tony Blair (HMT TB) and Prime Minister Davis Cameron (HMT DC). The abbreviation JM (in DOE JM, GOV JM) stands for Prime Minister John Major.

the hands of employers and trade unions. Among the more moderate critics of the minimum wage are employer organizations Institute of Directors and British Chamber of Commerce. Looking at the lower half of the table, one can see that trade unions are the strongest supporters of the National Minimum Wage, joined by the left-wing think tank Low Pay Unit, the commentators from the Guardian, and the Treasury under Prime Minister David Cameron. Between those poles, there is a broad spectrum of actors taking a moderate stance towards the minimum wage, among them the Liberal Democratic Party and the Conservative Party. The moderate spectrum also encompasses Prime Minister Tony Blair and a number of government ministries during his time as Prime Minister; the Low Pay Commission; two think tanks; the Department of Business under Prime Minister David Cameron; and the Confederation of British Industry, one of Britain's most influential business organizations.

Table 4.5 Support for the minimum wage by the most important actors in the British minimum wage policy subsystem. For the meaning of the actor abbreviations, see Table 4.4

Actor	Opposition to Minimum wage (percentage)	Mixed Position (percentage)	Support for minimum wage (percentage)
AEU	100	0	0
DOE JM	100	0	0
GOV JM	100	0	0
COC	67	33	0
GOV DC	67	33	0
IOD	67	33	0
TOR	42	46	12
TIM	38	38	25
DOB DC	33	33	33
IPD	33	33	33
TGWU	33	8	58
CBI	23	69	8
LIB	22	0	78
GOV TB	17	56	28

(continued)

Table 4.5 (continued)

Actor	Opposition to Minimum wage (percentage)	Mixed Position (percentage)	Support for minimum wage (percentage)
HMT TB	11	67	22
GUA	10	0	90
DOT TB	6	41	53
LAB	3	16	81
LPC	0	63	38
PMB	0	60	40
GBA	0	33	67
HMT DC	0	29	71
UNI	0	11	88
GMB	0	0	100
LPU	0	0	100
TUC	0	0	100
UNITE	0	0	100

This overall picture of trade union organizations and left-wing politicians and parties being supportive of the minimum wage, and right-wing politicians and parties opposing the minimum wage corresponds to the US minimum-wage policy subsystem. However, a major difference between the two subsystems is the number of moderate actors: While most actors and organizations in the US either take a clear stance for or against the minimum wage, 12 actors and organization were coded with statements supporting as well as statements opposing a higher minimum wage in the UK.

4.2.3 Over-Time Change

A more complete picture of the UK minimum-wage policy subsystem can be obtained when looking at different time periods separately. As mentioned above, qualitative accounts suggest that several actors have changed their position towards the National Minimum Wage after its introduction. This development is also visible in the data. Table 4.6 shows the overall support of major political actors for the minimum wage in two time periods. The first one encompasses the years leading up to the introduction of the NMW, 1990 to 1997. The second one encompasses the time since the introduction of the NMW, 1998 to 2015. Only actors for which the variable "minimum wage stance" was coded at least three times in the respective period are included.

While Table 4.6 includes only a relatively small number of actors in the first time period, the general trend that can be inferred is a markedly diminishing opposition against the minimum wage. Thus, two influential, economically conservative actors—the Conservative Party and the Confederation of British Industry—go from a decidedly negative attitude towards the minimum wage to a balanced position. Moreover, the anti-minimum wage Major Government is replaced by others having a much more supportive stance towards the minimum wage. Thus, the introduction of the National Minimum Wage is accompanied by a significant shift in the coalition structure of the minimum-wage policy subsytem. The result of this shift is less polarization in the sense that the number of moderate actors increases. Of the 11 actors in the upper part of Table 4.6, only the Liberal Democrats are coded with both statements supporting and opposing the minimum wage. In contrast, in the lower part of Table 4.6, 10 of 23 actors are coded with such positions.

Table 4.6 Minimum wage preferences of major actors in the British minimum wage policy subsystem, 1990–1997 and 1998–2015. For abbreviations, see Table 4.4

Actor	Opposition to Minimum wage (Percentage)	Mixed Position (percentage)	Support for minimum wage (percentage)
1990–1997			
AEU	100	0	0
DOE JM	100	0	0
GOV JM	100	0	0
TOR	100	0	0
CBI	67	33	0
TIM	33	67	0
LIB	25	0	75
TGWU	0	14	86
LAB	0	12	88
TUC	0	0	100
UNI	0	0	100

(continued)

Table 4.6 (continued)

Actor	Opposition to Minimum wage (Percentage)	Mixed Position (percentage)	Support for minimum wage (percentage)
1998–2015			
COC	67	33	0
GOV DC	67	33	0
IOD	67	33	0
TIM	40	20	40
DOB DC	33	33	33
IPD	33	33	33
TOR	29	57	14
LIB	20	0	80
GOV TB	18	59	24
CBI	17	74	9
HMT TB	11	67	22
LAB	10	25	65
DOT TB	7	47	47
LPC	0	61	39
PMB	0	75	25
GBA	0	33	67
HMT DC	0	29	71
GUA	0	0	100
UNI	0	15	85
GMB	0	0	100
LPU	0	0	100
TUC	0	0	100
UNITE	0	0	100

As was argued above, an actor's overall support of the minimum wage captures only a part of their beliefs regarding minimum wages. To capture the coalition structure when accounting for all coded variables describing what an actor thinks about the desirability and effects of minimum wages, a hierarchical clustering is conducted. To account for the sharp break that took place after the introduction of the NMW, this is done separately for the years from 1990 to 1997 and the period from 1998 to 2015. The results are presented in Figure 4.3, and roughly accord to what was concluded based on the overall actor positions towards the minimum wage. Before the introduction of the national minimum wage, cutting the dendogram at a height of approximately 1 delivers two main coalitions. The first coalition opposes the minimum wage and the Conservative Party, the Major Government, the CBI and the AEU. The second coalition supports the minimum wage and includes the Labour Party, the Liberal Democrats, and trade unions. The Times, identified with the conservative coalition in Table 4.11, is not part of the two coalitions.

After the introduction of the NMW, the picture changes markedly. While the pro-minimum wage coalition around Labour, the Liberal Democrats and trade unions persists, a new, moderate coalition emerges. This coalition contains parts of the Blair Government, the Low Pay Commission, the Conservative Party, the CBI, and the Business Department under Prime Minister Cameron. A smaller, third cluster consists of actors taking a more negative stance towards the NMW, namely the British Chamber of Commerce, the Institute of Directors, the British Government under Prime Minister David Cameron, and the Times. In terms of their beliefs, the actors are closer together than in the first half of the period of analysis: The three coalitions result from cutting the dendogram at a height of approximately .7. Three actors, The Guardian, The Times and George Bain, a researcher, are outside of this three-coalition structure.

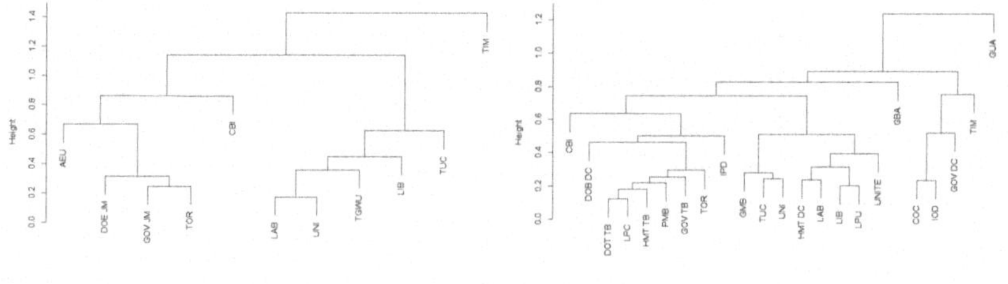

Figure 4.3 Dendogram of the coalition structure in the UK minimum-wage policy subsystem before (1990–1997; left) and after (1998–2015; right) the introduction of the NMW; distance measure: average Euclidean distance between clusters. For abbreviations, see Table 4.4

4.2.4 Coalition Beliefs

To get a better idea of what unites the actors that were grouped into the three coalitions, it is again instructive to summarize each coalition's beliefs. Tables 4.7 and 4.8 lists how often actors belonging to the different coalitions were coded expressing different beliefs regarding the desirability and effects of minimum wages. This is done separately for the periods from 1990 to 1997 and from 1998 to 2015. Again, only variables that were coded often enough to make a difference for the clustering are listed.

Table 4.7 Coalition beliefs in the UK minimum-wage policy subsystem, 1990–1997; members of the Pro Coalition: AEU, DOE JM, GOV JM, TOR, CBI; members of the Anti Coalition: LAB, UNI, TGWU, LIB, TUC. Reading example: "In 7 percent of the times in which an actor from the Pro Coalition was coded from a newspaper article, this actor made the statement that minimum wages alleviate poverty."

		Pro Coalition	Anti Coalition
Overall stance	Pro Minimum Wage	62%	5%
	Anti Minimum Wage	6%	44%
	Neutral Mixed Minimum Wage	10%	20%
	Not Specified	22%	33%
Employment	Employment Risk	4%	30%
	Employment Risk Min	3%	3%
Poverty	Poverty Benefit	7%	0%
	Poverty Benefit Min	0%	3%
Norms	Normative Benefit	4%	0%
Economy	Economic Risk	0%	3%
	Economic Risk Min	1%	3%

Before the introduction of the NMW, the main beliefs dividing the two coalitions are the overall support for the minimum wage, which is high for the Pro Coalition and low for the Anti Coalition, and the expected impact of the minimum wage on employment. While members of the Anti Coalition very frequently express fears that a minimum wage would reduce employment, such statements are rarely made by members of the Pro Coalition. Next to employment, other minimum-wage effects pale, with arguments about minimum wages' normative desirability and their beneficial impact on poverty playing a certain role among

Table 4.8 Coalition beliefs in the UK minimum-wage policy subsytem, 1998–2015; members of the Pro Coalition: GMB, TUC, UNI, HMT DC, LAB, LIB, LPU, UNITE; members oft he Middle Coalition: CBI, DOB DC, DOT TB, LPC, HMT TB, PMB, GOV TB, TOR, IPD; members of the Anti Coalition: COC, IOD, GOV DC. Reading example: "In 7 percent of the times in which an actor from the Pro Coalition was coded from a newspaper article, this actor made the statement that minimum wages alleviate poverty."

		Pro Coalition	Middle Coalition	Anti Coalition
Overall stance	Pro Minimum Wage	66%	15%	7%
	Anti Minimum Wage	2%	14%	43%
	Neutral/Mixed Minimum Wage	9%	34%	27%
	Not Specified	24%	37%	23%
Employment	Employment Risk	3%	15%	33%
	Employment Risk Min	5%	6%	7%
Poverty	Poverty Benefit	7%	1%	7%
	Poverty Benefit Min	0%	1%	3%
	Poverty Risk	0%	0%	3%
	Poverty Risk Min	0%	0%	3%
Norms	Normative Benefit	3%	1%	0%
Economy	Economic Risk	0%	9%	53%
	Economic Risk Min	3%	4%	3%
	Economic Benefit	2%	1%	3%

members of the supportive coalition. After the introduction of the National Minimum Wage, the beliefs of the Pro Coalition—which still mainly consists of trade unions, the Labour Party and the Liberal Democrats, stay roughly the same. A high overall support for the minimum wage is complemented by a lack of warnings about employments risks, and some statements regarding the normative desirability of minimum wages. The Anti Coalition is composed of different actors than before the introduction of the NMW. It is still united by a neutral-to-negative overall assessment of the minimum wage and the fear that it has a negative impact on employment. While there is no common view in the coalition regarding the effects of the minimum wage on poverty, there seems to be a strong feeling among the members of this coalition that the minimum wage poses a danger to businesses or the economy in general. Finally, the newly formed Middle Coalition reunites some actors from the former Anti Coalition and parts of the Blair and Cameron governments. It appears to be undecided when it comes to an overall evaluation of the minimum wage. Actors in this group share a certain discomfort when it comes to the employment effects of the minimum wage, but less so than the members of the Anti Coalition. Other than that, there is very little emphasis on the poverty effects and on the normative desirability of minimum wages. Compared to the Anti Coalition, there is only a weak concern with the effects of the minimum wage on businesses and the economy.

4.2.5 Summary: The British Minimum Wage Policy Subsystem

This section has presented the actors in the British minimum-wage policy subsystem, their minimum-wage related beliefs, and the coalitions they form. The overall actor structure has been shown to be roughly similar to what was found for the US. Thus, the most important actors in the subsystem are the major political parties, heads of government and government agencies, trade unions and employer organizations, and some think tanks and researchers. Trade unions and government departments play a greater role in the United Kingdom, while individual politicians—Members of Congress—are more important in the US. Regarding research-related actors, the UK stands out by the dominant position of the Low Pay Commission.

In both countries, the actors in the policy subsystem can be grouped into coalitions not only by their overall support for the minimum wage, but also according to their beliefs regarding minimum wage effects. There are two differences, however: First, while the coalition structure in the US subsystem is stable throughout the period of analysis, the UK subsystem experienced a substantial shift after the introduction of the NMW in 1997. Second, whereas the US minimum-wage policy subsystem is quite polarized, its British counterpart contains more moderate actors. Especially after the introduction of the NMW, formerly strong opponents of a statutory minimum wage gave up or at least moderated their critique of this policy, and the decidedly anti-minimum wage Government under John Major was replaced by more moderate Governments.

4.3 The German Minimum-Wage Policy Subsystem

Of the three countries in the sample, Germany was the last to introduce a general minimum wage in 2015. The period of analysis from 1992 to 2015, therefore, covers mostly the run-up to the introduction of the minimum wage, as well as the first year of its existence. As will be shown, the German minimum wage policy subsystem is closer to its UK counterpart than to the US. As in the UK, there is an over-time change in the coalition structure, and the polarization of the policy subsystem is comparatively low. Government-related organizations play an important role in brokering knowledge between the expert discourse and the policy subsystem.

4.3.1 Actors

An overview of the development of the German minimum-wage policy subsystem is provided by Nowak (2015), who describes the history of the introduction of the *Mindestlohn*. Per Nowak, the impetus for the introduction of a general, statutory minimum wage came in the late 1990s from a trade union organizing Food and Restaurant workers (*Gewerkschaft Nahrung-Genuss-Gaststätten*, NGG). It was taken up by the left-wing *Partei des Demokratischen Sozialismus* (PDS), which later formed party *Die Linke*. Over the next years, the demand spread into the broader trade union movement—many trade unions, seeking to protect the autonomy of wage-setting from the state, had initially been opposed to statutory minimum wages—and was eventually taken up by the center-left *Sozialdemokratische Partei Deutschlands* (SPD). The center-right party *Christlich Demokratische Union* (CDU) took a middle position, advocating regionally diversified minimum wages where no binding collective agreements existed. The economically conservative political party *Freie Demokratische Partei* (FDP) remained opposed to the minimum wage. The *Mindestlohn* was finally introduced in 2015, after SPD, CDU and *Christlich-soziale Union* (CSU) had formed a coalition government led by Chancellor Merkel.

Our own analysis of the German minimum-wage policy subsystem again starts by identifying the most important actors in the subsystem. These are defined as those organizations coded at least three times from the sample of newspaper articles. The results are presented in Table 4.9. Accordingly, the minimum-wage policy subsystem in Germany has 32 main actors, which can be divided into a few major subgroups. Among the most important actors are Germany's major political parties: the social democratic SPD; the conservative parties CDU, CSU, and their

Table 4.9 Most important actors in the German minimum-wage policy subsystem

Actor (abbreviation)	Times counted	Actor (abbreviation)	Times counted	Actor (abbreviation)	Times counted
Sozialdemokratische Partei Deutschland (political party; SPD)	83	Deutscher Gewerkschaftsbund (trade union federation; DGB)	10	Deutsche Post (company, DPO)	4
Christlich Demokratische Union (political party; CDU)	46	Chancellor Angela Merkel (BKA_AM)	8	Gewerkschaft Nahrung-Genuss-Gaststätten (trade union; NGG)	4
Ministry for Employment (BMA)	42	Die Linke (political party; LIN)	8	Vice Chancellor Franz Müntefering (VKA FM)	4
Die Union (political party; UNI)	35	Hauptverband der Deutschen Bauindustrie (employer organization; HDB)	7	IG Bergbau-Chemie-Energie (trade union; BCE)	3
Federal Government (BUN)	22	Süddeutsche Zeitung (newspaper; SZE)	7	Baugewerbeverband Mecklenburg-Vorpommern (employer organization; BGMV)	3
Freie Demokratische Partei (political party; FDP)	20	Bundesverfassungsgericht (court; BVG)	6	Deutsches Institut für Wirtschaftsforschung (policy advisory organization, DIW)	3
Christlich-soziale Union (political party; CSU)	18	IG Metall (trade union; IGM)	6	Deutsche Zoll- und Finanzgewerkschaft (trade union; DZF)	3

(continued)

Table 4.9 (continued)

Actor (abbreviation)	Times counted	Actor (abbreviation)	Times counted	Actor (abbreviation)	Times counted
Bundesvereinigung der Deutschen Arbeitgeberverbände (employer organization; BDA)	17	Bundesagentur für Arbeit (federal labor exchange office; BFA)	5	European Commission (EUK)	3
IG Bauen-Agrar-Umwelt (trade union; BAU)	16	Sachverständigenrat zur Begutachtung der gesamtwirtschaftlichen Entwicklung (policy advisory organization, SBE)	5	Frankfurter Allgemeine Zeitung (newspaper; FAZ)	3
Ministry for Economic Affairs (BMW)	15	Zentralverband des Deutschen Baugewerbes (employmer organization; ZDB)	5	Finanzkontrolle Schwarzarbeit (government agency; FKS)	3
Verdi (trade union; VER)	14	Chancellor Gerhard Schröder (BKA GS)	4		
Die Grünen (political party; GRÜ)	12	Ministry of Finance (BMF)	4		

parliamentary alliance, *Die Union*; economically conservative party FDP, as well as *Die Grünen*, and *Die Linke*. Next to political parties, trade unions and employer organizations play a major role. A number of them come from the construction sector, which was one of the first sectors where a statutory minimum wage was introduced in 1996 (Möller *et al.*, 2011). Another important group are the federal government, as well as several government departments, such as the Ministry for Employment, the Ministry of Economic Affairs, and the ministry of finance. The Chancellors Schröder (1998–2005) and Merkel (2005-) also appear in the list.

Research-related actors and organizations appear less often than in the data from the United Kingdom and the US. The two organizations that fall into this group are *Sachverständigenrat zur Begutachtung der gesamtwirtschaftlichen Entwicklung*, a group of economists appointed to advise the government in economic matters, and *Deutsches Institut für Wirtschaftsforschung*, a publicly funded research institution. This is in line with the classification of Germany as a country with a corporatist/consensual style of using scientific expertise, in which scientific expertise is mostly provided by publicly funded institutions.

4.3.2 Coalition Structure

Mapping the coalition structure of the German minimum-wage policy subsystem, the analysis again starts by plotting the overall support of the most important subsystem actors for the minimum wage. Table 4.10 lists the minimum wage preferences of all actors with at least three coded positions towards the minimum wage between 1992 and 2015. As above, government-related actors such as ministries were divided according to the government under which the statement was made: the coalition governments between CDU, CSU and FDP (UNI-FDP I from the beginning of the period of analysis to 1998 and UNI-FDP II from 2009 to 2013); between SPD and the Green Party (SPD-GRÜ between 1998 and 2005); and between CDU, CSU and SPD (UNI-SPD I from 2005–2009; and UNI-SPD II from 2013 ongoing).

The table shows a relatively large number of actors supporting the minimum wage. These include a number of actors related to the executive branch of government, trade union organizations such as Verdi, IG Bauen-Agrar-Umwelt, and NGG, and the left-of-center political parties SPD, Die Linke, and Die Grünen. Moreover, two employer organizations from the construction sector appear in the lower half of the table, who supported the introduction of minimum wages as a means to fend off cheaper competition from Eastern Europe. The range of actors taking a clear position against the minimum wage is relatively small. It includes economically conservative party FDP, the Ministry of Economic Affairs, the *Sachverständigenrat zur Begutachtung der gesamtwirtschaftlichen Entwicklung*, and the umbrella organization of Germany's employer associations, BDA. The trade union IG Metall also appears among the opponents of a minimum wage, a position based on the union's initial desire to protect wage bargaining from government interference. Between these poles, there is a relatively broad spectrum of actors taking a neutral or a moderately supportive/critical position towards the minimum wage, including the center-right political parties CDU and CSU, Chancellor Merkel, some ministries, and the commentators from the two newspapers from which the sample was drawn. Out of the 33 actors and organizations, 12 were coded as supporting the minimum wage at one point in time, and opposing it at another. Again, this indicates a low polarization in the sense that the boundary between supporters and opponents of the minimum wage is not clearly drawn.

Table 4.10 Minimum wage preferences of major actors in the German minimum wage policy subsystem, 1992–2015. For abbreviations, see Table 4.9

Actor	Opposition to minimum wage (percentage)	Mixed position (percentage)	Support for minimum wage (percentage)
BGMV	100	0	0
BMW UNI-SPD I	100	0	0
SBE	100	0	0
BDA	85	15	0
BMW UNI-FDP II	75	25	0
FDP	72	22	6
BUN SPD-GRU	67	0	33
IGM	50	50	0
UNI	46	33	21
CSU	39	31	31
BMA UNI-SPD II	33	0	67
BUN UNI-SPD I	33	33	33
FAZ	33	67	0
SZE	33	67	0
BKA_AM	30	20	50

(continued)

Table 4.10 (continued)

Actor	Opposition to minimum wage (percentage)	Mixed position (percentage)	Support for minimum wage (percentage)
CDU	27	15	58
BMA UNI-FDP I	20	0	80
DGB	11	0	89
BAU	8	8	83
SPD	7	5	88
BMA UNI-SPD I	0	0	100
BMA SPD-GRU	0	0	100
BVG	0	0	100
DZF	0	0	100
LIN	0	0	100
NGG	0	0	100
VKA_FM	0	0	100
VER	0	8	92
BMA UNI-FDP II	0	9	91
GRÜ	0	9	91
HDB	0	17	83
BUN UNI-FDP II	0	25	75
ZDB	0	25	75

As discussed above, the idea of a general, statutory minimum wage only gained track among major political actors during the period of analysis. Therefore, the analysis presented in Table 4.10 is repeated for two separate time periods. As point of separation, the year 2009 is chosen, the year in which the demand for a general minimum wage for the first time entered the election manifesto of Germany's major center-left party, the SPD (Sozialdemokratische Partei Deutschlands, 2009). The results of the analysis are shown in Table 4.11.

As can be seen, there is a marked change between the two periods. Thus, important actors formerly skeptical of minimum wages begin to support it, or at least give up their opposition. Most importantly, this concerns center-right political parties CDU and CSU, as well as Chancellor Merkel. Moreover, among those actors in support of the minimum wage, some increase their endorsement, for

Table 4.11 Minimum wage preferences of major actors in the German minimum wage policy subsystem, 1992–2008 and 2009–2015. For abbreviations, see Table 4.9

Actor	Opposition to Minimum wage (Percentage)	Mixed Position (percentage)	Support for minimum wage (Percentage)
1992–2008			
BGMV	100	0	0
BMW UNI-SPD I	100	0	0
SBE	100	0	0
BDA	88	11	0
UNI	73	18	9
BUN SPD-GRU	67	0	33
CSU	56	33	11
CDU	54	15	31
IGM	50	50	0
SZE	50	50	0
BUN UNI-SPD I	33	33	33
FDP	33	67	0
BKA_AM	29	14	57
GRÜ	25	0	75
BMA UNI_FDP I	20	0	80
DGB	20	0	80
SPD	11	3	87
BAU	10	10	80
BMA UNI-SPD I	0	0	100
BMA SPD-GRU	0	0	100
BVG	0	0	100
NGG	0	0	100
VKA_FM	0	0	100
HDB	0	17	83
VER	0	17	83
ZDB	0	25	75

(continued)

Table 4.11 (continued)

Actor	Opposition to Minimum wage (Percentage)	Mixed Position (percentage)	Support for minimum wage (Percentage)
2009–2015			
FDP	80	13	7
BMW UNI-FDP II	75	25	0
BDA	75	25	0
BMA UNI-SPD II	33	0	66
BKA_AM	33	33	33
UNI	23	46	31
CDU	10	15	75
BAU	0	0	100
BMA UNI-SPD I	0	0	100
DGB	0	0	100
DZF	0	0	100
GRÜ	0	0	100
LIN	0	0	100
VER	0	0	100
SPD	0	9	91
BMA UNI-FDP II	0	9	91
BUN UNI-FDP II	0	25	75
CSU	0	25	75

example the trade union federation DGB or the SPD. Of the 18 actors included in the period from 2009 to 2015, only three oppose the minimum wage.

As above, another coalition analysis taking into account all coded variables describing an actor's beliefs regarding the effects and desirability of the minimmum wage is performed using hierarchical clustering. This is done separately for the periods 1992–2008 and 2009–2015. The upper part of Figure 4.4 shows the coalition structure in the period from 1992 to 2008. Cutting the dendogram at a height of approximately .9 delivers two major coalitions. First, on the left part of the dendogram, is a coalition of actors that have been shown to support the minimum wage in Table 4.10. It consists mainly of trade unions, left-of-center parties, the Ministry of Employment, and employer organizations from

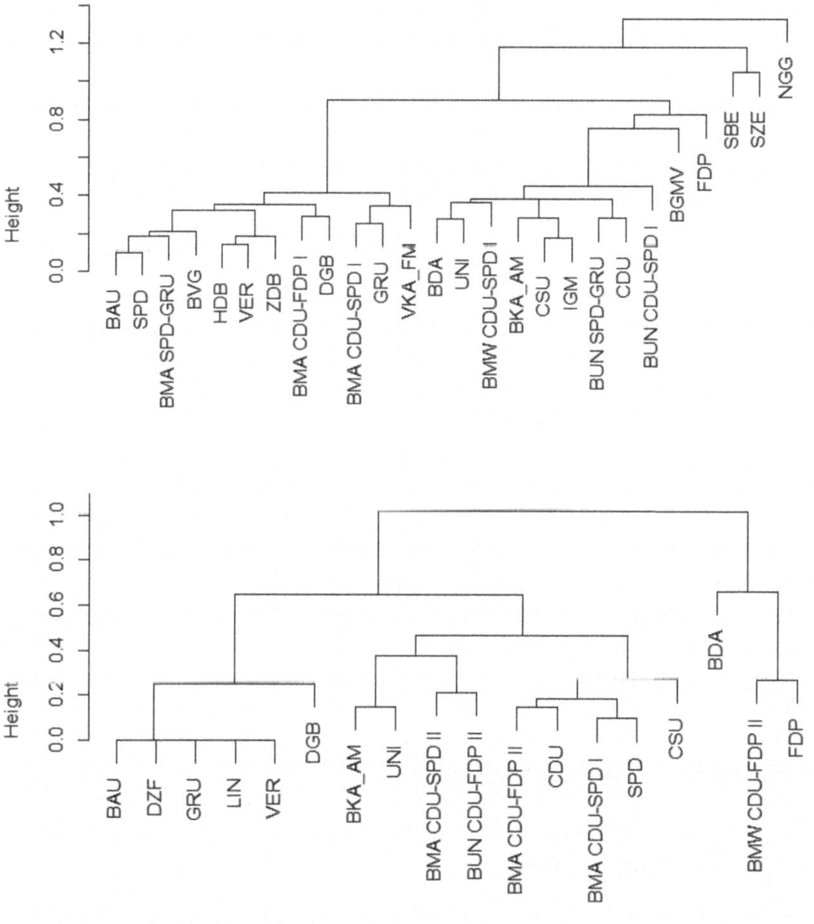

Figure 4.4 Dendogram of the coalition structure in the German minimum-wage policy subsystem, 1992–2008 (upper part) and 2009–2015 (lower part). Distance measure: average Euclidean distance between clusters. For abbreviations, see Table 4.9

the construction industry. A second coalition mainly consists of right-of center parties, some employer organizations and government actors, who have been shown to oppose minimum wages in Table 4.10. Three actors do not fit into this two-coalition structure: the *Sachverständigenrat zur Begutachtung der gesamtwirtschaftlichen Entwicklung*, the trade union NGG, and the commentators from the newspaper *Süddeutsche Zeitung*.

From 2009 onwards, this picture changes markedly. This is visible in the lower half of Figure 4.4. Here, cutting the dendogram at approximately .6 delivers three coalitions. First, the Pro Minimum Wage coalition continues to exist, consisting mainly of trade unions and left-of-center parties *Die Linke* and *Die Grünen.* A second cluster is composed of actors moderately in favor of the minimum wage: the political parties CDU, CSU, and SPD, along with a number of government actors. The third cluster are actors mostly opposing the minimum wage. These include the economically the FDP and the FDP-led ministry of economic affairs in the period from 2009–2013. The employer organization BDA is close to this coalition critical of the minimum wage.

In conclusion, the development of the subsystem coalition structure in Germany in the years *leading up* to the introduction of a general, staturory minimum wage approximately seems to match what happened in the UK *after* the introduction of the National Minimum Wage. Thus, the more the introduction of sectoral minimum wages proceeded, and the more the idea of a general, statutory minimum wage became an issue supported by left-of-center actors, the more the anti-minimum wage coalition began to crumble. While there was a relatively close coalition of actors being at least sceptical of minimum wages prior to the (somewhat arbitrarily chosen) breaking point of 2009, most of the actors of this coalition switched sides afterwards, forming their own cluster within the pro-minimum wage coalition. As in Britain, only a small number of actors really stayed opposed to the minimum wage.

4.3.3 Coalition Beliefs

Again, the beliefs of the coalitions identified above shall be explored, which is done separately for the time periods between 1992 and 2008, and from 2009 onwards (Tables 4.12, 4.13). In the former period, the two coalitions differ strongly on their overall stance towards the minimum wage. Regarding reasons for supporting or opposing minimum wages, the Pro Coalition advances benefits for businesses or the economy as a whole more often than other arguments. This is not wholly surprising. As was argued above, the introduction of sectoral minimum wages was at least partly seen as a measure to protect German businesses against low-wage competition from abroad. The Anti Coalition does not have common beliefs regarding the effect of minimum wages on the economy. Rather, next to a general opposition to the minimum wage, the common denominator of this group is the belief that minimum wages threaten employment. In the time period from 2009 to 2015, the Pro Coalition is still mainly united by its overall support for the minimum wage, which is even stronger than in the preceding period. Arguments by actors in this group about the risks and benefits of minimum wages are even rarer in this period. Given that the protectionist hue of the minimum wage debate was largely confined to the 1990s, it is unsurprising that less actors claim that the minimum wage is good for businesses. The few actors remaining in the Anti Coalition still are connected by their skeptical overall stance towards the minimum wage, as well as by the fear of negative employment effects. In contrast to the earlier period, there is now a strong feeling that a minimum wage would hurt businesses and the economy in general. The actors in the Middle Coalition resemble those in the Pro Coalition in that they rarely talk about the effects of minimum wages but are less steadfast in their support for the minimum wage.

Table 4.12 Coalition beliefs in the German minimum-wage policy subsystem, 1992–2008. Pro Coalition: BAU, SPD, BMA SPD-GRU, BVG, HDB, VER, ZDB; Anti Coalition: BDA, UNI, BMW CDU-SPD I, BKA_AM, CSU, IGM, BUN SPD-GRU, CDU, BUN CDU-SPD I, BGMV, FDP, BMA CDU-SPD I, GRU, VKA_FM

		Pro Coalition	**Anti Coalition**
Overall stance	Pro Minimum Wage	65%	8%
	Anti Minimum Wage	6%	47%
	Neutral/Mixed Minimum Wage	5%	17%
	Not Specified	24%	28%
Employment	Employment Risk	0%	13%
	Employment Benefit	4%	1%
Poverty	Poverty Benefit	2%	0%
Norms	Normative Benefit	3%	0%
Economy	Economic Risk	0%	4%
	Economic Benefit	8%	5%

Comparing the coalition beliefs in the German minimum-wage policy subsystem with those from the US or the UK, one can see that actors in Germany were more likely than actors in the other two countries to be quoted with statements about the normative desirability of minimum wages and their effect on employment, poverty, and the economy and businesses. If one looks at the coded

Table 4.13 Coalition beliefs in the German minimum-wage policy subsystem, 2009–2015. Pro Coalition: BAU, DZF, GRU, LIN, VER, DGB; Middle Coalition: BKA_AM, UNI, BMA CDU-SPD II, BUN CDU-FDP II, BMA CDU-FDP II, CDU, BMA CDU-SPD I, SPD, CSU; Anti Coalition: BDA, BMW CDU-FDP II, FDP

		Pro Coalition	Middle Coalition	Anti Coalition
Overall stance	Pro Minimum Wage	100%	52%	4%
	Anti Minimum Wage	0%	7%	65%
	Neutral/Mixed Minimum Wage	0%	16%	13%
	Not Specified	0%	25%	17%
Employment	Employment Risk	0%	2%	13%
Economy	Economic Risk	0%	1%	17%

arguments that *were* made by subsystem actors, however, the beliefs in the German subsystem roughly accord with the beliefs coded in the other two countries. The most important concerns of minimum-wage opponents are that they might threaten employment and businesses. Advocates of the minimum wage, in general, voice fewer arguments regarding the effects of minimum wages to support their cause. Only relatively rarely do they refer to beneficial effects of the minimum wage, for example on poverty. A reason for this could be that higher wages are seen as a good thing per se by many. While there is little reason for advocates of the minimum wage to argue why higher wages for low-wage earners are desirable, critics of the minimum wage will need good arguments for barring low-wage earners from raises.

4.3.4 Summary: The German Minimum Wage Policy Subsystem

The German minimum wage policy subsystem, as presented in this section, is similar to its UK counterpart. In Germany, as well as in the UK, the most important actors in the policy subsystem are political parties, the executive branch of government, trade unions and employer organizations. While the number of research-related actors in the data on the German policy subsystem is low, those that are present are publicly funded, conforming to the image of a consensual/corporatist policy subsystem.

The coalition structure is less polarized and more fluid than in the US. As in the UK, there are many actors who are neither in clear support of nor in clear opposition to the minimum wage. Moreover, many of the actors originally opposed to the introduction of a minimum wage changed their position around 2009, shifting towards moderate support of the minimum wage. As in the other two countries, the coalitions not only imply a common support or rejection of the minimum wage, but also shared beliefs regarding the effects of the minimum wage.

4.4 Conclusions

Preparing the ground for later analyses of how scientific knowledge from the expert discourse enters the media discourse on minimum wages and influences actors in minimum-wage policy subsystems (Chapters 5 to 7), Chapter 4 has presented insights about actors and coalitions in the minimum-wage policy subsystems of Germany, the United Kingdom, and the United States. The analysis for each country has begun by identifying the most important actors in the respective subsystem. Most of the main actor groups are common to all three subsystems. They include the major political parties, government-related actor organizations such as employment ministries and the head of the executive branch of government, interest groups representing labor and businesses, and researchers and research-related organizations. The importance of each group differs between the three countries. In the US, the representation of the minimum-wage policy subsystem in the mass media focuses on individual Congressional Representatives and Senators, a group missing in the other two countries. Conversely, in Germany and the UK, trade unions are much more present in the subsystem.

Regarding researchers and research-related actors, the differences between the three countries conform to the notion of a pluralistic style of using expertise in the US, and a corporatist/consensual style in Germany and the UK. Thus, while advocacy-oriented think tanks dominate in the US, the most important research-related actors in Germany and the United Kingdom are government-funded. Notably, the number of research-related actors in the German minimum wage policy subsystem is significantly smaller than in the other two countries.

Regarding the coalition structure of the subsystem, two different patterns emerge. The *first* was found in the US and involves the presence of two main coalitions, one strongly advocating and the other strongly opposing higher minimum wages, and a small number of actors—mostly connected to the executive branch of government—taking a moderating position between them. This coalition structure remained intact over the whole period of analysis. The *second* pattern is present in Germany and the UK, where the minimum-wage policy subsystem started out with two coalitions, one supporting and the other decidedly opposing the minimum wage. Over time, however, one can observe the disintegration of the anti-minimum wage coalition, with actors opposed to the minimum wage either disappearing from the subsystem or abandoning their opposition to it. The result are subsystems with a group of actors strongly supporting the minimum wage, another large group of actors mildly supporting or mildly opposing it, and a small group of actors decidedly opposing higher minimum wages.

Finally, the arguments dividing supporters and critics of the minimum wage are similar in all three countries. Thus, belief coalitions are not only bound together by a common support for or rejection of the minimum wage, but also by shared beliefs regarding its effects on poverty, employment, and the economy. While there is some variation between the three countries, critics of the minimum wage tend to underline its allegedly negative consequences on employment and the economy, while supporters rarely talk about its effects on employment and the economy, highlighting its alleged role in alleviating poverty instead.

Describing the minimum wage policy subsystems of Germany, the United Kingdom and the United States, this chapter has substantiated claims made in the previous chapter, on which the comparative research design of this research is built. It has demonstrated that minimum wage policy making in the three countries is comparable in the sense that it involves a similar set of actors, who form coalitions opposing or supporting the minimum wage based on similar arguments over the effects of minimum wages. However, it was also shown that the three countries offer the expected variation regarding styles of using scientific expertise and the coalition structures of the three countries.

Scientific Expertise in the Newspaper Discourse

5

The previous chapter has provided background information on the minimum wage policy subsystems of Germany, the United Kingdom, and the United States. Based on this, it is now possible to start testing the theoretical model formulated in Chapter 2. While the next chapter will be preoccupied with analyses of the influence of the expert discourse on the beliefs and preferences of political actors, this chapter is devoted to testing those hypotheses referring to the presence of scientific expertise in the newspaper discourse on minimum wages.

The chapter starts with an analysis of the expert discourse in the three countries, showing how many articles on minimum-wage effects were published at what point in time, which types of minimum-wage effects were of concern, and how these effects were evaluated. Then, the results of several analyses of the newspaper discourse in the three countries are presented. These were conducted to find out to what extent and how scholars and their research are present there. Finally, multivariate analyses will connect both datasets, answering questions about the relation between the expert discourse and its representation in the mass media.

5.1 The Expert Discourse on Minimum-Wage Effects

In the theoretical model, the expert discourse was conceptualized in two different ways. The first conceptualization is the international expert discourse, which

Electronic supplementary material The online version of this chapter (https://doi.org/10.1007/978-3-658-32746-0_5) contains supplementary material, which is available to authorized users.

F. Klein, *The Role of Scientific Expertise in Minimum Wage Policy Making*, Vergleichende Politikwissenschaft,
https://doi.org/10.1007/978-3-658-32746-0_5

includes scholarly articles published by researchers in any country and referring to minimum wage effects in any industrialized country. The second conceptualization is the domestic expert discourse of a country, which includes scholarly articles published by researchers working in that country or referring to minimum wage effects in that country. Chapter 2 argued that the question whether the international or domestic expert discourses are used by political actors is an empirical one. Therefore, in the following analyses, both possibilities will be considered and evaluated. The chapter starts by analyzing the three domestic expert discourses on minimum wages, and then describes the international expert discourse.

5.1.1 The US Expert Discourse

The US domestic expert discourse on minimum wages counts 370 articles between 1965 and 2014. As can be seen from Figure 5.1, the annual number of articles is relatively low for most years up to the 1980s, increases markedly during the 1990s and stays at a relatively high level thereafter. The increase in scholarly interest in minimum wages coincides with the publication of a number of much-noticed empirical studies in the early 1990s (e.g. Card and Alan B. Krueger, 1993). These challenged the consensus that higher minimum wages lead to lower employment and sparked a lively debate around the so-called new economics of the minimum wage (Burkhauser, Couch and Wittenburg, 2000).

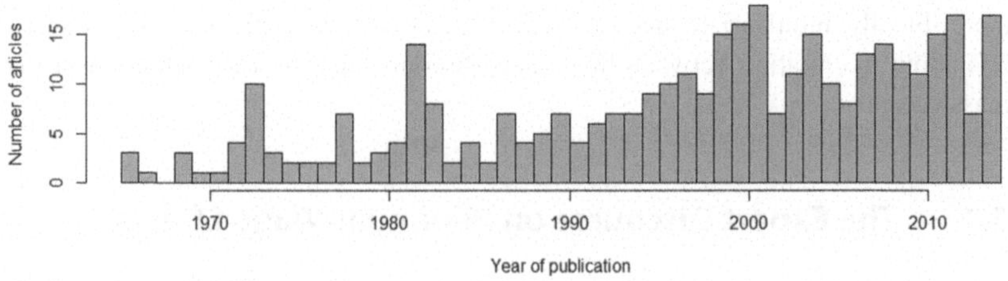

Figure 5.1 Annual number of articles in the US expert discourse

The types of minimum-wage effects that get most attention in the US expert discourse are those that are most discussed by the actors in the US minimum wage policy subsystem (see Chapter 4). The most important topics are minimum wage effects on employment and unemployment, which are analyzed in 225 of the 370 articles. Minimum-wage effects on poverty are analyzed in 70 articles, effects on the economy in 58 articles. Discussions of normative effects of minimum wages are neglectable. Moreover, 95 articles discuss minimum-wage effects on other variables that have not been coded, for example effects on high school dropout rates (e.g. Chaplin, Turner and Pape, 2003).

In addition to describing the types of minimum wage effects evaluated in the US expert discourse, the data also allows us to see *how* scientific research evaluates these effects. As shown in Table 5.1, a large majority (73%) of scientific articles in the US expert discourse finds that minimum wages reduce employment or increase unemployment. Most articles (67%) including results regarding minimum wage effects on poverty find that poverty is alleviated by higher minimum wages. Results on minimum wage effects on the economy are less certain, with 56 percent of all coded effects being undesirable, and 37 percent being desirable. The broad category of other effects is similarly split between negative and positive evaluations. This suggests that there are various other side effects of the minimum wage, which are evaluated differently in the expert discourse. Aggregating those variables into a single, overall evaluation of minimum wage effect (see Chapter 3), a majority of 59 percent of all articles in the US expert discourse finds mostly undesirable minimum wage effects, 18% find either no or a balanced effect, and 23 percent find mostly desirable minimum wage effects.

Table 5.1 Evaluation of minimum wage effects in the US expert discourse

	Undesirable minimum wage effect (%)	No/balanced minimum wage effect (%)	Desirable minimum wage effect (%)
Employment	73	18	10
Poverty	15	19	67
Economy	56	7	37
Other effects	58	12	31
Overall effect	59	18	23

A closer examination of the data suggests that this evaluation varies significantly over time. Thus, Figure 5.2 plots a five-years moving average of the fraction of articles in the US minimum wage policy subsystem that find a beneficial or a neutral effect of minimum wages on employment over time. The moving average is chosen to facilitate the identification of overall trends. Later analyses will show that political actors are influenced by such general trends rather than by the research results from a single year. As can be seen, a large majority of articles in the US expert discourse published up the early 1990s, with the exemption of a brief spike around 1980, finds undesirable minimum wage effects on employment and unemployment. From the mid-1990s onwards, the fraction of articles finding non-negative minimum wage effects on employment increases to approximately 30 to 40 percent. This is in line with the results from literature reviews regarding minimum wage effects on employment, suggesting that a new economics of the minimum wage, challenging the idea that minimum wage increases necessarily lead to less employment and more unemployment, developed in the 1990s (Burkhauser, Couch and Wittenburg, 2000). There is thus an agreement between our data and the findings from literature reviews. This supports the idea that the way the data set on the expert discourse was created is a valid indicator of how scientific research evaluates the minimum wage.

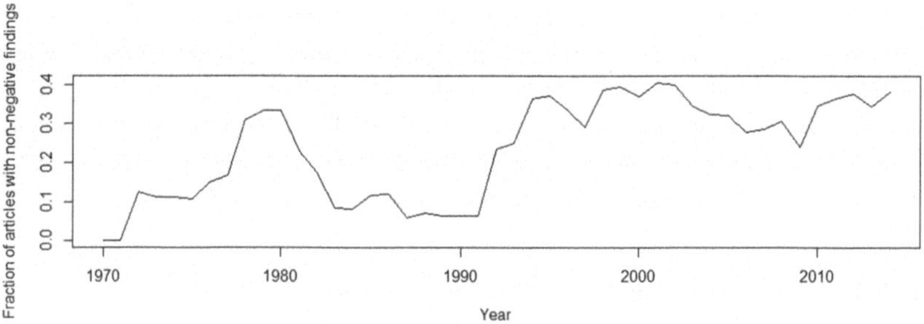

Figure 5.2 Fraction of articles in the US expert discourse that do not find undesirable effects of the minimum wage on employment or unemployment (five-years moving average)

As the evaluations of minimum wage effects on poverty, on the economy, and of other minimum wage effects show a similar pattern, the fraction of articles that do not find an undesirable overall effect of minimum wages increases over time (Figure 5.3). While the fraction of articles with a positive or neutral overall evaluation of minimum wage fluctuates between −0.1 and just below .40 up to the early 1990s, it rises thereafter. From the late 1990s until the end of the period of analysis, it oscillates around approximately .5.

5.1.2 The UK Expert Discourse

As in the US, the analysis of the British expert discourse starts five years before the period of analysis for this country, that is, between 1985 and 2014 (see

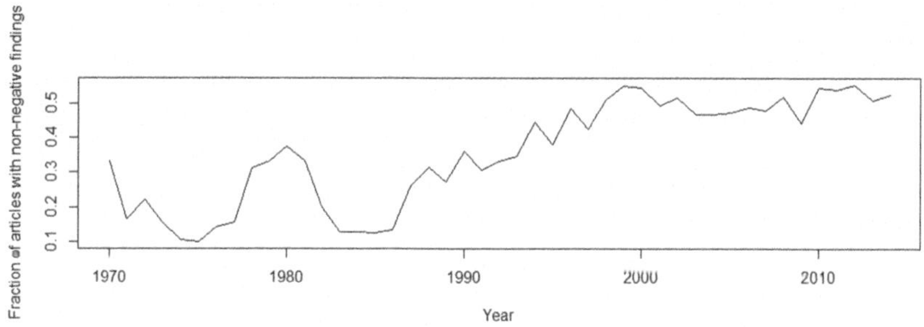

Figure 5.3 Fraction of articles in the US expert discourse that do not find an undesirable overall effects of minimum wages (five-years moving average)

Chapter 3). With 112 articles published in this time span, the UK expert discourse is significantly less voluminous than its US counterpart. This probably reflects the smaller number of universities and scholars in the UK. Judging by the number of articles published per year, the scholarly interest in minimum wage effects grew during the 1990s and reached its maximum in the early 2000s, shortly after the introduction of the National Minimum Wage. The number of articles published each year dropped afterwards but remained higher than during the 1990s (see Figure 5.4). The distribution of the types of effects analyzed in these articles resembles the one found in the US expert discourse. Fifty-three articles are concerned with the impact of minimum wages on employment and unemployment, 28 deal with minimum wage effects on poverty, 18 with effects on the economy, and 33 with other kinds of minimum wage effects.

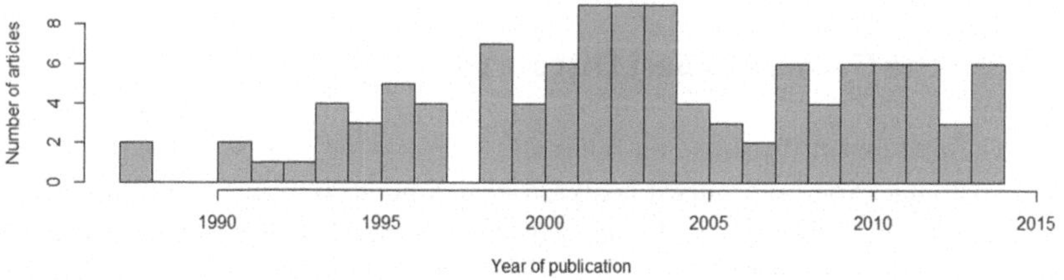

Figure 5.4 Number of articles published per year in the UK expert discourse

They way in which minimum wage effects are evaluated in the British expert discourse partly differs from the evaluation of minimum wages in the US expert discourse. As Table 5.2 shows, employment effects of minimum wages are evaluated much more favorably in the British expert discourse. The evaluation of minimum wage effects on poverty and the economy is similar in both expert discourses. Effects other than these are evaluated more favorably in the British expert discourse. This translates into a balanced overall evaluation of minimum wage effects, with 34 percent of all articles finding mostly undesirable minimum wage effects, 28 percent finding no, or a balanced number of positive and negative effects, and 38 percent finding mostly desirable effects.

Table 5.2 Evaluation of minimum wage effects in the British expert discourse

	Undesirable minimum wage effect (%)	No/balanced minimum wage effect (%)	Desirable minimum wage effect (%)
Employment	48	33	19
Poverty	11	14	75
Economy	59	12	29
Other effects	36	9	55
Overall effect	34	28	38

In contrast to the US expert discourse, there is no clear time trend in the UK, neither when looking at the evaluations of minimum wage effects on unemployment, poverty, the economy and other effects separately, nor when aggregating these evaluations into an overall evaluation of minimum wage effects. The fraction of articles that do not find an adverse overall minimum wage effect oscillates around a value of approximately .65 (see Figure 5.5).

5.1.3 The German Expert Discourse

The German expert discourse on minimum wages is the least voluminous of the three national expert discourses analyzed in this book. Between 1987 and 2014, it comprises only 54 articles. Figure 5.6 plots the number of articles by year of publication. It suggests that the scholarly interest in the minimum wage may be tied to the political debate around minimum wages. No articles were published prior to 1999, when a general minimum wage was not part of the political debate. The number of articles published annually was at two or below until 2005. Finally, it is at a level comparable to the UK for the time thereafter when the debate

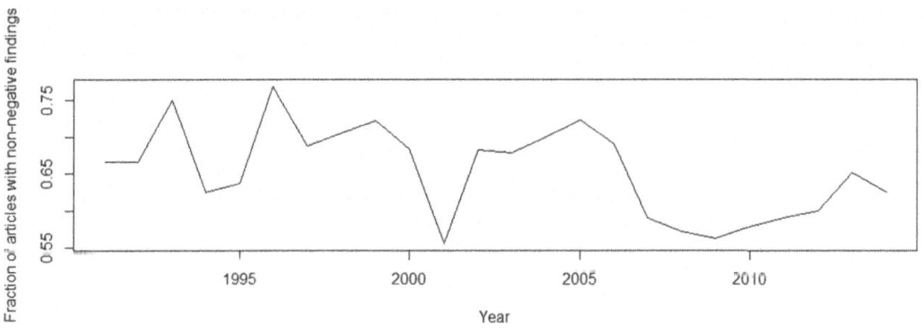

Figure 5.5 Fraction of articles in the British expert discourse that do not find an undesirable overall effect of minimum wages (five-years moving average)

around the extension of branch minimum wages and the introduction of a general minimum wage gained momentum.

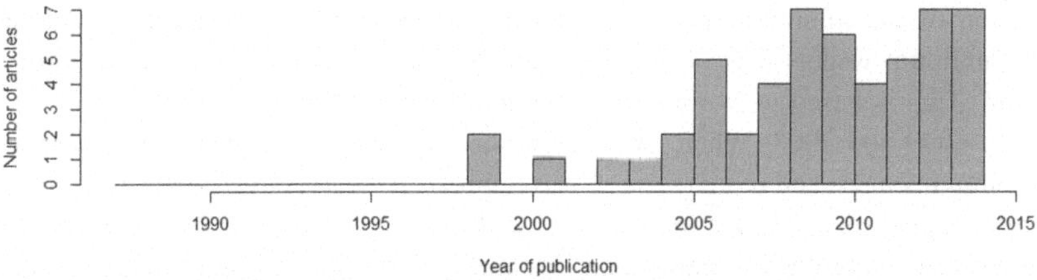

Figure 5.6 Number of articles per year in the German expert discourse

In terms of the type of minimum wage effects analyzed, the German expert discourse resembles the expert discourses in the United States and the United Kingdom. Thirty-four articles deal with minimum wage effects on employment, 11 analyze effects on poverty, six are preoccupied with effects on the economy, and 23 analyze other types of effects. Regarding *how* these effects are evaluated, the German expert discourse is closer to the US than to the British expert discourse. As shown in Table 5.3, minimum wage effects on poverty are mostly evaluated as being desirable, while minimum wage effects on employment, the economy, and other minimum wage effects are mostly seen as being undesirable. The overall evaluation of minimum wage effects in the German expert discourse, therefore, is unfavorable, with 58 percent of all articles finding mostly undesirable minimum wage effects, 21 percent finding no or a balanced number of desirable and undesirable effects, and a further 21 percent finding mostly desirable effects.

Table 5.3 Evaluation of minimum wage effects in the German expert discourse

	Undesirable minimum wage effect (%)	No/balanced minimum wage effect (%)	Desirable minimum wage effect (%)
Employment	74	24	3
Poverty	18	18	64
Economy	67	0	33
Other effects	61	0	38
Overall effect	58	21	21

While the low number of articles in the German expert discourse makes it impossible to identify separate over-time trends for the different minimum-wage effects reported in Table 5.3, an over-time change is visible in the overall evaluation of the minimum wage. As shown in Figure 5.7, the overall evaluation of minimum wages in the German expert discourse was strictly negative before 2004. This is based on a very small number of scholarly articles published between 1999 and 2003. When more researchers in Germany became interested in minimum wages, and more research was published, the overall evaluation of minimum wage effects became more favorable. From 2004 onwards, 40 to 50 percent of the articles in the German expert discourse do not find an undesirable overall effect of the minimum wage.

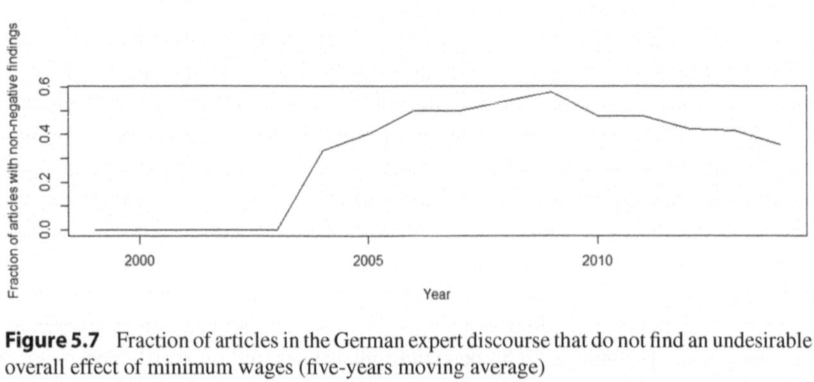

Figure 5.7 Fraction of articles in the German expert discourse that do not find an undesirable overall effect of minimum wages (five-years moving average)

5.1.4 The International Expert Discourse

As was argued above, the policy process in any given country might not only be influenced by the expert discourse in that country, but by all available research on the effects on minimum wages, that is, the international expert discourse. The sample of the international expert discourse on minimum wage effects comprises the three national expert discourses as well as research from other countries. It includes a total of 730 articles that were published between 1965 and 2014. These articles were written under the participation of authors working at institutions in 39 countries, and empirically analyze minimum wage effects in 31 different countries. The most important author countries are the United States (345 articles), the United Kingdom (105), Canada (59), Germany (54), and France (49). The most important countries for empirical analysis are the United States (246), the United Kingdom (71), Canada (47), Australia (20), France (20) and Germany (19). As Figure 5.8 shows, scholarly interest in the subject increased over time, reaching more than 30 published articles per year after 2010. In terms of the kinds of minimum wage effects analyzed, the international expert discourse shows approximately the same pattern as the three national expert discourses analyzed so far. Thus, 422 articles analyze effects on employment, 134 analyze effects on poverty, 125 analyze an impact on the economy, and 200 analyze other effects of minimum wages.

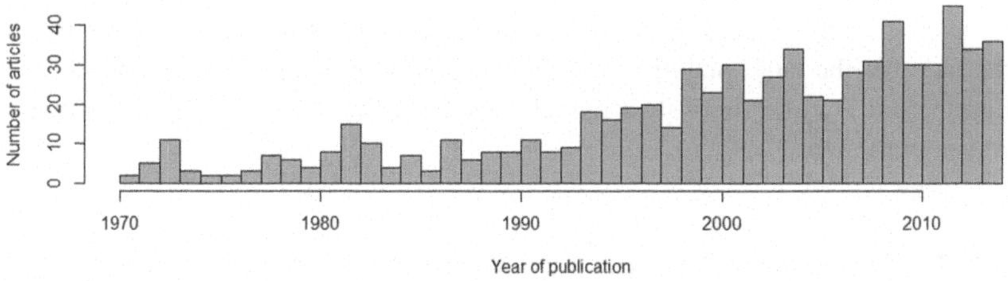

Figure 5.8 Number of articles published per year in the international expert discourse

In terms of how minimum wage effects are assessed, the international expert discourse is somewhere between the relatively unfavorable US and German expert discourses, and their relatively favorable British counterpart. As shown in Table 5.4, minimum wage effects on poverty are mostly assessed favorably. The assessment of minimum wage effects on the economy is balanced between undesirable and desirable effects, and employment and other minimum wage effects are mostly assessed to be undesirable. The overall evaluation of minimum wage effects in the international expert discourse is, consequently, rather negative. Fifty-two percent of all articles finding mostly undesirable effects, 21 percent finding no or a balanced number of desirable and undesirable effects, and 27 percent of all articles finding mostly desirable minimum wage effects.

Table 5.4 Evaluation of minimum wage effects in the international expert discourse

	Undesirable minimum wage effect (%)	No/balanced minimum wage effect (%)	Desirable minimum wage effect (%)
Employment	70	21	9
Poverty	12	17	71
Economy	47	7	46
Other effects	51	12	38
Overall effect	52	21	27

Over time, the evaluation of the minimum wage in the international expert discourse becomes more favorable. As shown in Figure 5.9, the fraction of articles in the international expert discourse that do not find an undesirable overall effect of minimum wages oscillates between approximately 10 percent and 30 percent from 1970 to 1990. It rises during the 1990s and rests between approximately 50 percent and 60 percent from 2000 to 2015. Especially in the years up to 1990, the plot strongly resembles the one from the US expert discourse. This reflects the fact that the large majority of scientific journal articles in the sample in this time period is either published by scholars from the US or refers to minimum wages in the US.

5.1.5 The Expert Discourse on Minimum Wages: Summary

So far, this chapter has given an overview of four expert discourses on minimum wage effects, three domestic ones (of Germany, the United Kingdom, and the United States) and an international one. The analysis has some notable results. *First*, there is a growing scholarly interest in minimum wages over time. Looking at the British and the German case, there are reasons to believe that scholarly interest is driven by political developments, namely the introduction of a minimum wage. This hypothesis will be tested in Chapter 6. *Second*, different types of minimum wage effects are evaluated differently. While minimum wage effects on

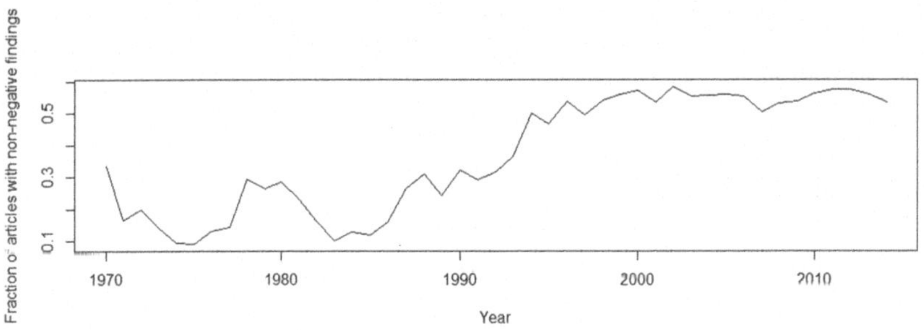

Figure 5.9 Fraction of articles in the international expert discourse that do not find an undesirable overall effect of minimum wages

poverty and inequality are widely seen as being beneficial, employment effects are being assessed unfavorably. The evaluation of other types of effects varies widely. *Third*, research results vary over time. Looking at the international and the US expert discourse, one can see that, between 1970 and the late 1990s, there has been a trend towards a more favorable evaluation of minimum wage effects. In Germany, the minimum wage was rarely an object research up to the mid-2000s. When the number of annual publications on the issue increased, the diversity of research findings grew with it, painting a no longer exclusively negative picture of the minimum wage. In the UK, no trend is clearly visible. *Fourth*, there are differences between the three countries being analyzed. Thus, the British expert discourse is more favorable in its evaluation of minimum wages than the other expert discourses.

5.2 Scientific Expertise in the Newspaper Discourse

Part of this chapter's efforts to shed light on the role of expert discourses in the policy process is to see to what degree scientific expertise enters the newspaper discourse on minimum wages. To this end, this section analyzes how often research-related actors—researchers at universities, think tanks, government institutions charged with providing expertise, or allusions to research in general—were coded from the newspaper articles from the three countries. The more often research-related actors are cited in newspaper articles, the more often will readers learn about the scientific evaluation of minimum wages, and the larger the role scientific expertise plays in the newspaper discourse. To understand whether the scientific expertise present in newspaper articles resembles the one from the expert discourse, this section also analyzes the statements about minimum wage effects with which research-related actors are cited in newspaper articles.

5.2.1 United States

In the case of the US, the analysis of the most important actors in the subsystem presented in the previous chapter has already suggested an important role for research-related actors. Among the most important actors in the subsystem are several university scholars. There are also think tanks active in the US minimum wage policy subsystem.

The closer analysis of the presence of scholars and think tanks in newspaper articles conducted in this chapter confirms the importance of research-related actors in the US newspaper discourse. Of the 1428 observations in the US newspaper data set—each one referring to a statement by an actor in the US minimum wage policy subsystem—123 are made by specified university-based researchers, and a further 48 refer to statements about research in general. Moreover, 75 observations refer to statements by actors connected to think tanks, and 22 refer to the Federal Minimum Wage Study Commission, the Council of Economic Advisors, and the Bureau of Labor Statistics. Together, these actors account for 266 observations, which amounts to about 19 percent of the sample. The left-hand side of Figure 5.10 shows the number of research-related actors coded per year. The right-hand side shows the total number of actors coded per year. One can see that the annual numbers of observations relating to researchers and think tanks approximately move in line with the overall number of actors coded. This suggests that research-related actors play a role in the US minimum wage policy subsystem over the entire period of analysis and are cited in newspaper articles whenever the issue is on the political agenda.

Taking a closer look at who is cited as an expert in the newspaper discourse suggests that a small number of scholars have a dominant position. Of the 171 observations referring to researchers at universities in the sample, 46 refer to academic research in general. Of the remaining 125 observations, 49 refer to a group of four highly cited economists at renowned universities: Alan Krueger (Princeton University), David Card (University of California, Berkeley), David Neumark (University of California, Irvine), and Lawrence Katz (Harvard University). In total, 60 scholars are cited, 58 of which were associated with US universities. Besides individual scholars, the newspaper articles cite 33 other knowledge-related actors. Of these, the Employment Policies Institute, the Federal

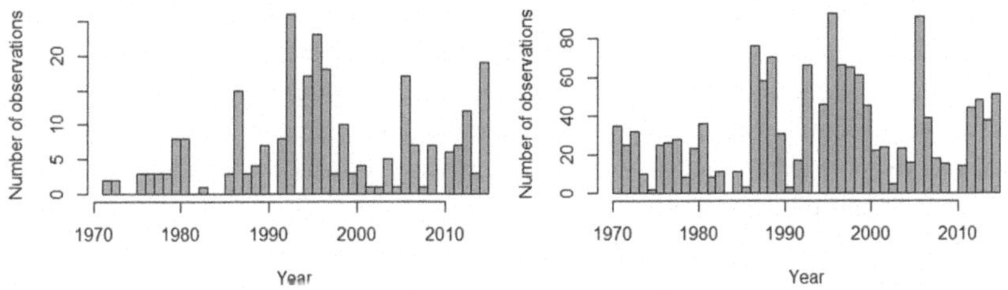

Figure 5.10 Annual number of research-related actors coded from US newspaper articles (left side); annual number of all actors coded from the US (right side)

Minimum Wage Study Commission, and the Economic Policy Institute are most visible.

Table 5.5 Evaluation of minimum wage effects by knowledge-related actors cited in US newspapers

	Undesirable minimum wage effect (%)	No/Neutral minimum wage effect (%)	Desirable minimum wage effect (%)
Employment	59	27	14
Poverty	31	36	33
Economy	42	37	22
Overall effect	52	27	20

Regarding the types of minimum-wage effects, there is a match between the questions the US expert discourse addresses and the questions experts cited in newspapers address. Minimum-wage effects on employment and unemployment play the largest role (coded 166 times), followed by effects on poverty (42 times) and the economy (41 times). As in the expert discourse, normative considerations play hardly any role (4 times). Moreover, the expert opinions presented in the mass media approximately match the findings from scientific research. As shown in Table 5.5, most research-related actors cited in newspaper articles claim that minimum wages have undesirable effects on employment and the economy. The evaluation of minimum wage effects on poverty by research-related actors cited in newspaper articles has no clear tendency and is more negative than the corresponding evaluation in the expert discourse. Overall, research-related actors cited in newspaper articles tend to provide a negative evaluation of minimum wages, similar to the overall evaluation in the US and the international expert discourse.

When the evaluation of minimum wage effects in the expert discourse changes, the expert opinions presented in newspaper articles change as well. Figure 5.11 demonstrates this with regard to the overall effect of minimum wages. As above, a five-year moving average is presented. Expert opinions cited in newspaper articles mostly pointed to undesirable minimum wage effects throughout the 1970s. A peak of positive and neutral statements happened in the early 1980s. Finally, from 1990 onwards, positive and neutral statements account for approximately 50 percent of all statements by research-related actors cited in US newspaper articles. This graph resembles the over-time development of the US expert discourse (Figure 5.3), but also the over-time development of the international expert discourse shown in Figure 5.9.

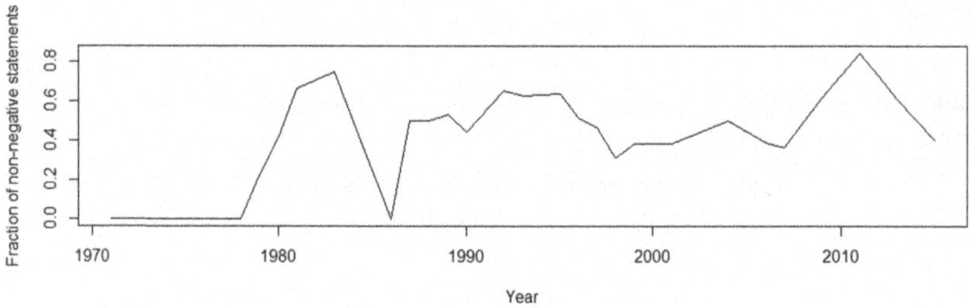

Figure 5.11 Fraction of statements by research-related actors in US newspapers that find that minimum wages have a neutral or desirable overall effect (five-years moving average)

5.2.2 United Kingdom

Compared to the United States, research-related actors are less important in the British newspaper discourse. Of the 706 observations in the data, about 9 percent—68 observations—refer to this actor group. Think tanks and university scholars are of about even significance, with 30 observations referring to university scholars and 26 to think tanks. The Low Pay Commission accounts for seven observations, the OECD for five.[1] As shown in Figure 5.12, experts were important in the newspaper discourse at three points in time during the period of

[1] As discussed in Chapter 3, the Low Pay Commission has a dual role in the British minimum wage policy process. On the one hand, it collects, commissions and evaluates research on the effects of the National Minimum Wage. On the other hand, it directly participates in

analysis. The first one is the election year 1992, during which Labour campaigned for the introduction of a minimum wage (Labour Party, 1992). The second one are the years before and after the introduction of the National Minimum Wage in 1997. The third one is the period from the mid-2000s to the end of the period of analysis, at a point in time at which significant raises of the National Minimum Wage were discussed (Wintour and Watt, 2013). Comparing the left-hand and the right-hand parts of Figure 5.12, one can see that the over-time distribution of references to research approximately follows the total number of actors coded per year. Thus, scientific expertise is part of newspaper reporting on minimum wages over the whole period of analysis.

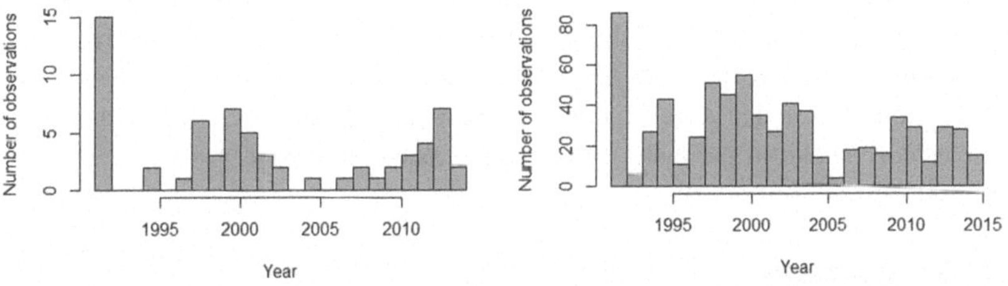

Figure 5.12 Annual number of research-related actors (left) and all actors coded from British newspaper articles

The diversity of research-related actors cited in British newspaper articles on minimum wages is lower than in the US. Of the 30 references to academic research, seven refer to unspecified researchers. The remaining 23 references are distributed among 15 individual actors, the most visible being George Bain, a British academic who was the first chair of the Low Pay Commission from 1997 to 2001. Compared to the US newspaper discourse, international scholars are more important. Four of the 15 actors are international researchers, among them David Card and Alan Krueger, two scholars who are important in the US expert discourse as well as in US newspaper articles. With respect to other research-related actors, 12 different organizations appear in the data, the most visible ones

setting minimum wage rates. In this chapter, we are only interested in the Commission's role in providing research-based policy advice. While it is not possible to neatly separate both roles, the solution chosen in this chapter is to count only those instances in which the Low Pay Commission is cited with an assessment of minimum wage effects as observations in which the organization provides research-based policy advice. Therefore, the number of seven *research-related* observations connected to the LPC is lower than the number of 46 observations connected to the LPC reported in Chapter 4.

being the Low Pay Commission followed by the Low Pay Unit and the OECD. The appearance of an international organization in this list differentiates the UK from the US.

In terms of the types of minimum wage effects on which research or think tank-related actors are quoted in newspapers, there is a strong focus on employment and unemployment (coded 31 times). Poverty (coded four times) and economic effects (coded six times), which are relatively important in the US expert discourse, are hardly relevant in the UK, and normative evaluations by research-related actors do not occur. The research-related actors cited in British newspapers evaluate minimum-wage effects on employment similar to the British expert discourse. Forty-two percent of them state that minimum wages reduce employment, 45 percent state that it has no effect on employment, and 13 percent state that it increases employment. While there is not enough data to identify an over-time development, the UK data will be included in later regression analyses testing to what extent and under which conditions the expert opinions cited in newspaper articles correspond to the main thrusts of the expert discourse.

5.2.3 Germany

Of the three countries analyzed, Germany is the one in which research-related actors are the least visible in newspaper articles. Of the 567 observations in the sample, 22 refer to university researchers and another 11 refer to think tanks—together less than six percent of the total number of actors. As shown in Figure 5.13, researchers did not play a role throughout most of the 1990s. During this time period, minimum wages featured prominently in the public debate but were still largely confined to the construction sector and designed to protect the German construction industry against cheaper competition from abroad. Moreover, as shown above, there was practically no German expert discourse on minimum wages during this period. Experts were more or less regularly part of the newspaper discourse in the 2000s, when minimum wages were extended to other branches and an introduction of a general minimum wage was discussed for the first time. They appear more frequently after 2010, in the years before the general minimum wage was introduced.

In contrast to the other two countries, the (few) citations of research-related actors are not concentrated on a small number of individuals and organizations. Of the 22 references to university researchers, 11 refer to unspecified researchers or research in general. The remaining 11 references are equally distributed among 11

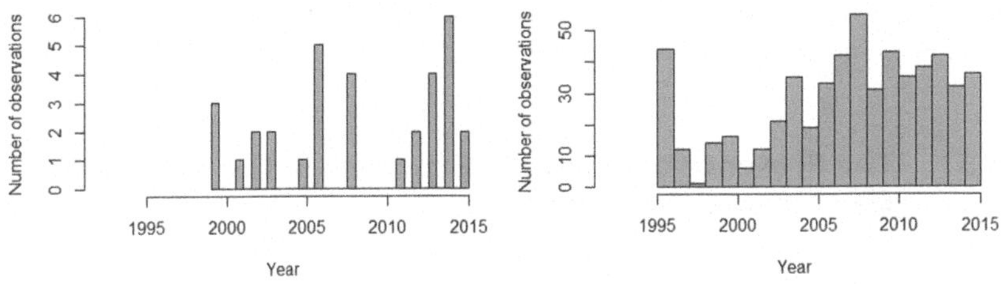

Figure 5.13 Annual number of research-related actors (left) and all actors coded from German newspaper articles

researchers, five of which are from universities outside of Germany. The 11 observations connected to think tanks are distributed over eight different organizations, the most visible of which is *Deutsches Insititut für Wirtschaftsforschung*.

The issues addressed by research-related cited in newspapers actors are similar to the US newspaper discourse. There are 19 references to the effect of minimum wages on employment, five references to economic effects, and three references to effects on poverty. Minimum wage effects are, moreover, assessed similarly by the publications in the German expert discourse and by research-related actors cited in German newspapers. Seventy-nine percent of research-related actors cited in newspaper articles state that the minimum wage hurts employment, while 21 percent say it has no effect on employment. As in the British case, there is not enough data to meaningfully identify an over-time development.

5.2.4 Experts and Expertise in Newspaper Articles: Summary

This section has described the presence of research-related actors in the newspaper discourses of the United States, the United Kingdom, and Germany. It was shown that, *first*, the presence of research-related actors varies strongly between countries, with 19 percent of all observations referring to this group in the United States, but only 6 percent in Germany. *Second*, how often university scholars and think tanks are quoted in newspaper articles seems to follow the general magnitude of the debate on minimum wages. *Third*, in all three countries, the statements by research-related actors presented in newspapers well represent the general tendencies of the expert discourse. Whether they resemble the international or rather the domestic expert discourse could not be established based on the analyses presented so far and will be further discussed below. *Fourth*, however, at least US newspapers rarely cite research-related actors from abroad, which is more common in the UK and Germany.

5.3 The Presence of Scientific Expertise in the Newspaper Discourse: Conditions

The previous sections have demonstrated that research-related actors do play an important role in the minimum wage policy subsystems of Germany, the United Kingdom and the United States. The hypotheses formulated in Chapter 2, however, go beyond stating that research from the expert discourse is present in newspaper articles. In addition, they specify the conditions under which this happens. To test those hypotheses, this section presents regression analyses that link the data on the expert discourse and the data on research-related actors in minimum wage policy subsystems. These analyses will also contribute to answering the question whether it is the international or rather the domestic expert discourse that enters the newspaper discourse.

5.3.1 Hypotheses and Operationalization

The theoretical model developed in Chapter 2 specifies conditions under which scientific expertise will be present in the public discourse on minimum wages. Scientific expertise was hypothesized to be more present in newspaper articles when more scientific articles on minimum wages are being published (H2.1). Moreover, Hypotheses H3.1 and H3.3 connect situations related to uncertainty about minimum wage effects—that is when the minimum wage is new, or when strong changes in the expert discourse occur—to a more intense public discussion of scientific expertise in newspapers. Lastly, scientific expertise was hypothesized to have a stronger presence in newspaper articles under the conditions of a pluralistic style of using expertise (H4.1), and in adversarial policy subsystems (H4.3). The regression analysis presented in this section tests these hypotheses.

The dependent variable of the analysis is the number of times a research-related actor was coded in the newspaper data from a given country in a given year. An example for one observation of the dependent variable is that, in all newspaper articles in the sample that were published in newspapers from the *United States* in the *year 1992*, a total of six research-related actors were coded. The data thus takes the structure of an unbalanced panel (Baltagi, 2008), in which each of the 93 observations—45 for the US, 25 for the UK, and 23 for Germany—relates to one country-year combination.

The explanatory variable connected to Hypothesis H2.1 is operationalized in two ways. *First*, it is operationalized as the number of scientific articles in the expert discourse published in one year. This variable captures a mechanism in which research results enter newspaper articles right after their publication, for example because journalists react to press releases by university departments. To make sure that the date by which a scholar is cited in a newspaper lies past the date a scientific study is published, this variable is lagged by one year. *Second*, such a direct way of popularizing research results can be contrasted with another, more indirect mechanism. In this mechanism, the fact that more researchers are interested in minimum wages leads to a higher presence of expertise in the newspaper discourse over the long term, for example because this makes it easier for journalists to find relevant scientific expertise when needed. To capture this indirect mechanism, a second variable is operationalized as a five-years moving average of the number of scientific articles in the expert discourse. For example, the level of scientific interest in minimum wages in 1995 in the US is calculated by summing up the number of articles in the US expert discourse that have been published in 1995, 1994, 1993, 1992, and 1991. Being less volatile than the number of articles published in one year, the five-years moving average better captures the idea of how many researchers are interested in minimum wages. Again, the variable is lagged by one year. As it is difficult to argue why the moving average should have a length of exactly five years, different lengths will be used as robustness checks if the variable is found to be significant. The same will be done for similarly arbitrary variables presented below. *Third*, for each country, two kinds of expert discourses are potentially relevant: the domestic and the international. Therefore, both are included in the model.

The first of the uncertainty-related hypotheses, H3.1, refers to an increased uncertainty about minimum wage effects in the years close to the introduction of a minimum wage. It is operationalized as a dummy variable that takes the value 1 in the five years preceding and following the introduction of the general minimum wage (2010–2015 for Germany; 1994–2004 for the UK). The second uncertainty-related hypothesis, H3.3, captures times in which strong changes in the expert discourse create uncertainty about minimum wage effects. The discussion above has identified two instances in which there were strong changes in the scientific evaluation of minimum wages. In the US expert discourse in the early 1990s, new studies pointed to a much more favorable average evaluation of minimum wage effects. The same happened in the German expert discourse in the second half of the 2000s. In the British expert discourse, such a sharp shift in the average

Table 5.6 Overview of the variables used in the regression analysis

Name	Description	Mean	Standard deviation
Research in news	Dependent variable (DV): Number of times researchers or think tanks were coded in the newspaper sample in a country in year t.	3.4	5.1
Domestic expert discourse	Number of articles in the expert discourse in a country in year t−1.	5.7	4.6
Domestic expert discourse, MA5	Five-years moving average of exp; summarizes the time span from t−5 to t−1.	25.6	20
International expert discourse	Number of articles in the international expert discourse in year t.	20.6	11.7
International expert discourse, MA5	Five-years moving average of int_exp; summarizes the time span from t−5 to t−1.	93.0	52.6
Actors coded	Total number of actors coded in the newspaper discourse a country in year t.	28.1	20.7
Article count	Total number of articles on minimum wages published in the analyzed newspapers in the respective year in the respective country. Normalized by dividing the number of articles by the maximum number of articles on minimum wages per year published in this country.	.21	.22
DE	Dummy variable for Germany		
UK	Dummy variable for the UK		
Minimum wage new	Dummy variable indicating years in which the minimum wage is new. Takes the value 1 from 1994–2004 in the UK, and 2010–2015 in Germany.		

(continued)

Table 5.6 (continued)

Name	Description	Mean	Standard deviation
Shift in evaluation	Dummy variable indicating rapid shifts in the evaluation of minimum wages in the expert discourse. Takes the value 1 between 1991 and 1997 for the US and 2003 and 2007 for Germany.		
Subsystem polarization	Mean distance between the actors from the coalition supporting the minimum wage and actors from the coalition opposing the minimum wage. Refers to the years t−5 to t−1.	1.28	.31

evaluation of the minimum wage was not observable. The shifts are indicated by a dummy variable taking the value 1 from 1991 to 1997 in the US and from 2003 to 2007 in Germany, and 0 otherwise.

Hypothesis H4.1 refers to different styles of using scientific expertise in the three countries. To evaluate what effect these different styles have on the intensity with which scientific expertise is publicly discussed in newspaper articles, country dummies are included into the regression. Hypothesis H4.3 refers to the coalition structure in the subsystem. Rather than designating the coalition structure in a policy subsystem as strictly adversarial or strictly cooperative, the coalition structure is operationalized as a continuum that describes how far the wage preferences of the main coalitions in the policy subsystem are apart. Thus, for a moving average of five years, the mean distance between the actors from the coalition supporting the minimum wage and actors from the coalition opposing the minimum wage is computed (see Appendix A5). A moving average of five years, rather than a simple average of one year, is chosen to express the idea that coalition structures do not change rapidly from one year to another.

Finally, two control variables are included. The first one, actors coded, measures the total number of actors coded in a country in one year. This variable is included because this analysis does not focus on what makes newspapers report about minimum wages, but on the factors that increase the importance of research-related actors *relative to* other actors in the policy subsystem. Moreover, the variable article count, describing the total number of articles on minimum wages published in the analyzed newspapers in a country in a year is included to control for the amount of attention paid to the issue. All variables are listed in Table 5.6.

5.3.2 Estimation

The choice of the estimation strategy is driven by two main properties of the data. *First*, the dependent variable is a count variable ranging, in theory, from 0 to infinity and containing relatively many zeros. A simple regression models for count data is Poisson regression which assumes equidispersion, that is, the equality of the mean and the variance of the dependent variable: $Var(y|x) = E(y|x)$. A test for equidispersion described in Cameron and Trivedi (2009, p. 575) indicates that the data used here not is overdispersed, meaning that the variance is not significantly larger than the mean.

The *second* important property of the data is that it is a panel. This means that it combines time-series and cross-sectional data, with the cross-section referring to the different units being observed over time—in this case, the three countries. An important advantage of panel data compared to pure cross-sectional data is that it allows to control for unobserved heterogeneity between the units (Baltagi, 2008, p. 6). This is important for our case. For example, different cultures of journalism or other variables might cause newspapers in one country to systematically include more information about researchers and research results than newspapers in another country. A widely used group of estimators being able to control for such unobserved individual heterogeneity are fixed effects estimators. Compared to other groups of estimators such as random effects estimators, fixed effects estimators require less strong assumptions (Cameron and Trivedi, 2009, p. 266). Moreover, one main problems connected to fixed effects estimators, a significant loss of degrees of freedom compared to random effects estimators (Baltagi, 2008, p. 17), is less of a concern for us, as there are only three units being observed.

Besides controlling for unobserved individual heterogeneity between the three countries, another important topic when dealing with panel data is serial correlation in the error terms. As panel data includes observations from the same unit over several time periods, these observations cannot be assumed to be independent from each other. This, however, is an assumption used in many regression methods for cross-sectional data, the violation of which leads to wrongly calculated standard errors. To compute appropriate standard errors, several options are available. Often, cluster-robust standard errors (Huber, 1967) are used, which, however, are only consistent if the number of clusters G is large. In our case, $G = 3$ (the three countries). Another possibility is percentile-t bootstrapping, which, however, is problematic when the regression includes dummy explanatory variables, as done here (Cameron and Miller, 2015, pp. 343–344). Wild bootstrap algorithms (Mammen, 1993) can avoid this problem, but do not work for Poisson or negative binomial regression. The estimation is therefore based on an approach described in Cameron and Miller (Cameron and Miller, 2015, p. 346): It is done using (inconsistent) cluster-robust standard errors, for which we correct by deriving the p-values using a t-distribution with G-1 degrees of freedom. The models were estimated using Stata's poisson command with cluster-robust standard errors.

5.3.3 Results

The results of the regression analysis are shown in Table 5.7. Model 1 is the full model with all variables specified in Table 5.1. As there is considerable multicollinearity between some of the variables included in Model 1, Model 2 was estimated, including less variables. It was derived by estimating Model 1, deleting the least significant variable, re-estimating the model, and re-iterating the process until all variables in the model reach the significance threshold of .05 value (Heij *et al.*, 2004, pp. 280–281). Being free of multicollinearity problems and including all variables with (statistically) significant explanatory power over the outcome, Model 2 is the more meaningful model.

Of the variables referring to the number of articles in the expert discourse, only the one describing the (lagged) five-years moving average of the number of articles in the international expert discourse is significant. If researchers publish more on minimum wages over the course of a few years, more scholars are cited in newspaper articles. The other variables related to the expert discourse lack statistical significance and are thus excluded from Model 2. The size of the effect of the international expert discourse, moreover, is small. The effect of one additional article in the international expert discourse on the estimated number of research-related actors cited in newspaper articles is about .4 percent of the size of the estimated difference in the number of research-related actors between German and US newspapers.

Of the two uncertainty-related variables, shift in evaluation and minimum wage new, both have the hypothesized positive sign, but neither of the two is statistically significant. The variable indicating situations of uncertainty linked to rapid shifts in the expert discourse is very close to statistical significance and has a substantially sizeable effect. The lack of statistical significance could be a result of the low number of observations rather than of a missing effect.

The two country dummies behave as hypothesized. Both in Germany and the UK, newspapers cite research-related actors significantly less often than in the US. The effect is more than twice as strong for Germany. Both variables are highly significant, statistically and substantially. The variable indicating the effect of subsystem polarization is far removed from statistical significance and is not included in Model 2.

Finally, the number of references to research-related actors in the sample is higher when the total number of actors that were coded is high. This is quite self-evident. In years in which newspapers write more about actors in minimum wage policy subsystems, they also write more about the research-related actors in the policy subsystems. The variable is significant both statistically and substantially.

Table 5.7 Poisson regression with cluster-robust standard errors; p-values (in parentheses) are corrected for the small number of clusters. Statistically significant coefficients (p<.05) are marked with a star

	Model 1	Model 2
	coefficient *(p-value)*	coefficient *(p-value)*
Domestic expert discourse	−0.002 *(.97)*	
Domestic expert discourse, MA5	−0.016 *(.19)*	
International expert discourse	−0.004 *(.88)*	
International expert discourse, MA5	0.011 *(.14)*	0.005 *(.04)**
Shift in evaluation	0.873 *(.07)*	0.814 *(.05)*
Minimum wage new	0.204 *(.63)*	
Subsystem polarization	0.188 *(.69)*	
DE	−1.865 *(.01)**	−1.215 *(.01)**
UK	−1.091 *(.03)**	−0.484 *(.01)**
Actors coded	0.024 *(.01)**	0.0261 *(.01)**
Article count	−0.002 *(.65)*	
Constant	0.081	−0.059
Pseudo-R2	*.45*	.43
N	*93*	93

5.3.4 Robustness Check

The expert discourse variable used in Model 2 (Table 5.7) is a five-years moving average of the number of scientific articles published in the international expert discourse. As discussed above, the decision to use a five-years moving average is somewhat arbitrary. While the idea behind this variable is to capture the current scientific interest in minimum wages, this could also be done with moving averages that are a bit shorter or longer. To ensure the robustness of Model 2 (that is, the more meaningful model on which the conclusions from this chapter are based), it was re-estimated using four-years and six-years moving averages instead. The results are documented in Appendix A5 (Table A5.1). The re-estimation leads to similar results. For the four-years moving average, the effect of the variable International Expert Discourse is a little bit stronger and significant, for the six-years moving average it is a bit weaker and just below the 5 percent threshold of significance.

5.3.5 Conditions of the Presence of Scientific Expertise in the Newspaper Discourse: Summary

This section has presented the results from a Poisson regression, in which different variables were used to predict the number of references to research-related actors in the newspaper discourse. The analysis was designed to test several hypotheses from the theoretical model developed in Chapter 2.

Hypothesis H2.1 predicts a higher overall use of scientific expertise when more articles on minimum wages are published. The results confirm this hypothesis only for the international expert discourse. Moreover, this effect is very weak and, thus, should be of little practical relevance.

Hypotheses H3.2 and H3.4 predict a higher overall use of scientific expertise in situations in which political actors can be expected to be uncertain about the effects of the minimum wage. The variable connected to hypothesis H3.2, referring to uncertainty caused by the fact that the minimum wage is new, has the expected sign, but is statistically insignificant. The variable connected to hypothesis H3.4, which refers to uncertainty caused by rapid changes in the scientific evaluation of minimum wage effects, also has the expected positive sign. It is statistically insignificant but comes close to the five percent significance threshold.

Finally, the analysis indicates that research-related actors are much less visible in the two countries with a consensual/corporatist style of using scientific expertise than in the US, where there is a pluralist style of using expertise. In contrast, the polarization of a policy subsystem has no effect on the presence of scientific expertise in the newspaper discourse.

5.4 Explaining Which Expertise is Present in the Newspaper Discourse

In addition to knowing *under what circumstances* scientific expertise is used by actors in minimum wage policy subsystems, there is also an interest in knowing *which* expertise is used. Is it the one described by the data set on the expert discourse on minimum wage? Or is it only parts of the expert discourse that enter newspaper articles, or a completely different set of expertise? To claim the former, we should be able to show that the statements by research-related actors in newspaper articles are broadly representative of the research results from the expert discourse. It is also important to specify *which* expert discourse is used. Is it the domestic or the international one?

Relevant information for answering these questions has already been presented earlier in this chapter. The analyses presented above show which scholars are cited in newspapers, and compare the evaluation of different minimum wage effects in the domestic expert discourse and by research-related actors cited in newspapers. In this section, the results from a more fine-grained regression analysis are presented. This is done for the evaluation of minimum wage effects on employment, where there is most data available.

5.4.1 Hypotheses and Operationalization

The theoretical model from Chapter 2 provides two hypotheses regarding which kind of expert knowledge is discussed in newspaper articles: H1.1 states that research results from the domestic expert discourse will enter newspaper reporting on minimum wages, while H1.3 states that knowledge from the international expert discourse enters the newspaper discourse. Both hypotheses are tested here.

The dependent variable in this regression analysis is the evaluation of minimum wage effects on employment by research-related actors cited in newspaper articles. One observation refers to one research-related actor who says something about how minimum wages influence employment, and is cited in one newspaper article. This gives a total of 182 observations, 143 of which refer to the United States, 17 to Germany and 22 to the UK. The dependent variable can take the values "−1", "−.5", "0", ".5", "1", where "−1" denotes a plain negative evaluation of minimum wage effects on employment "–.5" a limited negative evaluation, "0" the statement that the minimum wage has no effect on employment, ".5" a limited positive evaluation, and "1" a plain positive evaluation (see Chapter 3). The value ".5" does not occur in the data.

Table 5.8 Variables used in the regression analysis

Variable name	Description	Mean	Standard Deviation
Evaluation by scholars in newspapers	Dependent variable; evaluation of minimum wage effects on employment by a research-related actor at time t.	–.44	.71
International expert discourse	Mean evaluation of minimum wage effects on employment in the international expert discourse in at t-1.	–.61	.24
Domestic expert discourse	Mean evaluation of minimum wage effects on employment in the domestic expert discourse at t-1.	–.60	.47
International Expert discourse, MA5	Mean evaluation of minimum wage effects on employment in the international expert discourse in the years t-5 through t-1.	–.58	.15
Domestic expert discourse, MA5	Mean evaluation of minimum wage effects on employment in the domestic expert discourse in the years t-5 through t-1.	–.56	.23
DE	Dummy variable for Germany		
UK	Dummy variable for the UK		
Left paper	Dummy variable for left-wing newspapers		

Regarding explanatory variables, the focus is on the expert discourse on minimum wages. The variables International Expert Discourse and Domestic Expert Discourse refer to the mean evaluation of minimum wage effects on employment in the international and the domestic expert discourse. For example, for the variable International Expert Discourse in 1998, the mean evaluation of minimum wage effects on employment in all scientific articles published in 1998 is computed. As above, five-years moving averages of the evaluation of minimum wage effect on employment are included. This is done to capture a use of research that is oriented towards the general thrust of the expert discourse of the past years, rather than just the most recent research results. As in the previous regression analysis, all variables related to the expert discourse are lagged by one year.

Finally, as it seems plausible that left-wing newspapers cite more pro-minimum wage scholars than right-wing newspapers, the dummy variable Left Paper indicates whether an observation has been coded from the New York Times, the Guardian, or Süddeutsche Zeitung. The variables included in the analysis are listed in Table 5.8.

5.4.2 Estimation Method

The estimation method is, first, determined by the nature of the dependent variable (DV). As argued above, the DV is an ordinal rather than an interval variable. An appropriate method to deal with ordinal dependent variables is ordered logit regression (Heij *et al.*, 2004, pp. 474–477), which will be used.

As in the previous regression analysis, the estimation must deal with unobserved heterogeneity. The estimation presented in Table 5.7 used data aggregated at the country-year level and included dummy variables for the three countries. As the present analysis uses disaggregated data at the level of individual actors, it does not only have to deal with unobserved heterogeneity among countries. Since what a researcher quoted in a newspaper says at one point in time will almost certainly be correlated with what the same researcher says at later points in time, random effects at the level of the individual researcher are included. Compared to including dummy variables for every single actor, the random effects model has the advantage of including less variables and preserving more degrees of freedom. A Hausman test of fixed effects versus random effects clustering (Cameron and Trivedi, 2009, pp. 266–267) on the data suggests the appropriateness of the random effects model. In addition, as recommended by Cameron and Miller (2015), cluster-robust standard errors are used to address a possible serial correlation in the error terms within the random effects clusters.

The model was estimated using Stata's xtologit command, which uses a proportional odds model (Liu and Agresti, 2005, pp. 3–5). The pseudo-R^2 statistic reported is Cragg and Uhler's (1970), computed using the fitstat command (Long and Freese, 2014).

5.4.3 Results

The results of the regression analysis are presented in Table 5.9. Given high multicollinearity between the variables describing the domestic and those describing the international expert discourse, no model simultaneously including both expert discourses could be estimated. Instead, Model 1 includes only the domestic, while Model 2 includes only the international expert discourse. A comparison of the Bayes Information Criterion (Heij *et al.*, 2004, p. 279) suggests that Model 2 is the more appropriate model. To increase the precision of this better model, a procedure described by Heij et al. (2004, pp. 280–281) was applied. The variable with the highest p-value was deleted, and the model was re-estimated. The two steps were iterated until the Bayes Information Criterion took its optimal value. This resulted in Model 3. Of the three models presented in Table 5.9, it fits the data best.

Looking at Model 1 and Model 2, one can see that all variables connected to the expert discourse have the expected positive sign, meaning that, when the expert discourse has a more favorable evaluation of minimum wage effects on employment, newspapers cite more research-related actors with statements that the minimum wage does not harm employment. While the five-years moving averages of the expert discourse are not statistically significant, the one-year average is statistically significant in Model 2, and close to statistical significance in Model 1. Moreover, the lower value of the Bayes Information Criterion suggests that Model 2 better describes the data.

In Model 3, the five-years moving average of the expert discourse and the UK country dummy were excluded due to a lack of statistical significance, to increase the precision of the estimation. The results do not differ substantively from Model 2. The more positive the evaluation of minimum wages in the international expert discourse, the more positive the evaluation of minimum wages by researchers cited in newspaper articles.

With regard to control variables, Model 3 suggests that statements by research-related actors in German newspapers paint a less favorable picture of minimum wage effects on employment than statements in British and US newspapers. Moreover, those newspapers assumed to have a center-left political position more often quote research-related actors saying that the minimum wage does not harm employment.

Finally, the low values of the pseudo-R^2 suggest that none of the three models does a good job at predicting how a research-related actor cited in a newspaper article evaluates minimum wage effects on employment. This reflects the fact that newspapers, faced with an expert discourse that does not provide clear answers

Table 5.9 Ordered logit regression with cluster-robust standard errors (one cluster relates to one individual researcher); p-values in parentheses. Statistically significant coefficients ($p < .05$) are marked with a star. Dependent variable: evaluation of minimum wage effect on employment by researchers cited in newspaper articles

	Model 1	Model 2	Model 3
	Coefficient *(p-value)*	Coefficient *(p-value)*	Coefficient *(p-value)*
International expert discourse		2.769 *(.00)**	2.480 *(.00)**
International expert discourse, MA5		3.440 *(.11)*	
Domestic expert discourse	1.959 *(.06)*		
Domestic expert discourse, MA5	2.089 *(.20)*		
DE	−2.109 *(.01)**	−2.577 *(.00)**	−2.151 *(.00)**
UK	−1.287 *(.37)*	.291 *(.66)*	
Left paper	1.105 *(.00)**	1.276 *(.00)**	1.021 *(.00)**
Cutpoint 1	−1.209	−2.344	−.228
Cutpoint 2	−.331	−1.453	.612
Cutpoint 3	3.461	2.403	4.283
BIC	358	354	351
Pseudo-R2	.07	.08	.07
N	181	181	181

on minimum wage effects on employment, tend to cite different positions on minimum wages.

5.4.4 Robustness Check

Reflecting the discussion from Chapter 3 about averaging ordinal data, the three models presented in Table 5.9 were re-estimated using recoded versions of the variables in the expert discourse. Rather than describing the mean evaluation of minimum wages in the scientific articles published in one year/five years, these describe the fraction of the scientific articles published in one year/five years that do not find undesirable minimum wage effects. The results are presented in

Appendix A5 (Table A5.2) and are similar to those presented in Table 5.9, leading to the same conclusions.

5.4.5 Explaining the Kind of Expertise Present in the Newspaper Discourse: Summary

This section has continued to analyze the way in which expert knowledge is presented in newspapers. While the preceding section has discussed the factors that influence *when* and *how often* experts and their research will be cited in newspaper articles, this section has analyzed the variables that influence *what kind of* expert opinions are presented in newspaper articles.

The analysis shows that the evaluation of minimum wage effects on employment in the expert discourse influences what statements by research-related actors are cited in newspaper articles. When research evaluates the minimum wage more favorably, so do researchers cited in newspaper articles. Their statements reflect the expert discourse on minimum wages.

Moreover, the analysis suggests that the international expert discourse is a better predictor of the scientific expertise cited in newspaper articles than the domestic expert discourse. While high multicollinearity between the variables describing the domestic and the international expert discourse makes it impossible to estimate both simultaneously, the models using the international expert discourse better fit the data.

5.5 Conclusion: Scientific Expertise in the Newspaper Discourse

This chapter has presented several analyses to determine the extent and the conditions under which research results from the expert discourse enter public discussions on minimum wages taking place in newspapers. The chapter started with a descriptive analysis of the expert discourse. As was shown, there is a sizeable international expert discourse on minimum wages. Of the three domestic expert discourses analyzed, the one in the US is largest, and the one from Germany smallest. Moreover, the annual number of publications has increased over time. While most scientific articles in the expert discourse discuss minimum wage effects on employment, analyses of minimum wage effects on poverty and the economy are also common. The evaluation of minimum wage effects differs between the three domestic expert discourses. Publications in the UK expert discourse were found to deliver a favorable evaluation of the minimum wage, whereas publications in the US and the German expert discourse were markedly more critical. In the US, where the data on the expert discourse was collected for the longest time period, there is clear evidence of an over-time shift in the average evaluation of minimum wage effects. Here, the overall evaluation of minimum wage effects became markedly less negative over time. In Germany, a similar shift happened in the mid-2000s.

Next, the presentation of scientific expertise in the coded newspaper articles was analyzed. Research-related actors account for a relevant portion of all actors coded from newspaper articles. There are, however, differences between the three countries. In the US, researchers account for 17 percent of all actors coded, while the figure for Germany is six percent. The research-related actors and organizations that were cited are largely domestic. International actors and organizations, such as the OECD or scholars from other countries, were more often cited in German and British newspapers than in the US. Even there, however, they make up only for a minority of the research-related actors cited. Moreover, the evaluation of minimum wage effects by research-related actors cited in newspaper articles approximately reflects the evaluation of minimum wage effects in the expert discourse. Together, these findings suggest that there is a public discussion of minimum wage-related scientific expertise, and that this expertise reflects the research presented in scientific journals.

Afterwards, the results of two regression analyses were presented. The first one was conducted to identify the conditions under which journalists cite research-related actors. The results confirm the previous finding that US newspapers cite research-related actors significantly more frequently than German and British newspapers. Moreover, when the number of articles in the international expert discourse increases, research-related actors are cited slightly more often in newspaper articles. There is weaker evidence for an increased visibility of research-related actors when there are strong shifts in the expert discourse.

The second regression analysis was conducted to get additional knowledge about the kind of expert knowledge cited in newspaper articles. The expert opinions regarding minimum wage effects on employment cited in newspaper articles are positively related to the evaluation of minimum wage effects in the expert discourse. When the expert discourse evaluates minimum wages more positively, so do the research-related actors cited in newspapers. This corroborates the earlier finding that the research results presented in newspaper articles reflect those published in scholarly journals. While the domestic and the international expert discourse both have power in explaining what expertise is presented in newspaper articles, a model using the international expert discourse was found to fit the data better than a model using the domestic expert discourse.

These results can be used to evaluate several of the hypotheses formulated in Chapter 2. *First*, hypothesis H1.1 states that research from the domestic expert discourse enters the public discourse on minimum wages taking place in newspapers. Hypothesis H1.3 states that it is the international expert discourse which is discussed publicly. The results from this chapter suggest that both expert discourses play a role, but do not provide a clear answer regarding which one is more important. On the one hand, domestic minimum wage scholars and other domestic research-related actors are cited in newspaper articles much more often than international ones. On the other hand, the regression analyses point to the importance of the international expert discourse. Research-related actors are more often cited in newspapers when the number of articles in the international expert discourse increases. Moreover, the evaluation of minimum wage effects on employment in the international expert discourse predicts the evaluation of minimum wages by research-related actors cited in newspaper articles better than the domestic expert discourse, even if only slightly so. In sum, these findings seem to be best compatible with a situation in which both findings from the domestic and from the international expert discourse enter the newspaper discourse.

Second, hypothesis H2.1 states that the public discussion of scientific expertise in newspapers is more intense when more scientific articles on minimum wages are published. The regression analysis presented in Table 5.5 confirms this result: The more articles there are in the international expert discourse, the more often are research-related actors cited in newspaper articles. The correlation, however, is so weak that it doesn't matter much in practice.

Third, hypothesis H3.1 states that more scientific expertise enters newspaper reporting when the minimum wage is new, as uncertainty among political actors is high. Based on the analyses from this chapter, there is no support for this hypothesis: While the number of research-related actors cited in newspaper articles is slightly higher when the minimum wage is new, this effect is weak and statistically not significant. *Fourth*, hypothesis H3.3, also dealing with uncertainty, predicts more scientific expertise entering newspaper articles when new research results unsettle long-standing beliefs about how minimum wages work. Indeed, as shown in Table 5.5, the number of research-related actors in newspaper articles increases in such situations, even though the p-value of this effect is just above the 5 percent threshold.

Fifth, hypothesis H4.1 states that, under the conditions of a pluralistic style of using scientific expertise, the public discussion of scientific expertise in newspaper articles will be more intense than under the conditions of a consensual/corporatist style. This chapter has delivered support for this hypothesis. It was shown that research-related actors are much more visible in US newspapers, where there is a pluralistic style of using scientific expertise. While this result conforms to the expectations from hypothesis H4.1, it should be interpreted with caution. Thus, besides styles of using scientific expertise, there are many other differences between the three countries, which could also be responsible for the different numbers of research-related actors cited in newspaper articles. For example, a plausible alternative explanation would attribute the difference to different journalistic norms prevalent in the US.

Finally, hypotheses H4.3 states that the public discussion of scientific expertise is more intense in policy subsystems with an adversarial advocacy coalition structure. The analyses presented in this chapter have offered no support for this hypothesis. The number of research-related actors cited in newspaper articles is unaffected by the advocacy coalition structure.

The Influence of the Expert Discourse on Political Actors

6

The previous chapter has analyzed the presence of scientific expertise in the newspaper discourse, which was argued to often reflect or incite the political use of expertise. This chapter is concerned with the use of scientific expertise for policy-oriented learning across belief systems, analyzing the influence of expert discourses on political actors' beliefs and policy preferences. As before, the analyses are not only concerned with the extent of such an influence, but also with context variables that determine whether the expert discourse influences political actors' beliefs and preferences.

Methodologically, these questions are approached in different ways. The analysis starts by simply comparing the assessment of different minimum wage effects in the expert discourse with their evaluation by political actors. A connection between expert discourses and political actors' beliefs would appear plausible if both evaluations were similar. This comparison, however, can neither illuminate the direction of causality nor the conditions of expert influence. Therefore, several regression analyses are presented below, testing whether an actor's position towards the minimum wage at a given point in time depends on the expert discourse in the previous time period. In line with Granger (1969), causality is assumed if—after controlling for all relevant variables—knowledge of the expert discourse at one point in time helps to predict an actor's policy preference at a later point in time.

Electronic supplementary material The online version of this chapter (https://doi.org/10.1007/978-3-658-32746-0_6) contains supplementary material, which is available to authorized users.

F. Klein, *The Role of Scientific Expertise in Minimum Wage Policy Making*, Vergleichende Politikwissenschaft,
https://doi.org/10.1007/978-3-658-32746-0_6

Finally, to complete the picture of the relation between expert discourses and actor preferences, two further regression analyses are conducted to clarify whether there are reverse causal links going from the newspaper discourse and the minimum-wage policy subsystem to the expert discourse. The analyses test for two different forms of influence. *First*, they test whether an increased interest for minimum wages in the newspaper discourse leads to an increased interest in the topic in the expert discourse. S*econd*, they test whether the evaluation of minimum wages in the expert discourse is influenced by how actors in minimum wage policy subsystems evaluate the minimum wage.

6.1 Comparing Beliefs and Preferences

This section compares the average evaluations of different minimum wage effects by experts and actors in the three minimum wage policy subsystems. As mentioned above, a connection between expert discourses and political actors' beliefs would only appear plausible if both evaluations are similar. The results of the comparison for the three countries are presented in Table 6.1.

The table shows that, overall, there is a good deal of agreement between the evaluation of minimum wages in the expert discourse and by political actors. Regarding the evaluation of minimum wage effect on poverty, in all three countries, a large majority of the coded scientific articles evaluate minimum wages favorably. This evaluation is matched by political actors' assessment of the same question. In all three countries, most political actors assume a favorable effect of the minimum wage on poverty. The agreement between expert discourse and actors in minimum wage policy subsystems also holds for the evaluation of minimum wage effects on employment and the economy. For those two effects, the modal value of the evaluation of the minimum wage in the expert discourse is "−1" ("adverse effect") in all three countries. This evaluation is matched by political actors in the three countries, who mostly evaluate the effects of the minimum wage on employment and on the economy unfavorably. The only exception here is the evaluation of minimum wage effects on the economy in Germany. While the German expert discourse has a mostly negative view on such effects, a slight majority (52.3%) of political actors in Germany assume a favorable effect on the economy, while a relatively strong minority (45.5%) agrees with the expert discourse.

The agreement between the expert discourse and political actors is much weaker when it comes to the overall evaluation of the minimum wage. In the United States as well as in Germany, the domestic expert discourse presents a mostly negative view of the minimum wage, while most political actors support minimum wages. The fact that the agreement between scientific research and political actors is weaker for the overall evaluation of minimum wages is not surprising. The overall evaluation in the expert discourse is a composite measure derived from adding up all evaluations of different minimum wage effects in one article (see Chapter 3). Political actors will, however, often base their overall position towards the minimum wage on considerations other than minimum wage effects on employment, poverty and the economy. For example, a political party might choose to support the minimum wage because it is popular with voters, not because it has beneficial effects. To what extent the expert discourse also influences the overall preference of political actors will be a matter of further analyses in this chapter.

Moreover, even though there is a relatively high agreement between the evaluation of minimum wage effects by the expert discourse and political actors *on average*, one must keep in mind that this does not mean that each single actor equally agrees with the expert discourse. For example, as was shown in the analysis of coalition beliefs in Chapter 4, actors from the US anti-minimum wage coalition are very frequently cited in newspaper articles, stating that minimum wages harm employment. This claim is very much in line with the expert discourse. In contrast, this same statement was only made by 1 percent of the actors from the US pro-minimum wage coalition (see Chapter 4, Table 4.3). A further examination of the data presented in Chapter 4 shows that this pattern also holds for evaluations of minimum wage effects on poverty and the economy, and is also valid for the other two countries (see Chapter 4, Tables 4.7, 4.8, 4.12, 4.13). Political actors supporting the minimum wage rarely talk about its harmful effects, political actors opposing the minimum wage are quiet regarding its beneficial ones.

At the same time, political actors rarely actively contradict the expert discourse. For example, while actors from the US pro minimum wage coalition rarely state that the minimum wage harms employment, they also rarely state that minimum wages are good for employment. Again, similar patterns are visible for other minimum wage effects and for the other two countries (see Chapter 4, Tables 4.3, 4.7, 4.8, 4.12, 4.13). Political actors, rather than openly opposing the scientific evaluation of a specific minimum wage effect, often choose not to publicly address the issue when the expert discourse contradicts their own policy preference.

In sum, comparing the evaluation of minimum wages in the expert discourse with the evaluation of minimum wages by actors in minimum wage policy subsystems suggests two main conclusions. *First*, there is a clear correlation between the

Table 6.1 Evaluation of minimum wage effects and total evaluation of the minimum wage in the expert discourse and by actors in minimum wage policy subsystems. For example, in the US expert discourse, 14.3 percent of all coded scientific articles (corresponding to 10 articles) evaluate the effect of the minimum wage on poverty as unfavorable (−1). Of the UK political actors coded from the newspaper articles, 4.8 percent (corresponding to 4 actors) evaluate the effects of the minimum wage on employment as favorable (1). Note: to get a clearer presentation, the categories −.5 and −1 as well as the categories .5 and 1 were merged for the data referring to political actors

		Minimum wage effect on poverty			Minimum wage effect on the economy			Minimum wage effect on employment			Total evaluation of minimum wages		
		−1	0	1	−1	0	1	−1	0	1	-1	0	1
US	Expert discourse	*14.3% (10)*	*18.6% (13)*	*76.1% (47)*	*55.2% (35)*	*8.6% (5)*	*36.2% (21)*	*72.9% (164)*	*17.8% (40)*	*9.3% (21)*	*58.6% (201)*	*18.1% (62)*	*23.3% (80)*
	Political actors	*12.2% (11)*	*14.4% (13)*	*73.3% (66)*	*70.7% (99)*	*21.4% (30)*	*7.9% (11)*	*75.1% (166)*	*19.5% (43)*	*5.4% (12)*	*35.8% (321)*	*16.9% (152)*	*47.3% (425)*
UK	Expert discourse	*10.7% (3)*	*14.3% (4)*	*75.0% (21)*	*55.6% (10)*	*11.1% (2)*	*33.3% (6)*	*49.1% (26)*	*32.1% (17)*	*18.9% (10)*	*34.0% (33)*	*28.9% (28)*	*37.1% (36)*
	Political actors	*2.6% (1)*	*23.1% (9)*	*74.4% (29)*	*60.3% (47)*	*28.3% (22)*	*11.5% (9)*	*64.4% (67)*	*31.7% (33)*	*4.8% (4)*	*24.3% (107)*	*24.9% (110)*	*50.8% (224)*
DE	Expert discourse	*18.2% (2)*	*18.2% (2)*	*63.6% (7)*	*66.7 (4)*	*0.0% (0)*	*33.3% (2)*	*73.5% (25)*	*23.6% (8)*	*2.9% (1)*	*57.7% (30)*	*21.1% (11)*	*21.1% (11)*
	Political actors	*0% (0)*	*23.1% (3)*	*76.9% (10)*	*45.5% (20)*	*2.3% (1)*	*52.3% (23)*	*76.6% (36)*	*8.5% (4)*	*14.9% (7)*	*28.1% (107)*	*13.6% (52)*	*58.3% (222)*

evaluation of minimum wage effects in the expert discourse and the beliefs about the effects of minimum wages that political actors publicly express in newspapers. *Second*, this correlation is not obvious regarding the overall position towards the minimum wage.

6.2 Explaining Actors' Preferences with the Expert Discourse

A simple comparison, however, can only provide a first impression of possible causal connections between the expert discourse and the beliefs and preferences of political actors. It neither accounts for control variables nor clarifies the direction of possible causal connections. Do changes in the expert discourse lead to changes in actor preferences, or do actor preferences influence the expert discourse? The regression analyses presented in this section provide better insights into these questions. They also make it possible to identify conditions of expert influence.

The regression analyses are designed to explain political actors' positions towards the minimum wage with the expert discourse, as well as with a range of other control variables. In principle, this could be done for each of the four aspects of an actor's position towards the minimum wage analyzed above—beliefs regarding minimum wage effects on employment, the economy and poverty, and the overall preference towards the minimum wage. However, the analysis will only be done for actor's overall preference. On the practical side, this is because the number of statements by political actors that refer to minimum wage effects tend to be relatively rare compared to statements referring to the overall desirability of the minimum wage. From a theoretical point of view, the analysis in the previous section above has suggested that an expert influence on actors' overall policy preferences is a hard case compared to an expert influence on beliefs regarding minimum wage effects on employment, poverty, and the economy. One can thus expect that any expert influence found on the overall policy preference of political actors indicates that expert discourses also influence how political actors perceive minimum wage effects on poverty, the economy and employment.

In the analyses presented in this section, one observation refers to one instance in which a political actor has been coded from the newspaper articles that were analyzed and has revealed their preference towards the minimum wage. This preference is the dependent variable of the analysis. As discussed in Chapter 3, it takes the values "−1","0", and "1" with a negative value indicating opposition against and a positive value indicating support for the minimum wage.

6.2.1 Hypotheses and Operationalization

The theoretical model from Chapter 2 specifies several hypotheses regarding the influence of scientific expertise on the political actors' policy preferences. The most general hypotheses in the theoretical model expect that policy-oriented learning from the expert discourse occurs and is relevant for political actors' minimum wage preferences. Thus, Hypothesis H1.2 states that the domestic expert discourse influences political actors' minimum wage preferences, while Hypothesis H1.4 states that their preferences are influenced by the international expert discourse. The explanatory variables to test these hypotheses describe the evaluation of minimum wages in the expert discourse. The evaluation in the domestic expert discourse which is hypothesized to influence political actors at time t is operationalized as the *mean of the overall evaluation* (see Chapter 3) of minimum wages in all scholarly journal articles in this country's expert discourse published in the year t−1. Moreover, a five-years moving average of this variable is included, considering scientific articles published in the years t−5 to t−1. Additionally, the same one-year and five-years moving averages were computed for the international expert discourse. The different time lags are included to test whether political actors are influenced by the latest research results or by the research results published in recent years.

As discussed in Chapter 3, the variable describing a scientific article's overall evaluation of minimum wages lumps together minimum wage effects on employment, the economy, poverty, and other effects. Therefore, using the expert discourse's overall evaluation of minimum wage to explain political actors' policy preferences implies that these actors equally care about the different minimum wage effects researched in the expert discourse. In practice, however, some minimum wage effects might be more important for political actors' preference formation than others. This could be tested by separately analyzing the influence of those parts of the expert discourse researching minimum wage effects on employment, the economy, poverty, and so on. Given the limited number of scientific articles on minimum wage effects on variables other than employment, especially in Germany and the United Kingdom, this is not feasible. Therefore, the analyses in this chapter focus on whether the entirety of the expert discourse influences political actors' minimum wage preferences, and not on the question which parts of the expert discourse are most influential.

The theoretical model specifies several conditions of the influence of scientific expertise on political actors' minimum wage preferences. These hypotheses are tested using interaction terms between the variables measuring the overall evaluation of minimum wage in the expert discourse, and variables that indicate the degree to which these conditions are present. The *first* set of conditions refers to the expert discourse itself. Thus, hypothesis H2.2 predicts an expert influence to be stronger when more scientific articles on minimum wage effects are published. As in Chapter 5, this is operationalized as the number of scientific articles in the respective expert discourse in the respective time period. Hypothesis H2.3 states that expert influence is higher when the coherence in the expert discourse is high. The variable to test this hypothesis is operationalized as the variance of the overall evaluation of minimum wages in the articles of the respective expert discourse in the respective time period. If the articles in the expert discourse come to wildly different evaluations of the minimum wage, the variance is high, and less influence is expected.

The *second* set of hypotheses regarding the conditions of expert influence refers to uncertainty, with H3.2 predicting a stronger influence when the minimum wage is new, and H3.4 predicting a stronger influence in times in which new research results upset traded knowledge about the effects of minimum wages. As in Chapter 5, both hypotheses are operationalized as dummy variables.

Third, the environment in which minimum-wage policy making takes place was hypothesized to be relevant. The influence of the expert discourse on the minimum wage preferences of political actors is expected to be higher under the conditions of a consensual/corporatist style of using scientific expertise, as opposed to a pluralistic style (H4.2). The two different styles of using expertise are operationalized by including a country dummy for the US (the country with a pluralistic style). Furthermore, expert influence was hypothesized to be stronger when the coalition structure in the policy subsystem is collaborative, as opposed to adversarial (H4.4). As in Chapter 5, this variable was operationalized as the five-years moving average of the mean distance between the actors from the coalition supporting the minimum wage and actors from the coalition opposing the minimum wage (see Appendix A5).

Fourth, actors belonging to organizations without strong negative or positive preferences vis-à-vis minimum wages were hypothesized to be more likely to be influenced by the expert discourse (H5.1). This hypothesis is operationalized with a dummy variable that takes the value 1 for all actors belonging to organizations for which the mean of all positions towards the minimum wage with which the organization was coded lies in the range from −.5 to .5.

In addition to variables included to test hypotheses from the theoretical model, a number of control variables which are expected to predict an actor's position towards the minimum wage are included. The include socio-economic variables—GDP growth, unemployment rates, and low pay rates (OECD, 2015)—and country dummies. Moreover, a different minimum wage policy preference is expected for different types of actors. These actor types are left and right-wing political parties, trade unions, employer organizations, companies, and actors from the executive branch of the national/federal government—mostly ministries and heads of governments. The latter group was divided into a left-wing executive and a right-wing executive, depending on whether the Head of Government was affiliated with a left-of-center or a right-of-center political party.[1] Finally, two control variables were included to account for the idea that political actors might be less likely to publicly reveal their true preference regarding the minimum wage shortly before elections. Thus, the dummy variable election takes the value 1 for years with national elections.[2] The interaction term of the variable election and the expert discourse captures the idea that, in election years, political actors might orient their public statements about minimum wages more towards voter preferences and less towards the expert discourse. A complete list and description of the variables included into the analysis is shown in Table 6.2.

6.2.2 Estimation Method

As discussed in Chapter 3, the dependent variable—an actor's position on the minimum wage—is ordinal in nature. It can take three different values—"−1", "0", "1"—whose substantive meaning can be ordered from most negative to most supportive. The distances between the categories, however, are not necessarily equal. In parallel to the procedure used to estimate the regression presented in Table 5.5, the model is thus estimated using an ordered logistic regression model (Heij *et al.*, 2004, pp. 474–480).

As in previous estimations, the panel properties of data need to be accounted for. Unobserved heterogeneity between the three countries is dealt with through the inclusion of country dummies. Given that an organization's minimum wage policy preference at one point in time is likely to be correlated with the same organization's policy preference at another point in time, clustering at the level of the organization to which an actor belongs should be considered. A Hausman test of fixed effects versus random effects clustering (Cameron and Trivedi, 2009, pp. 266–267) shows that a random effects model is appropriate to do so. In addition, as recommended by Cameron and Miller (2015), cluster-robust standard

[1] In Germany, where coalition governments are common, the determination whether a federal ministry was left-of-center or right-of-center was done according to the party affiliation of the minister.

[2] Congressional and presidential elections in the US, general elections in the UK, and *Bundestagswahlen* in Germany.

Table 6.2 Variables included into the regression analysis

Variable name	Description	Mean	Standard deviation
Minimum wage stance	Dependent variable; the actor's position towards the minimum wage at time t.	.21	.88
International expert discourse	Mean evaluation of minimum wage effects on employment in the international expert discourse in at t−1.	−.25	.30
Domestic expert discourse	Mean evaluation of minimum wage effects on employment in the domestic expert discourse at t−1.	−.26	.42
International expert discourse, MA5	Mean evaluation of minimum wage effects on employment in the international expert discourse in the years t−5 through t−1.	−.29	.27
Domestic expert discourse, MA5	Mean evaluation of minimum wage effects on employment in the domestic expert discourse in the years t−5 through t−1.	−.24	.31
Variance of expert discourse	Variance of the evaluation of minimum wages in the articles of the domestic expert discourse; refers to the years t−5 to t−1.	.66	.24
Volume of expert discourse	Number of scientific journal articles in the domestic expert discourse; refers to the years t−5 to t−1.	29.93	20.25
Unemployment	Unemployment rate at time t (in percent)	6.56	1.76
Low pay	Percentage of low paid workers at time t	21.66	2.70
GDP growth	Annual growth of the gross domestic product at time t in percent.	2.58	1.91

(continued)

Table 6.2 (continued)

Variable name	Description	Mean	Standard deviation
US	Dummy variable for the United States.		
UK	Dummy variable for the UK.		
Minimum wage new	Dummy variable indicating years in which the minimum wage is new. Takes the value 1 from 1994–2004 in the UK, and 2010–2015 in Germany).		
Shift in evaluation	Dummy variable indicating rapid shifts in the evaluation of minimum wages in the expert discourse. Takes the value 1 between 1991 and 1997 for the US and 2003 and 2007 for Germany.		
Moderate actor	Dummy variable indicating moderate organizations. Takes the value 1 if the mean of all positions towards the minimum wage with which this organization was coded lies in the range from −.5 to .5.		
Subsystem polarization	Mean distance between the actors from the coalition supporting the minimum wage and actors from the coalition opposing the minimum wage. Refers to the years t−5 to t−1.	1.27	.32
Left party	Dummy variable taking the value 1 for actors speaking for a left-of-center political party.		
Right party	Dummy variable taking the value 1 for actors speaking for a right-of-center political party		

(continued)

errors are used to address a possible serial correlation in the error terms within the random effects clusters.

Table 6.2 (continued)

Variable name	Description	Mean	Standard deviation
Left executive	Dummy variable taking the value 1 for actors speaking for an organization that is part of the executive branch of a federal government headed by a politician affiliated with a left-of-center political party.		
Right executive	Dummy variable taking the value 1 for actors speaking for an organization that is part of the executive branch of a federal government headed by a politician affiliated with a right-of-center political party.		
Trade union	Dummy variable taking the value 1 for actors speaking for a trade union.		
Employer organization	Dummy variable taking the value 1 for actors speaking for an employer organization.		
Company	Dummy variable taking the value 1 for actors speaking for a company.		
Election	Dummy variable taking the value 1 in years with national elections (Congress, Presidential, General Election, Bundestagswahl)		
Experts * variance	Interaction term of Domestic Expert Discourse, MA5, and Variance of Expert Discourse.	−.12	.16
Experts * volume	Interaction term of Domestic Expert Discourse, MA5, and Volume of Expert Discourse.	−8,43	8.90
Experts * us	Interaction term of Domestic Expert Discourse, MA5, and US.	−.25	.29

(continued)

Table 6.2 (continued)

Variable name	Description	Mean	Standard deviation
Experts * mw new	Interaction term of Domestic Expert Discourse, MA5, and Minimum Wage New.	.01	.07
Experts * shift	Interaction term of Domestic Expert Discourse, MA5, and Shift in Evaluation.	−.04	.14
Experts * moderate	Interaction term of Domestic Expert Discourse, MA5, and Moderate Actor.	−.06	.20
Experts * polarization	Interaction term of Domestic Expert Discourse, MA5, and Subsystem Polarization.	−.33	.45
Experts * election	Interaction term of Domestic Expert Discourse, MA5, and Election.	−.07	.20

As before, the model was estimated using Stata's xtologit command, which uses a proportional odds model (Liu and Agresti, 2005, pp. 3–5). The pseudo-R^2 statistic reported is Cragg and Uhler's (1970), computed using the fitstat command (Long and Freese, 2014).

6.2.3 Results

Before the full model with all variables from Table 6.2 is discussed in Table 6.4, two smaller models are reported in Table 6.3. These estimate the influence of expert discourses on political actors' minimum wage policy preferences without interaction variables The motivation for this is to test whether it is the international or the domestic expert discourse that influences political actors, and whether the one-year average or the five-years moving average are most influential.

6.2.3.1 Models without Interaction Effects

Model 1 from Table 6.3 therefore includes four expert discourse variables (domestic and international; one-year and five-years moving average), as well as the control variables from Table 6.2: the actor type, the country dummies, and the three variables indicating socio-economic circumstances. Most importantly, the results show a significantly positive impact of the five-years moving average of the domestic expert discourse on actors' minimum wage preferences. The effect of the international expert discourse is, surprisingly, negative, but relatively far removed from statistical significance.

Table 6.3 Influence of the expert discourse without interaction effects. Dependent variable: minimum wage stance. A star marks statistically significant results (p<.05)

	Model 1	Model 2
	Coefficient *(p-value)*	Coefficient *(p-value)*
Domestic expert discourse	.537 *(.10)*	
International expert discourse	−.548 *(.44)*	
Domestic expert discourse, MA5	1.083 *(.04)**	.879 *(.03)**
International expert discourse, Ma5	−1.000 *(.17)*	
Unemployment	−.282 *(.00)**	−.237 *(.00)**
Low pay	.218 *(.23)*	
GDP growth	−.032 *(.50)*	
US	−3.163 *(.01)**	−1.581 *(.00)**
UK	−.919 *(.22)*	
Left party	1.681 *(.03)**	1.746 *(.02)**
Right Party	−2.884 *(.00)**	−2.775 *(.00)**
Left executive	−1.928 *(.01)**	−1.936 *(.01)**
Right executive	−2.466 *(.00)**	−2.472 *(.00)**
Trade union	3.506 *(.00)**	3.414 *(.00)**
Employer organization	−4.040 *(.00)**	−4.065 *(.00)**
Company	−4.069 *(.00)**	−4.177 *(.00)**
Cutpoint 1	−1.400	−4.958
Cutpoint 2	.165	−3.349
Number of observations	1451	1497
Bayes Information Criterion	2301	2338
Pseudo-R2	.38	.37

Regarding the socio-economic variables, Model 1 suggests that higher unemployment goes along with less support for the minimum wage, while economic growth and low pay rates seem to have no statistically significant influence. Regarding actor types, trade unions are most supportive of the minimum wage, followed by left-wing political parties. Companies and employer organizations are most critical of the minimum wage, right-wing political parties are moderately critical. Actors connected to the executive branch of government tend to be more moderate compared to other actor types. The coefficient of actors connected to the executive branch of a left-wing government is smaller than the coefficient of a left-wing actors. Similarly, the coefficient of actors connected to the executive branch of a right-wing government is larger than the coefficient of right-wing actors. The reason for this may be that a head of government or a secretary of labor is more strongly coerced to make compromises than a trade union or a representative of an opposition party. Finally, actors from the US are generally more critically towards the minimum wage than actors from Germany and the UK.

To increase the precision of the analysis, the procedure of iteratively deleting the variable with the highest p-value and then re-estimating the model until the Bayes Information Criterion takes its optimal value (Heij *et al.*, 2004, pp. 280–281) was applied. The result is Model 2, which preserves the basic results from Model 1 but is more precise and, therefore, the more adequate model.[3]

For the following analyses, three main conclusions from Models 1 and 2 are relevant. *First*, there is a correlation between the expert discourse and political actors' minimum wage preference, suggesting that policy-oriented learning across belief systems from the expert discourse happens. *Second*, the expert discourse which is relevant for political actors is the domestic one, not the international one. Further analyses will therefore deal the conditions under which the *domestic* expert discourse influences political actors' policy preferences. *Third*, the five-years moving average of the evaluation of minimum wage effects has more explanatory power than the one-year average. It will be used in the following analyses.

6.2.3.2 Models with Interaction Effects

Due to the high number of variables and the high number of interaction terms, estimating a full model with all variables listed in Table 6.2 poses problems of

[3]The higher Bayes Information Criterion value for Model 2 is based on the fact that Model 1 encompasses fewer observations. This is because data on the low pay variable is not available over the whole period of analysis.

multicollinearity. This means a high correlation among the explanatory variables that can strongly increase the confidence intervals of the affected coefficients, making the estimation imprecise. A preliminary analysis of variance inflation factors suggested problems related to multicollinearity with several variables.

6.2.3.2.1 Dealing with Multicollinearity

Problematic in this sense is, *first*, the low pay variable, which is strongly correlated with the US country dummy (r = .83). Low pay is a control variable and not in the center of the analysis performed in this chapter, whereas the US country dummy is important. Therefore, it is possible to follow the advice found in many statistics textbooks (e.g. Kronthaler, 2016, p. 256) and to omit the variable. In terms of interpreting the results, this means that it is difficult to tell whether different levels of support for the minimum wage in the US are related to higher numbers of low-paid workers there, or to other factors. While this difficulty in principle also concerns the interaction variable between the US country dummy and the expert discourse, there is no theoretical reason to assume that the proportion of low-paid workers in a country mediates the influence the expert discourse has on political actors.

Second, there are multicollinearity problems involving some of the interaction terms listed in Table 6.2. There is a high correlation between the variables Domestic Expert Discourse, MA5 and Experts * Variance. Moreover, there is substantial correlation between the interaction variable Experts * Variance and the other interaction terms listed in Table 6.2. Furthermore, there is a strong correlation between the variables Domestic Expert Discourse, MA5 and Experts * Polarization. Finally, there is a strong correlation between the variables Shift in Evaluation and its interaction term with the expert discourse, Experts * Shift.

The high correlation between some of the interaction terms and other variables in the model makes it impossible to estimate a model including all interaction terms from Table 6.2. To alleviate the multicollinearity problem, a three-step procedure is followed. First, the model is estimated without the variables Variance of Expert Discourse and Experts * Variance, Shift in Evaluation and Experts * Shift, and Subsystem Polarization and Experts * Polarization. Next, insignificant variables are eliminated from this first model according to the procedure used above, delivering a second model with less variables (Heij *et al.*, 2004, pp. 280–281). Finally, the hitherto omitted variables are added to this smaller model one by one, allowing an estimation with high but still acceptable degrees of multicollinearity.

6.2.3.2.2 Results

Therefore, Model 3 from Table 6.4 includes all explanatory variables from Table 6.2, except the interaction terms involving multicollinearity problems discussed in the previous subsection. Model 4 is then derived by iteratively deleting the variable with the highest p-value and then re-estimating the model until the Bayes Information Criterion takes its optimal value (Heij *et al.*, 2004, pp. 280–281). The results from both models are consistent with each other, but Model 4 is more precise.

Regarding policy-oriented learning from the expert discourse, both Model 3 and Model 4 suggest that that the expert discourse strongly influences political actor's minimum wage policy preferences. When compared to Models 1 and 2, the coefficient of the variable Domestic Expert Discourse, MA5, is much larger in Models 3 and 4. The expert discourse is now one of the strongest predictors of an actor's minimum wage preference. It is both statistically and substantially highly significant.

To understand why the coefficient of Domestic Expert Discourse, MA5, has become so large, it is instructive to look at the interaction terms describing the circumstances under which experts influence political actors' minimum wage preferences. Thus, expert influence is much smaller in the US, with a coefficient of 1.372 (4.585 − 3.213). This difference between expert influence in the US on the one hand, and in Germany and the UK on the other hand is statistically significant. Expert influence is also significantly smaller in election years. Moreover, the results indicate that, in the five years preceding and following the introduction of the minimum wage, expert influence is not positive, but *negative*, with a coefficient of −3.157 (4.585 − 7.742). When the minimum wage is new, a more positive evaluation of minimum wages in the expert discourse is correlated with a more negative evaluation of minimum wages by political actors. Again, this effect is statistically significant. This is a surprising result, which squarely contradicts the expectation formulated in hypothesis H2.5. It will be further explored below.

Two other variables describing the conditions of expert influence on political actors' minimum wage policy preferences that were formulated above do not have a significant effect in Models 3 and 4. Expert influence apparently does not depend on how many scientific studies of minimum wage effects are published. In contrast to what was expected, the corresponding variable, Experts * Volume, has a negative sign and is far removed from statistical significance. The analysis also suggests that actors with moderate views on the minimum wage—not clearly in favor, not clearly opposed—are not more likely to be influenced by the expert discourse than any other actor. Contrary to what was expected, the corresponding variable, Experts * Moderate, has a negative sign and is far removed from statistical significance. However, as shown in the simulations below (see Section 6.2.6), moderate actors are still more likely to change their position on the minimum wage due to expert influence. This is because moderate belief change resulting from learning from the expert discourse will not turn a steadfast opponent of the minimum wage into a supporter but might be enough to "tip the balance" for a moderate minimum wage sceptic.

Regarding control variables, the results are mostly as expected. Left-wing actors are more in favor of the minimum wage than right-wing actors, with actors connected to the executive branch of government being having more moderate views than others. The only difference to Models 1 and 2 is that the variable describing the effect of unemployment on political actors' minimum wage policy preferences has lost its statistical significance.

As discussed above, Models 5, 6 and 7 conform to Model 4, but add the variables omitted so far due to multicollinearity: Shift in Evaluation and Experts * Shift (Model 5), Variance of the Expert Discourse and Experts * Variance (Model 6), and Subsystem Polarization and Experts * Polarization (Model 7). The results of Model 5 suggest that there is little support for the hypothesized link between uncertainty due to a rapidly changing evaluation of minimum wages in the expert discourse and an increased expert influence. The corresponding variable, Experts * Shift, has the expected positive sign, but is far removed from statistical significance. However, the lack of significance of this variable may partly be due to the level of multicollinearity, which is still high in Model 5. Therefore, hypothesis H2.5 should not be completely discarded. To thoroughly test it, additional data would be necessary. Regarding the other variables, Model 5 generally delivers the same conclusions as Model 4. Only the variable Experts * US, describing expert influence in the United States, is statistically significant in Model 4 and insignificant in Model 5. Again, this is probably due to the relatively high degree of multicollinearity in Model 5. The lower Bayes Information Criterion suggests that Model 4 is superior to Model 5, and should be used for interpreting the data.

The picture is similar for Model 6. It conforms to Model 4, but includes the variables designed to test whether coherence in the expert discourse furthers its influence on political actors' minimum wage policy preferences: Variance of the Expert Discourse and the interaction term Experts * Variance. Contrary to expectations, Experts * Variance has a positive sign, meaning that more disagreement among experts increases expert influence. With a p-value of .45, the coefficient is not statistically significant. Regarding the other variables, Model 6 generally suggests the same conclusions as Model 4. A difference is that the variable describing the evaluation of minimum wages in the expert discourse is statistically

Table 6.4 Influence of the expert discourse with interaction variables. Dependent variable: minimum wage stance. A star marks statistically significant results (p<.05)

	Model 3	Model 4	Model 5	model 6	Model 7
	Coefficient *(p-value)*				
Domestic expert discourse, MA5	3.733 *(.00)**	4.536 *(.00)**	3.846 *(.02)**	3.454 *(.07)*	3.152 *(.22)*
Volume of expert discourse	.581 *(.42)*				
Variance of expert discourse				1.448 *(.65)*	
Unemployment	−.031 *(.77)*				
GDP growth	.105 *(.13)*				
US	−1.698 *(.03)**	−1.870 *(.00)**	−1.763 *(.00)**	−1.946 *(.00)**	−1.811 *(.00)**
UK	.446 *(.49)*				
Minimum wage new	−.103 *(.75)*	−.279 *(.39)*	−.225 *(.57)*	−.427 *(.22)*	−.199 *(.51)*
Shift in evaluation			.090 *(.95)*		
Left party	1.984 *(.01)**	1.935 *(.01)**	1.960 *(.01)**	1.923 *(.01)**	1.980 *(.01)**
Right Party	−3.279 *(.00)**	−3.077 *(.00)**	−3.077 *(.00)**	−3.081 *(.00)**	−3.069 *(.00)**
Left executive	−1.736 *(.01)**	−1.609 *(.02)**	−1.539 *(.03)**	−1.570 *(.02)**	−1.679 *(.01)**
Right executive	−2.861 *(.00)**	−2.777 *(.00)**	−2.799 *(.00)**	−2.825 *(.00)**	−2.745 *(.00)**
Trade union	4.131 *(.00)**	4.240 *(.00)**	4.284 *(.00)**	4.249 *(.00)**	4.298 *(.00)**
Employer organization	−4.301 *(.00)**	−4.241 *(.00)**	−4.269 *(.00)**	−4.256 *(.00)**	−4.217 *(.00)**
Company	−4.198 *(.00)**	−4.223 *(.00)**	−4.203 *(.00)**	−4.247 *(.00)**	−4.218 *(.00)**
Moderate Actor	.313 *(.59)*				

(continued)

insignificant in Model 6, with a p-value of .06. Again, this can be ascribed to the substantial amount of multicollinearity in the model. The lower Bayes Information

Table 6.4 (continued)

Subsystem Polarization					−.519 *(.38)*
Election	−.306 *(.18)*	−.310 *(.15)*	−.304 *(.16)*	−.307 *(.17)*	−.369 *(.12)*
Experts * volume	−.371 *(.85)*				
Experts * variance				1.809 *(.44)*	
Experts * US	−2.432 *(.02)**	−3.155 *(.00)**	−2.479 *(.15)*	-3.469 *(.00)**	−3.387 *(.00)**
Experts * mw new	−7.281 *(.00)**	−7.829 *(.00)**	−7.297 *(.00)**	−8.444 *(.00)**	−7.487 *(.00)**
Experts * shift			.787 *(.67)*		
Experts * moderate	−.254 *(.70)*				
Experts * Polarization					.974 *(.57)*
Experts * election	−1.867 *(.00)**	−1.828 *(.00)**	−1.795 *(.00)**	−1.849 *(.00)**	−1.936 *(.00)**
Cutpoint 1	−3.219	−3.982	−3.906	−2.952	−4.510
Cutpoint 2	−1.542	−2.316	−2.239	−1.285	−2.828
Number of observations	1497	1497	1497	1497	1494
Bayes Information Criterion	2363	2321	2334	2335	2328
Pseudo-R2	.41	.39	.40	.40	.40

Criterion suggests that Model 4 is superior and should be used for interpreting the data.

Finally, Model 7 tests how subsystem polarization mediates the influence of expert discourses on political actors' minimum wage policy preferences. In contrast to the expectation that more polarization would make policy oriented learning across belief systems less likely, the interaction term Experts * Polarization has a positive sign, and is statistically not significant. Due to the high multicollinearity in the model, the variable describing the effect of the expert discourse also loses its statistical significance. Apart from that, Model 7 suggests the same conclusions as Model 4. The lower Bayes Information Criterion points to the fact that Model 4 is the better model.

6.2.3.3 Robustness checks

Above, Model 4 was established to be the most adequate representation of the data. To ensure that the conclusions drawn from the model are robust against small changes in model specification, additional analyses were conducted. *First*, to address the concerns regarding averaging over ordinal data discussed in Chapter 3, the model was re-estimated using an alternative version of the variable Domestic Expert Discourse, MA5. The alternative version does not describe the average evaluation of minimum wages in the expert discourse, but the share of scientific articles in the expert discourse which either find positive or neutral minimum wage effects. The results are reported in Appendix A6, Table A6.13. As can be seen, they correspond to the results from Table 6.4.

Second, Model 4 was re-estimated using four-years and six-years moving averages of the expert discourse, instead of the five-years moving average originally used. This was done to avoid basing central conclusions from this Chapter on an arbitrary specification of one variable (see Chapter 5). The results are also presented in Table A6.13 (Appendix A6) and support the robustness of Model 4. Re-estimating the model using a four-years moving average of the evaluation of minimum wages in the expert discourse delivers results practically identical to those of Model 4. Using a six-years moving average, it was not possible to include the interaction term Experts * US due to high multicollinearity (see Appendix A6). Estimating the model without the interaction term suggests a statistically significant expert influence which is weaker in election years and reverses in the five years prior to and following the introduction of a minimum wage. Again, this conforms to the results from Model 4.

6.2.4 What Happens When the Minimum Wage is New?

A surprising result of the preceding analyses is that expert influence on political actors' minimum wage policy preferences has a negative sign in the five years prior to and after the introduction of the minimum wage. During this time, when experts find less negative effects of minimum wages, political actors are more likely to oppose the minimum wage. This subsection investigates how this result comes about. To do so, this section first identifies the data points which are "responsible" for the large negative coefficient of the variable Experts * MW New in Table 6.4, Model 4. Then, additional information is brought in to make better guesses as to why these actors' policy preferences do not conform to the initial expectations. This is done first for the UK and then for Germany.

6.2.4.1 United Kingdom

In the UK, the expert discourse exhibited a favorable evaluation of the minimum wage during the five years before and after the introduction of the National Minimum Wage, taking values from 0 to .33 (see Chapter 5, Figure 5.5). In this case, a negative expert influence means that actors who were supposed to express support for the minimum wage failed to do so. To identify the actors "responsible" for the negative sign of the expert discourse variable, one should thus look at those actors who are more critical towards the minimum wage than one would have expected based on a model in which expert influence has a positive sign for all years.

To identify those actors, Model 2—in which expert influence is positive in all years—was re-estimated and used to predict the expected minimum wage preference of each actor coded in the five years prior to and after the introduction of the minimum wage. Table 6.5 compares this prediction with the observed minimum wage preferences. This is done for all organizations in the UK minimum wage policy subsystem whose minimum wage preference was coded at least 5 times during the period from 1992 to 2002.

Comparing the predicted probabilities with the observed minimum wage preferences shows that the trade unions listed in Table 6.5—Transport and General Workers' Union, Trades Union Congress and Unison—are homogeneously in support of the minimum wage, thus conforming to expectations. Another interest group listed in the table, the Confederation of British Industry, shows a more favorable evaluation of the minimum wage than expected. The remaining organizations listed in Table 6.5 fall in two broad categories: political parties, and bodies connected to the Labour government under Prime Minister Tony Blair. Both actor groups are less supportive of the minimum wage than expected. Actors who were coded to be connected to the Government of the United Kingdom in general, the Department of Trade and Industry, the Treasury, and the Low Pay Commission were all expected to mostly support the minimum wage, but were mostly coded as having a neutral or mixed position towards the minimum wage. The Labour Party and the Conservative Party, as well, underperformed regarding their support for the minimum wage.

Re-reading the newspaper articles from which these positions were coded reveals that at least the actors connected to the Labour party and the Labour government were in no way opposed to or impassionate about the minimum wage. Instead, the statements in which Labour-related actors do not or only reluctantly support the minimum wage usually appear as a reaction to other actors' calls for a considerably higher minimum wage. Prior to the introduction of the minimum wage, trade unions pushed for a high minimum wage, and the Labour government tried to balance the demands of business representatives and trade unions

Table 6.5 Actors in the British minimum wage policy subsystem which were coded at least five times between 1992 and 2002, their predicted minimum wage preference, and their observed minimum wage preference (total numbers in parentheses)

Organization		Minimum wage preference		
		Favorable	Neutral	Unfavorable
Confederation of British Industry	Observed Predicted (mean)	7% (1) 11%	73% (11) 27%	20% (3) 62%
Department of Trade and Industry (Blair)	Observed Predicted (mean)	46% (5) 55%	46% (5) 31%	9% (1) 14%
Government of the United Kingdom (Blair)	Observed Predicted (mean)	9% (1) 49%	73% (8) 32%	18% (2) 19%
Her Majesty's Treasury (Blair)	Observed Predicted (mean)	0% (0) 55%	80% (4) 31%	20% (1) 14%
Labour Party	Observed Predicted (mean)	82% (36) 96%	16% (7) 3%	2% (1) 0%
Liberal Demoracts	Observed Predicted (mean)	80% (4) 83%	0% (0) 13%	20% (1) 4%
Low Pay Commission	Observed Predicted (mean)	27% (4) 56%	73% (11) 31%	0% (0) 14%
Transport and General Workers' Union	Observed Predicted (mean)	88% (7) 99%	13% (1) 1%	0% (0) 0%
Conservative Party	Observed Predicted (mean)	0% (0) 32%	56% (10) 37%	44% (8) 32%
Trades Union Congress	Observed Predicted (mean)	100% (15) 100%	0% (0) 0%	0% (0) 0%
Unison (trade union)	Observed Predicted (mean)	85% (11) 92%	15% (2) 6%	0% (0) 2%

(Macaskill and Milne, 1998). After the introduction, the situation was similar. Trade unions as well as Labour backbenchers pushed for a significant raise of the minimum wage while the Blair government hesitated, citing fears over adverse economic consequences (Guardian, 2000; Maguire and Elliott, 2000). In the data set, this push by left-wing actors for higher minimum wages is visible as an increase in the mean number of actors that were coded as supporting the minimum wage during this time period to just under 10 per year, as compared to approximately 6 in the remaining years.[4]

It is plausible to understand the enthusiasm of trade unions and other left-wing actors for higher minimum wages at least partly as a reaction to the positive evaluation of minimum wage effects in the expert discourse. Supporters of a quick and strong raise of the National Minimum Wage were cited in newspapers claiming that the minimum wage could be raised significantly because it had not caused unemployment to rise (Gow, 2002; see, for example, Stewart, 2002). It makes sense to argue that such claims were at least facilitated by the expert discourse, as the evaluation of minimum wages in the British expert discourse was largely positive around the time of its introduction (see Figure 5.8).

The negative sign of the variable Experts * MW New could thus be the product of an indirect effect of the expert discourse. The positive evaluation of the National Minimum Wage by scholars could have motivated actors in favor of higher minimum wages to increase their pressure for a minimum wage hike. This could have forced more moderate supporters of the minimum wage to publicly speak out against strongly increasing the minimum wage.

6.2.4.2 Germany

The same procedure employed above is used to identify the relevant actors in Germany. In the German expert discourse, in the five years prior to the introduction of the minimum wage, the mean evaluation of the minimum wage is slightly negative, ranging from −.31 to −.11 (see Chapter 5, Figure 5.7). Thus, the actors "responsible" for the negative sign of the expert discourse variable in Germany are those showing a more favorable preference towards the minimum wage than otherwise expected. To identify those actors, Table 6.6 compares the observed preferences of those organizations in the German minimum wage policy subsystems that were coded at least 5 times between 2009 and 2014 with their predicted minimum wage preference according to Model 2.

Model 2 accurately predicts a highly favorable minimum wage preference for the three left-wing political parties Die Grünen, Die Linke, and Sozialdemokratische Partei Deutschlands, as well as for the trade union Verdi. The prediction for the economically conservative political party Freie Demokratische Partei is less accurate, with observed statements being less supportive of the minimum

[4]This is not an artefact of a generally increased attention to the minimum wage. This can be seen by comparing the trend in the number of statements supporting the minimum wage with the trend in the number of statements opposing the minimum wage. In contrast to the former, the latter stays approximately constant over time.

Table 6.6 Actors in the German minimum wage policy subsystem which were coded at least five times between 2009 and 2014, their predicted minimum wage preference, and their observed minimum wage preference

Organization		Minimum wage preference		
		Favorable	Neutral	Unfavorable
Federal Ministry of Employment (Merkel II)	Observed Predicted (mean)	91% (10) 36%	9% (1) 33%	0 31%
Christlich Demokratische Union/Christlich-Soziale Union	Observed Predicted (mean)	61% (22) 23%	28% (10) 37%	11% (4) 40%
Freie Demokratische Partei	Observed Predicted (mean)	7% (1) 23%	13% (2) 36%	80% (12) 41%
Die Grünen	Observed Predicted (mean)	100% (7) 96%	0% (0) 3%	0% (0) 1%
Die Linke	Observed Predicted (mean)	100% (5) 96%	0% (0) 3%	0% (0) 1%
Sozialdemokratische Partei Deutschlands	Observed Predicted (mean)	95% (19) 96%	5% (1) 3%	0% (0) 1%
Verdi	Observed Predicted (mean)	100% (7) 99%	0% (0) 1%	0% (0) 0%

wage than predicted. As, in the German case, the expert discourse provides a negative assessment of the minimum wage, these observations cannot explain the negative sign of the expert discourse in Germany between 2009 and 2014. There are two actor groups which are much more in favor of the minimum wage than expected under Model 2. The first one comprises the conservative political parties Christlich Demokratische Union/Christlich-soziale Union (CDU/CSU). The second one is the Federal Ministry of Employment, which, under the second Merkel government from 2009 to 2013, was led by CDU politician Ursula von der Leyen.

As will be discussed in detail in Chapter 7, the CDU/CSU changed its stance towards the minimum wage between the years 2005 and approximately 2009, becoming much more open to the introduction of branch minimum wages, or even of a general minimum wage. This change occurred more or less in parallel with the change in the German expert discourse, which showed a very unfavorable evaluation of the minimum wage in 2005, changing to nearly neutral in 2009 (see Chapter 5). Thus, over the whole period of analysis, the CDU/CSU's position seems to have evolved in parallel with, rather than in opposition to the expert discourse. The qualitative analyses from Chapter 7 even suggest that the CDU/CSU accepted the introduction of a general minimum wage partly because of the change in the expert discourse. Therefore, the German case does not provide a sensible interpretation for the negative sign of the expert discourse variable.

6.2.4.3 The Uncertainty Puzzle—Conclusions

It does not make sense to interpret the strongly negative coefficient of the variable Experts * MW New in a way that, when the minimum wage is new, some actors would consciously adjust their position towards the minimum wage in a way to contradict the expert discourse. In the UK, the Labour government did not adjust its position at all—it continued supporting a moderate minimum wage. This position just appeared to be more conservative when trade unions and other actors started to demand a rapid increase of the newly introduced National Minimum Wage. In Germany, the CDU/CSU's turn towards the minimum wage happened in parallel to the changing German expert discourse, not against it.

While the qualitative analysis rejects the idea of political actors adjusting their policy preferences in a way to contradict the expert discourse, the cases of Germany and the UK do not offer a common alternative explanation for the negative sign of the variable Experts * MW New. The British case suggests a mechanism in which a positive evaluation of minimum wages in the expert discourse encourages left-wing actors to demand minimum wage hikes that more moderate backers of the minimum wage are not willing to support. This mechanism, however, does not hold for Germany.

6.2.5 Explaining Actors' Preferences with the Expert Discourse: Summary

The results of the analyses presented so far allow a preliminary evaluation of several hypotheses from the theoretical model developed in Chapter 2. *First*, the results suggest that there is an influence of the domestic expert discourse on the minimum wage policy preferences of political actors. The international expert discourse, in contrast, has no independent effect. This supports hypothesis H1.2 and refutes hypothesis H1.4.

Second, properties of the expert discourse do not affect the strength of this influence. Thus, neither a higher number of scientific articles on minimum wage effects nor more agreement among those articles increases expert influence. Hypotheses H2.2 and H2.3 are therefore rejected.

Third, the influence of the expert discourse on the preferences of political actors is not higher in situations in which actors can be expected to be particularly uncertain about the effects of minimum wages, that is, when the minimum wage is new or when new research results upset traded knowledge about minimum wage effects. Hypotheses H3.2 and H3.3 are therefore rejected. Indeed, a *negative* correlation was found between the evaluation of minimum wages in the expert discourse and the preferences of political actors in the five years preceding and following the introduction of a minimum wage. A closer re-analysis of the data suggested, however, that this correlation should not be interpreted as a causal connection in the sense that a better evaluation of minimum wage effects in the expert discourse directly causes political actors to take a more critical stance towards the minimum wage.

Fourth, different styles of using scientific expertise are correlated with different levels of influence of expert discourses. As expected, expert influence is weaker in the United States, that is, under the conditions of a pluralistic style of using expertise. Hypothesis H4.2 is, therefore, confirmed. In contrast, different coalition structures in the policy subsystem do not mediate the influence of the expert discourse on political actors in the expected way, leading us to reject hypothesis H4.4. *Fifth*, there was no support for hypothesis H5.1, predicting that actors without a strong preference for or against the minimum wage are more likely to be influenced by the expert discourse.

6.2.6 Interpretation of Results: A Simulation

So far, this chapter has analyzed the influence of the expert discourse on political actors' minimum wage policy preferences. The analyses presented above show that the evaluation of minimum wage effects in the expert discourse influences the policy preferences of political actors, and that the strength of this influence varies under different conditions.

To illustrate what the link between expert discourses and actors' policy preferences means in practice, this section presents a simulation. To this end, a few actors from each country are selected to demonstrate how their minimum wage preference would be expected to be influenced by the expert discourse. The simulation is based on Model 4, Table 6.4.

6.2.6.1 United States

In the United States, the organizations most likely to support the minimum wage are trade unions. If the overall evaluation of minimum wages in the expert discourse takes the neutral value 0, their latent preference takes the value of 2.370 (see Table 6.4, Model 4). This value is derived by adding the intercept for actors in the US (−1.870) to the intercept for trade unions (4.240). To identify the stance towards the minimum wage in which this is likely to translate, one needs to compare the latent preference with the two cutpoints estimated in Model 4, −3.982 and −2.316. A value above the upper cutpoint suggests that an actor supports the minimum wage most of the time. A value between the two cutpoints suggests that an actor takes a mixed position most of the time. A value beneath the lower cutpoint suggests that an actor is critical of the minimum wage most of the time. While the exact distribution of the estimated preference will be detailed below, for now it suffices to note that the latent preference for trade unions is much higher than the upper cutpoint when the expert discourse takes the neutral value 0. This suggests a strong support for the minimum wage.

Actors affiliated with a left-wing political party—in the sample, these were mostly Democrats in Congress—are also likely to support higher minimum wages, with a latent preference of 0.065. Actors affiliated with the executive branch of a federal government under a Democratic president have a latent preference of −3.479, indicating a mixed or neutral position towards minimum wage hikes. Actors affiliated with the executive branch of a federal government under a Republican President (latent preference: −4.647) are expected to oppose higher minimum wages. The same is true for right-wing political parties (mostly Republicans in Congress; latent preference: −4.947), employer organizations (latent preference: −6.111) and businesses (latent preference: −6.093).

This picture changes when considering that the overall evaluation of minimum wages in the US expert discourse generally takes a value lower than 0. To illustrate the effect, the estimated preference of the aforementioned actor groups is simulated for two years. The first year is 1985, when the overall evaluation of minimum wages in the US expert discourse was overwhelmingly negative (−.81). The second year is 2001, when research termed the new economics of the minimum wage (Burkhauser, Couch and Wittenburg, 2000) had led to a more positive evaluation (−.11).

The simulation results are presented in Table 6.7. While the expert discourse equally influences all actors' *latent* preferences, the likelihood with which a shift in the expert discourse changes *observed* preferences—whether an actor supports the minimum wage—differs between actor types. It is small for those actors who either strongly support or strongly reject minimum wages. Actors affiliated with trade unions are predicted to support higher minimum wages with a probability of 97 percent in 1985 and 99 percent in 2001. Likewise, actors representing companies or employer organizations support higher minimum wages with a probability of 1 percent in 1985 and 2 percent in 2001.

Conversely, expert influence on observed preferences is stronger for those actors who are in-between strong support of and strong opposition to the minimum wage. It is most pronounced for actors who are part of the executive branch of government under a Democratic president ("left executive"). In 1985, only a minority of actors in this group is predicted to take a favorable (9%) or neutral (26%) position on the minimum wage, with opposition to the minimum wage being expected in 65 percent of cases. In 2001, this picture looks markedly different. Actors in this group are now expected to oppose the minimum wage with a probability of only 42 percent and have a significantly higher probability of supporting it (21%) or taking a neutral position (37%) than before.

Table 6.7 Predicted minimum wage policy preferences for different actors groups in the US minimum wage policy subsystem, 1985 and 2001. Based on the estimation in Model 4, Table 6.4. Reading example: In 1985, an actor affiliated with a trade union is predicted to support the minimum wage with a probability of 97 percent, to take a neutral position with a probability of 2 percent, and to oppose the minimum wage with a probability of 1 percent

	Minimum wage preference 1985 (predicted probability in percent)			Minimum wage preference 2001 (predicted probability in percent)		
	Favorable	*Neutral*	*Unfavorable*	*Favorable*	*Neutral*	*Unfavorable*
Trade union	97	2	1	99	1	0
Left party	78	17	5	90	8	2
Left executive	9	26	65	21	37	42
Right executive	3	11	86	8	23	70
Right party	2	9	89	6	19	76
Company	1	3	96	2	7	91
Employer organization	1	3	96	2	7	91

The effect of election years is similar to the one of a more favorable evaluation of minimum wages in the expert discourse. In Model 4, the coefficient of the expert discourse variable in normal years is 1.381 (4.536 – 3.155). In election years, the coefficient changes to –.447 (1.381 – 1.828), that is, close to 0. As the overall evaluation of minimum wages in the US expert discourse is always negative, the meaning of this lower coefficient is that all actors are more likely to support higher minimum wages. As with the effect of the shift in the expert discourse between 1985 and 2001, the strongest preference changes are predicted for actors affiliated with those actors who are in-between strong support of and strong opposition to the minimum wage.

6.2.6.2 Germany

Assuming an evaluation of minimum wages in the expert discourse of 0, those German organizations predicted to have a latent support for the minimum wage significantly above the upper cutpoint of −2.316, and thus expected to mostly support the minimum wage, are trade unions (latent preference: 4.240) and left-wing political parties (latent preference: 1.935). Actors affiliated with the executive branch of a left-wing government are also predicted to mostly support the minimum wage, but less clearly (latent preference: −1.609). Actors affiliated with the executive branch of a right-wing government are expected to mostly have a neutral position on the minimum wage, with their latent preference (−2.777) being between the two cutpoints. Actors representing companies and employer organizations are predicted to mostly oppose higher minimum wages, although less strongly than their US counterparts (latent preferences: −4.223, −4.241).

To illustrate the effect that the expert discourse has on observed preferences, the predicted probabilities of supporting higher minimum wages are compared for two points in time. The first one is 2003, when the German expert discourse was at an evaluation of minimum wage effects of −1. The second one is 2012, when the evaluation was at −.22. The results of the simulation are presented in Table 6.8.

As shown, expert influence is generally stronger in Germany than in the US. Except for trade unions, who support the minimum wage regardless of what scientific research finds, the change in the expert discourse affects the policy preferences of all actor groups. For some actor groups, the effect of the shift in the German expert discourse is to harden or soften an existing preference for or against the minimum wage. For example, left-wing political parties are predicted to mostly support the minimum wage even in 2003. For them, the shift in the German expert discourse happening until 2012 has the effect of strengthening their existing support. Similarly, companies and employer organizations are predicted to mostly oppose the minimum wage in 2003 as well as in 2012. However, their opposition is expected to be significantly less firm in 2012. For other actor groups, the shift in the German expert discourse has the effect of altogether changing their position towards the minimum wage. Actors connected to the executive branch of left-wing or right-wing governments are predicted to strongly oppose the minimum wage in 2003, and to mostly support it in 2012. The same is true for right-wing political parties.

The effect of election years in Germany is similar to the one in the US. This is because the expert discourses in both countries generally evaluates minimum wage effects negatively. As the coefficient of the expert discourse variable gets smaller, political actors, especially those most affected by the expert discourse, are more likely to support higher minimum wages.

Table 6.8 Predicted minimum wage policy preferences for different actors groups in the German minimum wage policy subsystem, 2004 and 2008. Based on the estimation in Model 4, Table 6.4

	Minimum wage preference 2003 (predicted probability in percent)			Minimum wage preference 2012 (predicted probability in percent)		
	Favorable	*Neutral*	*Unfavorable*	*Favorable*	*Neutral*	*Unfavorable*
Trade union	88	9	2	100	0	0
Left party	43	37	20	99	1	0
Left executive	2	8	90	76	19	6
Right executive	1	3	97	49	34	16
Right party	1	2	97	42	37	21
Company	0	1	99	19	36	45
Employer organization	0	1	99	18	36	46

6.2.6.3 United Kingdom

The pattern of expert influence in the UK is still different. On the one hand, while the coefficient of the expert discourse variable is the same as in Germany, the over-time variation of the expert discourse is smaller. On the other hand, different actors are affected.

Assuming an overall evaluation of minimum wages in the expert discourse of 0, the predicted observed minimum wage preferences for the different types of organizations are the same as in Germany. Given that the overall evaluation of minimum wage effects in the British expert discourse, in contrast to its German and US counterparts, is positive, the average British actor is more supportive of the minimum wage than the average German actor.

To illustrate the effect of changes in the minimum wage, the years 2004 and 2011 are compared. In this period, the overall evaluation of minimum wages in the British expert discourse slightly decreased from .05 to −.13. The fact that this drop is considerably smaller than the change in the expert discourse used in the simulations for the US and Germany is illustrative of the generally smaller over-time variance of the British expert discourse.[5]

The estimation results are presented in Table 6.9. They illustrate two features of the influence of the British expert discourse on political actors' observed minimum wage policy preferences. *First*, the differences in political actors' predicted policy preferences between the years 2004 and 2011 are relatively small. For most actors, the less favorable evaluation of minimum wages in the expert discourse in 2011 means that their support for the minimum wage slightly declines, or their opposition slightly hardens. Even though the coefficient of the expert discourse variable has the same size in the UK and in Germany, the British expert discourse causes less over-time change in political actors' evaluation of the minimum wage. The reason for this is the smaller over-time variance of the British expert discourse.

Second, the actors most affected by the expert discourse differ from those in the other two countries. In Germany and in the US, the actors whose support for the minimum wage was most likely to be affected by the expert discourse were actors related to the executive branch of government. In the United Kingdom, the actor group that is most affected by the expert discourse are right-wing political parties. Moreover, left-wing political parties' observed minimum wage preferences are influenced by the expert discourse in Germany and the US, but unaffected in Britain. The reason for these differences is that the political actors in the UK are generally more favorable of the minimum wage than those in Germany and the US. As a result, British right-wing political parties neither have a clear predicted preference for or against the minimum wage, and relatively small changes in the expert discourse suffice to push them from support to rejection. In contrast, British

[5]This over-time shift is not the strongest in the British expert discourse: In 1994, the overall evaluation of minimum wage effects in the British expert discourse was .33, considerably higher than the .05 used here. The effect of the expert discourse on political actors' policy preferences, however, is complicated by the fact that the minimum wage is new during this time, which changes the coefficient of the expert discourse variable (see Table 6.4, Model 4). Even if one ignored those concerns, the difference between an evaluation of .33 in 1994 and −.13 in 2011 is still significantly smaller than the shifts present in the US and the German expert discourses.

left-wing political parties are so strongly biased in favor of the minimum wage that a slightly less positive evaluation of minimum wage effects in the expert discourse has no influence on their policy preference.

Table 6.9 Predicted minimum wage policy preferences for different actors groups in the British minimum wage policy subsystem, 2004 and 2011. Based on the estimation in Model 4, Table 6.4

	Minimum wage preference 2004 (predicted probability in percent)			Minimum wage preference 2011 (predicted probability in percent)		
	Favorable	*Neutral*	*Unfavorable*	*Favorable*	*Neutral*	*Unfavorable*
Trade union	100	0	0	100	0	0
Left party	98	1	0	98	2	0
Left executive	63	27	10	54	32	14
Right executive	34	39	27	26	39	35
Right party	45	30	25	21	37	41
Company	11	29	61	8	23	69
Employer organization	11	28	61	8	23	70

Finally, this discussion also allows us to identify what happens in election years. As in the other two countries, the influence of the expert discourse gets smaller in election years. As the evaluation of minimum wages in the British expert discourse has a positive sign in most years, the effect of an election year is the same as the effect of a less favorable evaluation of minimum wages in the expert discourse. Thus, in election years, political actors connected to right-wing political parties and the executive government are predicted to lessen their support for the minimum wage. In contrast, trade unions and left-wing political parties are unaffected and remain steadfast supporters of the minimum wage.

6.3 Reversing the Influence: Explaining the Expert Discourse

The last parts of the theoretical model from Chapter 2 which have not been tested yet are the possible reverse influences of the media discourse and the policy subsystem on the expert discourse. So far, the relationship between the expert discourse and the position of actors in minimum wage policy subsystems has been treated as a one-way street. The analyses in Chapters 5 and 6 have found that the expert discourse on minimum wages influences the media discourse, as well as the evaluation of minimum wages by the actors in minimum wage policy subsystems. However, these connections could also work in the opposite direction. Specifically, this section considers two kinds of reverse influences. *First*, does the fact that minimum wages are on the media agenda lead to an increase in scientific publications studying the effects of the minimum wage? *Second*, do the positions of actors in minimum wage policy subsystems influence the research results published in the expert discourse?

6.3.1 Predicting the Number of Articles in the Expert Discourse

This section starts by analyzing whether the degree to which minimum wages are on the media agenda influences the degree to which minimum wages are on the research agenda. Such a connection seems plausible, as researchers might become interested in minimum wages when minimum wages are an important part of the political debate, which they perceive through the mass media (H6.1). To study this effect, the analysis combines data on the expert discourse with data on the newspaper coverage of minimum wages.

6.3.1.1 Variables

In this analysis, the dependent variable is the prominence of minimum wages on the research agenda. It is operationalized as the annual number of scientific journal articles in the respective domestic expert discourse.

The main independent variable describes the prominence of minimum wages on the media agenda. It is operationalized as the annual number of newspaper articles on minimum wages in the respective country (from the newspapers listed in Chapter 3, and according to the selection criteria described there). As the research process leading to a publication of an article in a scientific journal often takes several years, different lags for the independent variable are tried. In accordance to the procedure from Chapter 5, the number of newspaper articles on minimum wages is normalized by dividing the number of articles in one country in one year by the maximum number of newspaper articles on minimum wages per year published in this country. This is done to account for the fact that the number of newspaper articles on the issue differs significantly between the three countries.

Moreover, country dummies are included to account for the different sizes of the research community in the three countries (and, thus, different expectations regarding the number of scientific journal articles published each year). Finally, a linear time trend captures potential over-time changes in academia, for example a growing pressure to publish. All variables are summarized in Table 6.10.

Table 6.10 Variables used in the regression analysis

Name	Description	Mean	Standard Deviation
Scientific agenda	Dependent variable; number of articles in the expert discourse in one country in year t.	5.67	4.61
Media agenda	Total number of articles on minimum wages published in the analyzed newspapers from the respective country in one year. Normalized by dividing the number of articles by the maximum number of articles on minimum wages per year published in this country. Different time lags of this variable are included.	.21	.22
DE	Dummy variable for Germany.		
UK	Dummy variable for the UK.		
Year	Linear time trend.		

6.3.1.2 Estimation Technique

The estimation problem is similar to the regression analysis presented in Chapter 5, Table 5.7. The dependent variable is a count variable, which is why Poisson regression is used. This decision is supported by a test for overdispersion (Cameron and Trivedi, 2009, p. 575), which suggests that the data is equidispersed.

Moreover, the data once again takes the structure of an unbalanced panel with a maximum of 96 observations—46 for the US, 26 for the UK, and 24 for Germany.[6] The observations are clustered in three groups—the three countries. Unobserved heterogeneity between those clusters is accounted for through the inclusion of country dummies. To deal with potential serial correlation of the error terms, the approach described in Cameron and Miller (Cameron and Miller,

[6]The actual number of observations will be lower due to the time lag of the independent variable article count, which forces us to exclude the earliest years for each country.

2015, p. 346) is followed. As in previous analyses, the estimation is performed using (inconsistent) cluster-robust standard errors, and p-values are derived using a t-distribution with G-1 degrees of freedom. The estimation was done using Stata's poisson command.

6.3.1.3 Results

Table 6.11 reports the results of the regression analysis. It displays two models. Model 1 contains all variables listed in Table 6.10. The variable Media Agenda, describing the number of newspaper articles published on minimum wages, is included with four different time lags: one year, three years, five years, and seven years. This makes it possible not only to test whether the political agenda influences the number of scientific articles published on minimum wages, but also to identify the time span over which such an influence takes place. As in the previous analysis, in order to avoid problems connected to multicollinearity and to increase the precision of the estimation, Model 2 is derived by iteratively deleting the variable with the highest p-value and re-estimating the model, until all remaining variables are significant (Heij *et al.*, 2004, pp. 280–281).

The estimation clearly indicates that the expert discourse is influenced by the media agenda, supporting hypothesis H6.1. Thus, the more articles newspapers publish about minimum wages, the more scientific articles evaluating minimum wages are published. This link is true for the short term. The coefficient of the Media Agenda variable lagged by one year is positive and statistically significant. This could indicate a mechanism by which the fact that minimum wages are on the political agenda motivates researchers to conduct smaller studies on minimum wage effects, which can be published relatively fast (for example evaluations of the effects of a minimum wage hike that just came into effect). As a result, when minimum wages are high on the political agenda in one year, scientific publications on minimum wages will be more frequent in the next year. The link between the media agenda and the research agenda also exists for the medium term. The significantly positive coefficient of the Media Agenda variable lagged by five years could point to situations in which a political interest in minimum wages motivates larger, longer-term research projects, whose results are only published a few years later.

The results for the other three variables in the model confirm conclusions that were drawn from the univariate analyses of the expert discourses in Chapter 5. The number of scientific articles on minimum wages is highest in the US, and lowest in Germany. Moreover, there has been a trend towards more publications on minimum wages over time.

Table 6.11 Poisson regression of the number of articles in the expert discourse on the number of articles on minimum wages in newspapers and further variables. A star marks statistically significant results (p<.05)

	Model 1	Model 2
	Coefficient *(p-value)*	Coefficient *(p-value)*
L1: Media agenda	.791 *(.03)**	.809 *(.05)**
L3: Media agenda	.510 *(.20)*	
L5: Media agenda	1.061 *(.03)**	1.087 *(.02)**
L7: Media agenda	.211 *(.38)*	
DE	−1.599 *(.00)**	−1.599 *(.00)**
UK	−.828 *(.00)**	−.818 *(.00)**
Year	.036 *(.00)**	.039 *(.00)**
Constant	−70.658	−75.443
Pseudo-R2	.31	.33
N	71	77

6.3.2 Influence on the Evaluation of Minimum Wages in the Expert Discourse

Besides the link between media attention and scientific attention to the minimum wage, the theoretical model hypothesized a possible influence of the way political actors evaluate the minimum wage, and its evaluation in the expert discourse (H6.2). The regression analysis presented in this subsection tests for the presence of such a link.

6.3.2.1 Variables

One observation in the analysis refers to one scientific article which is part of the British, German, or United States domestic expert discourse. The dependent variable is the overall evaluation of minimum wages in this article, which takes the values "−1" (negative), "0" (neutral), and "1" (positive).

The main independent variables describe the mean evaluation of minimum wages by all actors coded from the newspaper articles from the respective country but operationalize this concept in two different ways. *First*, the variable Actors' Evaluation is computed by taking the mean of all expressed positions towards the minimum wage coded from the newspaper data in one country in one year.

It is included into the regression analysis with the two different time lags which were shown to be relevant in the previous analysis: one year and five years before the scientific journal article to which the dependent variable refers was published. *Second*, the variable Actors' Evaluation, MA5, is a five-years moving average of all expressed positions towards the minimum wage coded from the newspaper data in one country. This variable, as well, is included with two different time lags, one and five years. The inclusion of both a simple average of one year and a five-years moving average captures two different paths of influence. On the one hand, a more direct influence could be based on political actors directly influencing research results. This mechanism is captured through the simple average of one year, which captures the policy preference of those actors potentially influencing research in a given year. On the other hand, a more indirect influence could exist, in which a general change of society's perspective on the minimum wage influences research results. This mechanism is captured by the five-years moving average, which is less volatile and better suited to describe the general political mood.

Moreover, several other variables potentially explaining the evaluation of minimum wages in the expert discourse are included as control variables. These include country dummies as well as three socio-demographic variables used in previous estimations: unemployment, poverty, and economic growth rates. All variables are summarized in Table 6.12.

6.3.2.2 Estimation Method

Like the estimation reported in Tables 6.3 and 6.4, the dependent variable is ordinal. Therefore, the estimation is done as an ordered logit regression (Heij *et al.*, 2004, pp. 474–480). Similar to previous estimations, the observations are grouped into three clusters—the three national expert discourses, for which dummy variables are included. To deal with potential serial correlation of the error terms within those clusters, the approach described in Cameron and Miller (Cameron and Miller, 2015, p. 346) is followed. The estimation is performed using (inconsistent) cluster-robust standard errors, and p-values are derived using a t-distribution with G-1 degrees of freedom. The estimation was performed using Stata's ologit command.

6.3.2.3 Results

The results of the estimation are presented in Table 6.13. As in previous estimations, two different models are reported: Model 1 is the full model with all independent variables listed in Table 6.7. Model 2 is the more precise one and

Table 6.12 Variables in the regression analysis

Name	Description	Mean	Standard Deviation
Experts' evaluation	Dependent variable; overall evaluation of the minimum wage in one scientific article published in year t.	−.28	.85
Actors' Evaluation	Mean evaluation of minimum wages by all actors coded in the newspaper articles from one country from one year. Included with two different lags: one year and five years.	.24	.35
Actors' Evaluation, MA5	Five-years moving average of the mean evaluation of minimum wages by all actors coded in the newspaper articles from one country from one year. Included with two different lags: one year and five years.	.18	.15
DE	Dummy variable for Germany.		
UK	Dummy variable for the UK.		
Unemployment	Unemployment rate (in percent). Included with two different lags: one year and five years.	6.45	1.73
Low pay	Percentage of low paid workers. Included with two different lags: one year and five years.	22.76	2.20
GDP growth	Annual growth of the gross domestic product in percent. Included with two different lags: one year and five years.	2.29	2.16

has been derived from Model 1 by gradually deleting the variable with the highest p-value and then re-estimating the model, until all remaining variables were significant (Heij *et al.*, 2004, pp. 280–281).

The estimation clearly rejects hypothesis H6.2, which states that the expert discourse is influenced by how actors in minimum wage policy subsystems evaluate

Table 6.13 Ordered logit regression explaining the overall evaluation of minimum wages in scientific journal articles. A star marks statistically significant results (p<.05)

	Model 1	Model 2
	Coefficient *(p-value)*	Coefficient *(p-value)*
L1: Actors' evaluation	−.226 *(.64)*	
L5: Actors' evaluation	−.265 *(.55)*	
L1: Actors' evaluation, MA5	1.591 *(.29)*	
L5: Actors' evaluation, MA5	.953 *(.97)*	
L1: Unemployment	.061 *(.56)*	
L5: Unemployment	−.035 *(.64)*	
L1: GDP growth	−.013 *(.89)*	
L5: GDP growth	−017 *(.67)*	
L1: Low pay	.177 *(.23)*	
L5: Low pay	.162 *(.10)*	.239 *(.01)**
DE	1.929 *(.06)*	1.423 *(.01)**
UK	1.624 *(.04)**	1.476 *(.00)**
Cutpoint 1	5.523	5.926
Cutpoint 2	6.430	6.877
Pseudo-R2	.03	.02
N	421	469

the minimum wage. Thus, none of the four variables describing the evaluation of minimum wages by actors in minimum wage policy subsystems is statistically significant, or even close to significance. Minimum-wage research, according to this analysis, is independent of what society thinks of minimum wages.

Regarding control variables, the proportion of low wage workers in a country, lagged by five years, has a significant positive effect on the evaluation of minimum wages in the expert discourse. In contrast, a similar effect does not occur with regard to GDP growth or unemployment rates. Finally, researchers in Germany and the United Kingdom are more likely to positively evaluate the minimum wage than scholars from the United States. Given the findings from the descriptive analysis of the expert discourse in Chapter 5, this is no surprise: the three national expert discourses take very different trajectories over time. Overall, the pseudo-R^2 of only 2 percent shows that the employed variables do a very poor job at predicting how a scientific journal article evaluates the minimum wage.

From the reverse analysis, predicting the expert discourse with the media agenda and the preferences of political actors in minimum wage policy subsystems, two main conclusions can be drawn. *First*, when minimum wages are high on the political agenda, they will also be more important in the research agenda. *Second*, while developments in society have an influence on whether minimum wages are researched, there is no influence the results of this research.

6.4 Conclusion

While the previous chapter has dealt with the presence of scientific expertise in the newspaper discourse on minimum wages, this chapter has analyzed the influence of the expert discourse on the minimum wage policy preferences of political actors such as interest groups or political parties. This has been interpreted as a measure for policy-oriented learning across belief systems from the expert discourse. Summing up the various results presented above, we can get a good picture of this relation and evaluate the relevant hypotheses from the theoretical model.

The analysis started by comparing statements about the desirability and the effects of minimum wages made by political actors with research results from the expert discourse. In terms of minimum wage effects, the comparison shows that there is a relatively strong agreement between experts and other political actors, at least on average. Although there is substantial variation among actors, most of them do not openly disagree with the central conclusions from the expert discourse. When political actors make statements about minimum wage effects in newspaper articles, they are mostly in agreement with the expert discourse, saying that minimum wages tend to reduce employment/increase unemployment, are likely to reduce poverty/inequality, and are probably harmful to the economy. This close match does not extend to the overall evaluation of minimum wages. Non-surprisingly, policy preferences are also influenced by factors other than the expert discourse.

To get a more precise picture of the extent to which there is an influence of scientific expertise on political actors' minimum wage preferences, a series of regression analyses was conducted. These show that the scientific research has a considerable influence on whether actors support the minimum wage. There is clear support for hypothesis H1.1, stating that political actors' minimum wage preferences are influenced by the domestic expert discourse. In contrast, hypothesis H1.4, stating that political actors are influenced by the international expert discourse, is refuted. The analysis also show that the expert discourse is not the strongest predictor of an actor's minimum wage preference. Thus, the most important variables influencing an actor's stance towards the minimum wage describe the type of organization the actor belongs to. With some exceptions, trade unions and left-wing political parties are steadfast supporters of the minimum wage, while employer organizations, companies and right-wing political parties mostly oppose the minimum wage.

As in Chapter 5, the analyses not only focused on whether there is an expert influence, but also on the conditions under which this influence is stronger or weaker. The results from the regression analyses show that, *first*, properties of the expert discourse do not mediate expert influence. According to the results presented above, neither the number of scientific studies evaluating minimum wages published nor the degree to which these studies come to similar conclusions about the effects of minimum wages matters for how strong expert influence is. Hypotheses H2.2 and H2.4 are, therefore, rejected.

Second, the variables that were intended to indicate political actors' uncertainty about minimum wage effects did not have the expected effect. Neither in the five years before and after the introduction of the minimum wage, nor in time periods in which new research results upset long-held knowledge about minimum wage effects, is there a stronger influence of the expert discourse on political actors' minimum wage preferences. The statistical analysis even indicated that, in the five years prior to and after the introduction of the minimum wage, expert influence is negative. An additional qualitative analysis suggested that this correlation cannot simply be interpreted as a causal connection in which political actors actively refute the findings from research. While it seems possible that the two variables taken as indicators of political actors' uncertainty did not really capture uncertainty, at least so far, there is no support for hypotheses H3.1 and H3.3.

Third, different styles of using scientific expertise are strongly correlated with the strength of the influence of scientific expertise on political actors. Experts exert more influence over political actors' policy preference in Germany and the United Kingdom than in the United States. This confirmed the expectations formulated in Chapter 2. These were based on the reasoning that experts will exert less influence if the use of expertise in a country is strongly politicized, as is the case in countries with a pluralist policy-making style. Hypothesis H4.2 is, therefore, supported by the data.

Fourth, the analyses in this chapter offer no compelling evidence for hypothesis H4.4, stating that the influence of the expert discourse on political actors' minimum wage preferences is higher in policy subsystems with a collaborative advocacy coalition structure. While the corresponding variable in Model 6.7 has the expected positive sign, it is not statistically significant. This might be because there is no connection between coalition structure and cross-coalition learning from scientific expertise, but it might also result from the still relatively high multicollinearity in the model. Therefore, hypothesis H4.4 cannot be supported, but should neither be rejected based on the analyses from this chapter.

Fifth, actors belonging to organizations that neither strongly oppose nor strongly support the minimum wage are not more likely to be influenced by the expert discourse (H5.1). Instead, what was found is that the expert discourse has an equal influence on the latent preferences of all different actor groups. Thus, there is no support for the hypothesis that actors reject the conclusions of scientific expertise as wrong just because they do not fit their world view. The analysis also showed that many actors have such a strong bias for or against the minimum wage that even a moderate change in their latent preference caused by a change in the expert discourse is very unlikely to turn a supporter of the minimum wage into a critic, or vice versa. It is in this sense that moderate actors are more likely to be influenced by the expert discourse. Which actors are most likely to fall into that category depends on the specific constellation of the minimum wage policy subsystem.

Finally, the analysis was reversed to get a better idea of the full relation between expert discourses, the media discourse and actors in minimum wage policy subsystems. The results suggest that, *first*, the research agenda is partly driven by the media agenda. If minimum wages are high on the media agenda, more scientific articles on the subject are published in the following years. This supports hypothesis H6.1. While the amount of research assessing minimum wage effects is influenced by the media agenda, the evaluation of minimum wages in the expert discourse is independent of the evaluation of minimum wages by subsystem actors in previous years. Therefore, hypothesis H6.2 is refuted. This result shows that there is a clear temporal order in the correlation between the evaluation of minimum wage effects in the expert discourse and political actors' policy preferences. The former influences the latter, not vice versa.

Evaluating the Validity of the Quantitative Analysis

7

In the preceding chapters, quantitative data was analyzed to make inferences about the role of scientific expertise in minimum wage policy making. Of the methods employed, many are new. Coding newspaper articles to identify actors in policy subsystems, and these actors' beliefs, is a method that was recently developed by Heikkila et al. (2016). Combining this data with data gathered by coding scientific journal articles to show how scientific expertise enters the newspaper discourse, or influences political actors, has not been done before. The reliance on new methods spurs questions about the validity of the results presented in previous chapters. Thus, these results can only be accepted if it can be shown that the operationalization of the key variables from the quantitative analyses is valid. Moreover, it should be possible to show that the correlations found in previous regression analyses point to the causal connections as which they were interpreted.

This chapter, therefore, completes the previous analyses with three qualitative case studies of actors in the German minimum wage policy subsystem. Rather than presenting a complete picture of the German minimum wage policy subsystem with its coalitions, actors, and beliefs, these case studies test the validity of central claims made in the previous chapters. *First*, they test whether the key variables used in the quantitative analyses were operationalized in a way to measure what they are intended to measure. Regarding the expert discourse on minimum wages, this means showing that the expertise used by political actors is related to the expert discourse that was coded from scientific journal articles. Regarding the data coded from newspaper articles, it needs to be shown that the

---

Electronic supplementary material The online version of this chapter (https://doi.org/10.1007/978-3-658-32746-0_7) contains supplementary material, which is available to authorized users.

F. Klein, *The Role of Scientific Expertise in Minimum Wage Policy Making*, Vergleichende Politikwissenschaft,
https://doi.org/10.1007/978-3-658-32746-0_7

actors' policy preferences drawn from this data accurately describe their actual preferences.

Second, the case studies test the validity of the central conclusion from the previous chapter. The regression analyses from Chapter 6 showed that there is a correlation between the evaluation of minimum wages in the expert discourse and the policy preferences of political actors. This correlation was interpreted as evidence for a causal process in which political actors learn from the expert discourse and adjust their policy preference accordingly. While the quantitative data did not allow us to directly observe such learning processes, the qualitative analyses from this chapter make it possible to test for their presence.

7.1 Evaluating the Validity of the Quantitative Analyses

7.1.1 Case Selection

In the case studies, one case refers to one organization—such as a political party or an interest group—in a minimum wage policy subsystem. While, in principle, it would also be possible to focus on single actors such as individual politicians within a political party, most of the analyses in the previous chapters focused either on the policy subsystem as a whole, or on the organizations in the subsystem. Sticking to Gerring's (2004, p. 342) definition of a case study as "an intensive study of a single unit for the purpose of understanding a larger class of units," the units analyzed in this chapter are political organizations, whose development will be followed over time.

The organizations to be analyzed were picked in a way to allow achieving the goals formulated above. Most demanding in this respect is finding out whether the correlation between the evaluation of minimum wages in the domestic expert discourse and political actors' policy preferences points to a causal connection based on policy-oriented learning. This means testing the validity of the most general claim derived from the regression models presented in Tables 6.3 and 6.4. For such designs, Lieberman (2005) suggests analyzing cases which, on the one hand, exhibit a large variation on the key independent variable and, on the other hand, are apparently well explained by the quantitative model. Another strategy proposed by Lieberman is to analyze cases less well explained by the quantitative model to identify reasons for which model fit is imperfect. The case selection here combines the two approaches: It selects cases exhibiting a high variation in the key independent variable—the expert discourse—some of which are well explained by the quantitative model, others less well.

To identify cases for which there is a strong variation in the independent variable, this chapter focuses on the strongest shift in the expert discourse available in our data. In Germany, between the years 2003 and 2012, the mean overall evaluation of minimum wage effects in the domestic expert discourse changed from highly critical (−1) to approximately neutral (−.22). In the same time period, three major actors in the German minimum wage subsystem, trade union federation *Deutscher Gewerkschaftsbund* (DGB), the largest center-left party, *Sozialdemokratische Partei Deutschlands* (SPD), and the coalition of the largest center-right parties, *Christlich Demokratische Union Deutschlands* and *Christlich-soziale Union Deutschlands* (CDU/CSU), changed their support for the minimum wage. While all three of them (more or less strongly) rejected the introduction of a general minimum wage in 2003, they (more or less strongly) supported its introduction in 2012. For all three cases, there is thus a correlation between the main independent and the dependent variable.

For the CDU/CSU, this correlation follows expectations. As center-right political parties in Germany, they are expected to oppose the minimum wage when the expert discourse negatively evaluates minimum wage effects, and to tacitly support it when experts' evaluation is approximately neutral (see below). For the SPD, the quantitative model also predicts an over-time observed preference change, but not a shift as strong as observed. As discussed in detail below, the SPD would be expected to fully support the minimum wage when experts' evaluation is neutral (as it did), but to still moderately support the minimum wage when experts' evaluation is negative (which it did not). Therefore, the quantitative model suggests that there are factors other than the expert discourse that explain why the SPD's initial position on the minimum wage was so negative. Finally, the DGB would be expected to be unaffected by the expert discourse, unequivocally supporting the minimum wage no matter what experts say. Therefore, based on the quantitative model, the existence of other factors explaining the DGB's critical stance towards the minimum wage before 2005 seems likely (Table 7.1).

Studying these three cases will also contribute to the other goals of the qualitative analysis formulated above. The analysis of the minimum wage preference of the three organizations will show whether their preferences are well described by the data coded from newspaper articles. It will also become clear whether the expertise that reaches political actors is well described by the data on the expert discourse that was coded from scientific journal articles. The three cases are summarized in Table 7.1, which also summarizes the interest in each case.

Table 7.1 Case selection

Actor	Minimum wage support 2003	Minimum wage support 2012	Correlation between support and expert discourse	Expected correlation between support and expert discourse	Interest in case
DGB	Mix of rejection/support	Support	Yes	No	Test validity of expert discourse and newspaper data. Verify whether no expert influence on the policy preferences of trade unions is plausible.
SPD	Mostly rejection, some support	Support	Yes	Yes, moderate.	Test validity of expert discourse and newspaper data. Verify whether a moderate expert influence based on policy-oriented learning is plausible.
CDU/CSU	Rejection	Moderate support	Yes	Yes, strong	Test validity of expert discourse and newspaper data. Verify whether a strong expert influence based on policy-oriented learning is plausible.

7.1.2 Identifying a Causal Connection Between the Expert Discourse and Policy Preferences

The most demanding goal of the qualitative analysis is to test whether there is a causal influence of the expert discourse on the minimum wage preferences of political actors, which is based on policy-oriented learning. Thus, it can be simply observed whether the minimum wage preference of an organization accords to what was coded from the newspaper articles. In contrast, showing that policy-oriented learning from the expert discourse is responsible for an organization's preference change is not as easy as it might seem. All three organizations are likely to have been in contact with scientific information. Therefore, simply asking people from these organizations whether this information played a role for their organization's preference formation bears the risks that interviewees unconsciously exaggerate the role scientific research played in the process.

Therefore, the strategy chosen was to identify observable implications (King, Keohane and Verba, 1994, pp. 11–12) of the hypothesized expert influence on the organization's minimum wage preference. For the case study, information about the three organizations' preference formation was gathered to judge whether these implications can be observed or not. Only if all observable implications are present can an expert influence be plausibly assumed.

The *first* condition for assuming causality between the shift in the expert discourse and the change in the actor's minimum wage preference is that the preference shift visible in the quantitative data actually happened, that is, that the measurement of the dependent variable is valid. Therefore, for all three actors, is necessary to show that they were more critical of the minimum wage in 2003 than in 2012.

Second, causality between the expert discourse and the organization's position on the minimum wage can only be assumed if the shift in the organization's preference was at least partly based on a changing evaluation of minimum wage effects by the organization. The expert discourse delivers information about minimum wage effects on employment, poverty, and other issues. If it is supposed to be influencing an organization's minimum wage preference, this can only happen if this kind of information plays any role for this organization's preference formation. Likewise, if the organization's assessment of minimum wage effects did not evolve together with the change in the expert discourse, the idea of an expert influence is not plausible.

Third, if the shift in the organization's preference resulted from a changing evaluation of minimum wage effects, it is necessary to show that organization's assessment of minimum wage effects was based on scientific sources. The theoretical model from Chapter 2 does not assume political actors to have direct access to the expert discourse. Therefore, it is not necessary to show that the actors have read the scientific journal articles of which the German expert discourse consists. Rather, it is necessary to show that they have used sources drawing on the scientific state of the art on minimum wage effects. Such sources include scientific research published outside of academic journals, policy papers giving recommendations based on reviewing academic research, and meetings with researchers.

Fourth, the general message the organization drew from these scientific sources should be in line with our data on the expert discourse. To argue that a shift from negative to neutral in the expert discourse led to a change in an organization's minimum wage policy preference only makes sense if the organization also perceived this shift. In other words, it is necessary to show that the shift in the expert discourse not only happened in our data set, but also that the organizations potentially influenced by the shift perceived the scientific evaluation of minimum wage in 2012 to be more favorable than in 2003.

While none of the four conditions proves an expert influence on the organizations minimum wage preference in itself, together they constitute what the process tracing literature has called a *doubly decisive test* (Collier, 2011). If all four of them are true, it is safe to argue that the organization's minimum wage preference was influenced by the expert discourse. In contrast, if one of them is not fulfilled, the organization's minimum wage preference was not influenced by the expert discourse. In the presentation of the case studies, these four criteria will be evaluated for each of the three organizations.

7.1.3 Data

The analysis mostly draws on two sources of information. On the one hand, publicly available sources giving insights about an organization's position on the minimum wage, and the minimum wage-related discussions within this organization were analyzed. These include newspaper articles, election manifestos, and other documents published by the organization itself or by other, related organizations. On the other hand, semi-structured interviews were conducted with people who held offices that were important for the minimum wage preference formation of their respective organization. For each organization, a minimum of three interviews were conducted. If the information from those interviews in combination with the publicly available data was not sufficiently clear or contradictory, further interviews were done until an unambiguous picture had emerged. For the DGB, the interviews partners were the two officials responsible for managing the DGB's minimum wage campaign and one official responsible for minimum wage-related questions at the DGB's member union Verdi, one of the early voices calling for a minimum wage within the DGB. For the SPD, interviews were conducted with two former SPD members of the German *Bundestag*, both of whom also served as *Parlamentarische Staatssekretäre* at the Federal Ministry of Labour and Social Affairs (previously Ministry for Economics and Labour) during the period of analysis. Moreover, a current SPD member of the *Bundestag* engaged in social and economic policy was interviewed. Furthermore, interviews were conducted with two SPD staff members who were responsible for coordinating minimum wage policy, one of them for the SPD's parliamentary group in the *Bundestag*, the other at the SPD party central. Finally, a staff member working on minimum wage-related issues at the *Friedrich-Ebert-Stiftung* was interviewed, a foundation with close ties to the SPD and an important role in providing information on minimum wage policy for the party. For the CDU/CSU, interviews were conducted with a member of the *Bundestag* who is the CDU/CSU's parliamentary group's longstanding rapporteur on minimum wage policy. Moreover, a staff member coordinating the issue of minimum wage policy for the CDU/CSU's parliamentary group in the *Bundestag* was interviewed. Finally, two staff members working on minimum-wage related issues at the *Konrad-Adenauer-Stiftung* were interviewed, a foundation with close ties to the CDU and an important role of providing information on policy for the party. The list of interviewees is documented in Appendix A7. The interview guidelines were designed in a way to avoid suggesting to the interviewees that scientific expertise may have played a role in the preference formation of the organization.

Together, these information sources provide a clear picture of the minimum wage preference formation in all three organizations. Before the three case studies are presented, the next subsection gives a closer insight into the shift that happened in the German expert discourse between 2003 and 2012.

7.1.4 The German Expert Discourse, 2003–2012

As discussed in Chapter 5, the German expert discourse on minimum wage effects is composed of less articles than the British and the US expert discourses. The number of articles published per year has increased with the progression of the political debate about the introduction of a general minimum wage in Germany. For the years 2003 to 2005, during which the debate about the introduction of a general statutory minimum wage first surfaced, the data set on the German expert discourse contains only four scientific articles, all of them measuring minimum wage effects on employment. The fact that not all possible outlets for scientific research were covered in creating the data set—book chapters, for example, were not considered—means that the actual number of relevant publications might have been higher. Still, it seems safe to assume that, up to 2005, the number of publications dealing with minimum wages was low in Germany. According to the results from Chapter 6 (Table 6.4), however, this should not have diminished the influence of the expert discourse.

The number of scientific articles evaluating minimum wages increased faster after 2005. As results from the previous chapter suggest, this might have been a consequence of the increased political attention to the minimum wage. With the increasing number of scholars working, and work being published, on the issue, the evaluation of minimum wages in the expert discourse changed. *First*, this concerned the evaluation minimum wage effects on employment. While the few articles in the expert discourse published before 2005 unequivocally find that minimum wages either increase unemployment or decrease employment, those published between 2005 and 2012 are evenly split between articles finding negative effects on employment, and those not finding such effects. While the strength of the negative effects is not always specified, some publications quantify the adverse employment effect as weak (Feldmann, 2005; Bauer and Schmidt, 2007; Papps, 2012), while others find a substantial or even strong adverse impact (Feldmann, 2003; Clark, Kaas and Madden, 2006; Bauer *et al.*, 2009; Knabe and Schöb, 2009, 2011). A political actor trying to base his or her assessment of minimum wage effects on employment on the "average" evaluation of minimum wage effects in the expert discourse before 2005 would therefore likely conclude that minimum wages have adverse effects on employment, potentially strong. Based on the expert discourse from 2005 to 2012, the conclusion would rather be that while the existence of a substantial adverse impact on employment is possible, it is more likely to be weak, or even nonexistent.

The second important change in the German expert discourse after 2005 is that the diversity of subjects discussed in the scientific publications increases. Analyses of minimum wage effects on poverty and inequality enter the discussion and account for eight articles published between 2005 and 2012. Six of these find a beneficial impact of minimum wages. Moreover, five articles discussing minimum wage effects on the economy and economic growth were published between 2005 and 2012, two of which find beneficial, and three of which find adverse minimum wage effects. In the same time span, 18 articles analyzing other minimum wage effects such as effects on work effort (Kräkel and Schöttner, 2010) are in the data set, 12 of which find undesirable, and 7 of which find desirable minimum wage effects.

In sum, between 2003 and 2012, the German expert discourse became larger, more diverse regarding the kind of minimum wage effects being analyzed, and more favorable in its evaluation of the minimum wage. In terms of the overall evaluation of the minimum wage, these developments are visible as a strong shift over time. While the overall evaluation of minimum wages in the German expert discourse is at a maximally unfavorable −1 up to 2005, it takes a much more favorable value of −.22 in 2012.[1] This shift is the steepest in the entire data used for this book.

The next section analyzes the DGB's, SPD's and CDU/CSU's process of preference formation regarding the minimum wage. Doing so will allow us to see what role the changing evaluation of minimum wages in the German expert discourse on minimum wages played in this process.

7.1.5 The Expert Discourse and Preference Formation on the Minimum Wage

7.1.5.1 German Federation of Trade Unions

The German Federation of Trade Unions (DGB) is by far the largest trade union federation in Germany, its eight member unions having a combined membership of about 6.1 million. While these member unions—IG Bauen-Agrar-Umwelt (BAU, construction sector), IG Bergbau, Chemie, Energie (BCE, chemical industry), IG Metall (IGM, metalworking) Eisenbahn- und Verkehrsgerkschaft (EVG, transportation), Gewerkschaft Erziehung und Wissenschaft (GEW, education), Gewerkschaft Nahrung-Genuss-Gaststätten (NGG, food), Gewerkschaft der Polizei (GdP, police), and Vereinte Dienstleistungsgewerkschaft (Verdi, services)—did not always take a unified stance towards the minimum wage, their positions towards the minimum wage evolved in close coordination. In 2006, the eight trade unions together started a campaign under the DGB's roof for the introduction of a general minimum wage in Germany. For these reasons, the DGB and its member unions are discussed together here.

[1] These values refer to the variable Domestic Expert Discourse, MA5, as used in the estimation from Chapter 6 (Table 6.4).

7.1.5.1.1 Expectations and Quantitative Data

The quantitative data gathered from newspaper articles suggests that the trade unions' minimum wage preferences changed over time. Between 2003 and 2006, when the introduction of a general minimum wage was first a matter of intense public discussion in Germany, the trade unions took a divided stance towards the minimum wage. In the data set, some actors related to the DGB's member unions speak out against the minimum wage (20% of all coded trade-union related actors between 2003 and 2006), some take a mixed position (30%), and others support it (50%). After 2006, all coded statements of trade-union related actors are supportive of the minimum wage.

The direction of this preference change follows the shift in the German expert discourse which took place between 2003 and 2012. It does not, however, accord to the expectations derived from the regression analyses of the previous chapter. Based on Model 4 from Table 6.4, a trade-union related actor is expected to be supportive of the minimum wage with a probability of 88 percent, even if the expert discourse takes a maximally negative view towards the minimum wage. The correlation between the change in the expert discourse and the change in trade unions' preferences is puzzling and could be based on variables not included into the model. Alternatively, it could indicate that the conclusion that trade unions' positions towards the minimum wage are generally not influenced by the expert discourse is based on a false interpretation of the data. The following qualitative analysis helps to interpret this correlation.

7.1.5.1.2 Qualitative Analysis

The analysis of newspaper articles, interviews and other documents suggests that the quantitative analysis is accurate in describing the preferences of the DGB and its member unions. Thus, in 2003, the DGB's member unions were divided regarding their position towards the minimum wage. On the one hand, the trade unions organizing many low-paid service workers, most importantly Verdi and NGG, were pushing for the introduction of a general minimum wage. This was mostly based on the rationale that the existence of low-wage competitors makes it hard for trade unions to organize workers in these sectors. On the other hand, those trade unions mostly organizing the generally better-paid industrial workers, most importantly IGM, were skeptical of a minimum wage. The skepticism was mostly based on *Tarifautonomie*, a guiding principle in German industrial relations, according to which wage-setting should be performed by trade unions and employer organizations, without the interference of the state. From this perspective, a minimum wage appeared as a threat to this fundamental trade union right. This situation changed when, in May 2006, delegates from all of the DGB's eight member unions decided to campaign together for the introduction of a general and statutory minimum wage of €7.50 (later €8.50; interviews 1.2, 1.3).

The way in which trade unions discussed the minimum wage among themselves clearly suggests that the expert discourse did not play a role in this shift. When asked for the arguments that were important in the trade union debate about whether or not to introduce a minimum wage, the three interview partners from trade unions agreed that the central argument supporting the minimum wage was a growing low-wage sectors combined with a declining coverage of collective bargaining agreements. The central argument against the minimum wage was the preservation of *Tarifautonomie* (interviews 1.1, 1.2, 1.3). When prodded for the role that arguments related to the labor market effects of minimum wages played in the trade union debate—the central subject in the German expert discourse—two respondents stated that this argument did not matter (interviews 1.1, 1.2), and one respondent noted that trade unions had always agreed on the view that minimum wages would not cost jobs (interview 1.3). This view is supported by another interview partner who participated in early talks between trade unions and the SPD about the possible introduction of a minimum wage and claimed that discussions centered on the question of *Tarifautonomie.* (interview 2.4).

The shift from a mixed assessment of minimum wages to full-blown support thus appears to be a result of the increasingly strong perception that a growing low-wage sector would endanger the ability of trade unions to negotiate higher wages for their members, which finally took precedence over worries related to government interference in wage setting. An important building block in this growing minimum wage sector seem to have been the so-called Hartz-IV labor market reforms introduced under Chancellor Schröder in 2004, forcing the unemployed to take low-wage jobs, thus aggravating the problem of low-wage employment (interview 1.2).

The fact that the minimum wage effects discussed in the expert discourse did not matter for trade unions' preference shift does not mean trade unions did not pay attention to research. Rather, research was used politically to provide a foundation to the DGB's claim that the effects of the introduction of a general minimum wage would be beneficial (interview 1.2). Researchers from *Wirtschafts- und Sozialwissenschaftliches Institut* (WSI), a research institution connected to the DGB, conducted several studies dealing with minimum wages between 2003 and 2012 (Schulten, Bispinck and Schäfer, 2006; e.g. Bispinck, 2008). Some of these studies are also part of the sample of scientific journal articles that were coded as the expert discourse on minimum wage. Moreover, trade union Verdi commissioned a study evaluating the economic and labor market effects of a statutory minimum wage (Bartsch, 2007). Research results supporting a minimum wage were communicated to the public, for example by publishing the studies cited above on the DGB's web site. This web site also included interviews with researchers in favor of the minimum wage (Deutscher Gewerkschaftsbund, 2008, 2010). Some of the research commissioned by trade unions was also picked up by the mass media, consistent with the idea that there is a connection between the political use of scientific expertise and its presence in the media discourse (e.g. Brönstrup, 2006; Takács, 2007).

All interview partners were also aware of research results contradicting the rather optimistic forecasts from those studies. They mentioned, for example, a study published by the economic think tank *ifo Institut*, which is also among the articles coded as the German expert discourse (Knabe, Schöb and Thum, 2014). Another body whose expertise was perceived to be influential by the interviewees is the *Sachverständigenrat zur Begutachtung der gesamtwirtschaftlichen Entwicklung,* a body of economists tasked with advising the federal government (interviews 1.1, 1.2, 1.3). Based on a review of scientific studies, many of which are part of what was coded as the German or the international expert discourse, the *Sachverständigenrat* has provided advice regarding the introduction of a general minimum wage (Sachverständigenrat zur Begutachtung der Gesamtwirtschaftlichen Entwicklung, 2006, pp. 402–412). Moreover, one interviewee, a former university lecturer (*Privatdozent*) for economics, had in-depth knowledge about the minimum-wage related debate in the economics discipline (interview 1.3). Pessimistic forecasts about minimum wage effects on the economy and the labor market were, however, generally discarded as being based on false assumptions (interview 1.3) or as contradicting the experience that other European countries, especially the UK, had made with the introduction of a minimum wage (interview 1.2).

In sum, the policy preference of the German trade unions organized in the DGB is well described by the data coded from newspaper articles. The qualitative analysis confirms that there is a correlation between the development of the DGB's support for the minimum wage and its evaluation in the German expert discourse. However, it suggests that the DGB chose to embrace the introduction of a general minimum wage not because of the shift in the expert discourse, but because of growing problems related to low-wage employment. If not for cross-coalition learning, scientific expertise was used intensively to be able to better promote the demand for a minimum wage. The expertise that was used to promote the minimum wage, as well as the expertise which was perceived as important in providing arguments to the critics of the minimum wage, was often part of or built on the German or the international expert discourse. Several of the studies promoted by the DGB were picked up by newspapers, entering the media discourse on minimum wages.

7.1.5.2 Sozialdemokratische Partei Deutschlands

The SPD is Germany's largest center-left party, with a vote share of 38.5 percent in the federal elections of 2002, 34.2 percent in 2005, and 23.0 percent in 2009. It led the governing coalition with the Green Party under Chancellor Gerhard Schröder from 2002 to 2005 and was the smaller partner in the governing coalition with the Christian Democrats under Chancellor Angela Merkel from 2005 to 2009.

7.1.5.2.1 Expectations and Quantitative Data

As a center-left political party, the results of the quantitative analyses from Chapter 6 predict the SPD to generally support the minimum wage, although less strongly than trade unions. Based on Model 4 from Table 6.4, SPD politicians are predicted to support the minimum wage with a probability of 43 percent in 2003, when the German expert discourse was still overwhelmingly critical of the minimum wage, to take a mixed position on the minimum wage with a probability of 37 percent, and to be critical of the minimum wage with a probability of 20 percent. In 2012, when the evaluation of the minimum wage in the expert discourse was much more positive, the predicted probability for support was at 99 percent. In other words, according to the statistical model, one would expect the expert discourse to have moderately influenced the SPD, leading it to increase its support for the minimum wage from moderate to strong.

As in the case of the DGB and its affiliated trade unions, the newspaper data suggests that the SPD shifted its position on the minimum wage between 2003 and 2012. Thus, from 2003 to 2005, 50 percent of all statements by actors related to the SPD were critical of the minimum wage, and 50 percent were supportive of the minimum wage (N = 8). After 2005, all but two of the coded statements by actors related to the SPD supported the minimum wage (95%; N = 44). As above, this shift correlates with a positive change in the expert discourse, which started in the same year. Still, the SPD's minimum wage preference does not exactly correspond to the expectations. From 2003 to 2005, opposition to the minimum wage within the SPD was more frequent than expected, although this difference is not as striking as in the case of trade unions.

7.1.5.2.2 Qualitative Analysis

The qualitative analysis, first, suggests that the quantitative data is relatively precise in describing the shift in the SPD's minimum wage preference between 2003 and 2012. In 2003, a debate emerged within the SPD about introducing a minimum wage to compensate for the Hartz-IV labor market reforms, which were seen as harsh by many social democrats. During this debate, some prominent social democrats supported the introduction of the minimum wage, while others were opposed to it (Klüver, 2004). Faced with reluctance from trade unions (who were still struggling with the preservation of *Tarifautonomie*), the project was put on hold in late 2004 (DPA, 2004). A so-called project group of leading SPD politicians and trade union representatives was installed to discuss low-wage issues (*Projektgruppe Einkommensgestaltung im unteren Bereich*), from which a decision of the SPD leadership to support the introduction of a general minimum wage emerged in 2006 (Interview 2.4; Rosigkeit, 2006). In the following years, the SPD heavily pressurized the CDU/CSU for the introduction of branch minimum wages in several industries (Süddeutsche Zeitung, 2007), and included the demand for the introduction of a general minimum wage in its manifesto for the 2009 general election (Sozialdemokratische Partei Deutschlands, 2009).

The discussion within the SPD about whether or not to introduce a minimum wage clearly emerged before 2005, meaning that the rapid shift in the German expert discourse happening *after* 2005 was not the cause that put a reconsideration of the minimum wage on the SPD's agenda. For most interview partners, this cause was the introduction of the Hartz-IV labor market reforms, in combination with the longer-term trend of expanding low-wage employment. Also, pressure by trade unions NGG and Verdi was mentioned (interviews 2.1, 2.2, 2.3, 2.4).

However, according to the expectations from the statistical model, the scientific evaluation of minimum wages should have had some influence on the SPD's policy preference once the party had started reconsidering the minimum wage. As argued above, a precondition for such an influence is that questions regarding the effects of a minimum wage on employment and other variables played a role for the SPD. A first indicator for this is how often actors connected to the SPD publicly spoke about minimum wage effects. In the available newspaper data set, this is the case only three times between 2003 and 2012. This compares with 44 times in which an actor connected to the SPD voiced support or disapproval for the minimum wage during this time span. The interviews as well suggest that concerns about labor-market, economic, and inequality effects of minimum wages were not central for the SPD's preference formation. Rather, in the years prior to 2006, the most important argument within the SPD against the introduction of a minimum wage was a reluctance to interfere with the principle of *Tarifautonomie* (interviews 2.1, 2.3, 2.4). Once trade unions had achieved unanimity on this issue, supporting the minimum wage was also easier for the SPD.

If not central, minimum wage effects still were of some importance for the discussions within the SPD. While the picture that emerges from the interviews is not completely homogenous, the respondents agree that questions about the effects of minimum wages were part of the party's internal debate about the minimum wage between 2004 and 2006 (interviews 2.1, 2.2, 2.3,2.6). In 2005, unemployment numbers in Germany reached a record high, and the SPD-led government was careful in evaluating economic measures regarding their impact on employment and economic competitiveness (interview 2.1). In this context, at least for some SPD politicians dealing with economic and financial policy, minimum wages appeared undesirable (interviews 2.1, 2.2, 2.3). In 2004, the Federal Minister for Economics and Labour, SPD politician Wolfgang Clement, claimed that minimum wages were not commensurable with the overall goal of economic deregulation (Handelsblatt, 2004). In 2006, the Federal Minister of Finance, SPD politician Peer Steinbrück, voiced fears about job losses following the introduction of a minimum wage (DPA, 2006). On the other hand, such concerns were shared only by a minority within the SPD (interview 2.6). Also, there was change over time. In the years after 2006, statements by SPD politicians critical of the minimum wage ceased, and some of the former critics became convinced that a minimum wage would not have negative effects on employment or the economy (interview 2.3).

While questions related to the effects of minimum wages were only moderately important for the SPD's decision to support the minimum wage, there is strong support for the claim that the SPD's assessment of such effects was influenced by scientific research. When asked where knowledge about minimum wage effects came from, all interviewees prominently mentioned scientific sources. Particularly important among these were publicly funded economic research institutions, most importantly the *Institut für Arbeit und Berufsforschung* (IAB; interviews 2.1, 2.2, 2.3, 2.6), which published several empirical and theoretical studies of the effects of minimum wages between 2003 and 2012 (e.g. Rhein, 2003; König and Möller, 2007; Feil *et al.*, 2010; Möller, 2010). Of the minimum-wage related studies published by IAB researchers, several are also part of our sample of the German expert discourse. Moreover, the *Friedrich-Ebert-Stiftung* (FES), a foundation close to the SPD, commissioned a number of studies evaluating the potential effects of the introduction of a minimum wage in Germany (Bosch, Kalina and Weinkopf, 2009; Bosch, Weinkopf and Kalina, 2009; Ehrentraut *et al.*, 2011). These were judged to be important for the minimum wage-related discussion within the SPD by several interviewees (interviews 2.2, 2.3, 2.5, 2.6). While these studies are not themselves part of our sample of the expert discourse on minimum wages, they review literature from the German and the international expert discourse. Also, two of their authors—Gerhard Bosch and Claudia Weinkopf—have published other studies that are part of the German expert discourse. Another important source for assessing the potential impact of a minimum wage were the experiences of other European countries with the minimum wage, most importantly the United Kingdom. These experiences were assessed through academic literature (interview 2.4), but also on a trip to visit the British Low Pay Commission (interview 2.3). Finally, meetings with interest groups were important sources of information (interviews 2.3, 2.6).

The central messages the party took from these sources are roughly representative of the German expert discourse discussed above. While much of the research that interviewees described as most important was published after 2005 and paints a moderately positive picture of minimum wage effects, there is also evidence that earlier research was perceived to be more critical. Of the six interviewees, three reported that resistance among researchers against a minimum wage was strongest around 2005 and that the scientific evaluation became more positive thereafter (interviews 2.2, 2.5, 2.6). Another interviewee stated that, based on the information available, fears about negative minimum wage effects had become smaller within the SPD over time (interview 2.3). A fifth one, who was involved in minimum wage policy making only until 2007, had perceived scientific opinion on the minimum wage as uniformly negative, a perception in agreement with our data for most of the years before 2007 (interview 2.1). The experiences of a sixth interviewee, however, do not match this pattern. According to his perception, research had never pointed to strong negative minimum wage effects (interview 2.4).

Besides for learning about the effects of minimum wages, the SPD also used scientific studies politically. For example, the abovementioned study by Ehrentraut et al. (2011) was published on the web site of the SPD party group in the *Bundestag* (SPD-Bundestagsfraktion, 2013), and advertised in press releases (SPD-Bundestagsfraktion, 2011). Like this, it also entered several newspaper articles (Süddeutsche Zeitung, 2011; Creutzburg, 2013). Also on other occasions, SPD politicians publicly pointed to studies supporting their claim that a minimum wage would have no adverse effects (Schreiner, 2009; Kramme, 2013).

In sum, the qualitative analysis suggests that the change in the SPD's position on the minimum wage between 2003 and 2012 was mostly driven by rising numbers of low-wage employment on the one hand, and the wish to preserve *Tarifautonomie*, on the other hand. The issue was discussed in close coordination with the DGB, and it was the DGB's lack of support for the minimum wage which was mostly responsible for the SPD rejecting the introduction of a minimum wage in 2004. Yet, this is not the whole story. For some influential SPD politicians, assumed adverse labor market effects were a reason to initially reject the minimum wage. Statements pointing to negative minimum wage effects on employment or the economy subsided after 2006, at the same time at which the German expert discourse became more favorable towards the minimum wage. Based on the data presented in this section, it appears plausible that the changing assessment of minimum wage effects within the SPD is a result of the changed expert discourse. Scientific research was among the most important sources based on which minimum wage effects were assessed, and the conclusions the party took from this research are in line with our data on the German expert discourse. The results from the qualitative analysis are thus consistent with a limited expert influence on the SPD's minimum wage preference, which is based on learning from the expert discourse. Moreover, the qualitative analysis suggests that the SPD used scientific research politically to support its demand for the introduction of a general minimum wage.

7.1.5.3 Christian Democrats

The *Christlich Demokratische Union Deutschland* (CDU) and the *Christlich-Soziale Union in Bayern* (CSU) are Germany's main conservative parties and form a common parliamentary group in the *Bundestag* (CDU/CSU). CDU/CSU had a combined vote share of 38.5 percent in 2002, 35.2 percent in 2005, 33.8 percent in 2009, and 41.5 percent in 2013, and CDU party leader Angela Merkel has been serving as Chancellor since 2005, in coalition governments with the SPD (2005–2009 and since 2013) and *Freie Demokratische Partei* (FDP; 2009–2013).

7.1.5.3.1 Expectations and Quantitative Data

As center-right political parties, the CDU/CSU's position towards the minimum wage should be strongly dependent on the expert discourse. Based on Model 4 from Table 6.4, CDU/CSU politicians are predicted to oppose the minimum wage with a probability of 97 percent in 2003, when the evaluation of minimum wage effects in the expert discourse takes the value of −1, with a 2 percent chance for a mixed or neutral position and a 1 percent probability for support. In 2012, with a mean evaluation of minimum wages in the expert discourse of −.21, CDU/CSU politicians are predicted to oppose the minimum wage with a probability of just 21 percent, to take a mixed or neutral position with a probability of 37 percent, and to support it with a probability of 42 percent. Substantially, therefore, one would expect the expert discourse to have led the CDU/CSU to change its political position on the minimum wage from strong opposition to moderate support. This is the strongest expected influence of the three actors analyzed here.

As with the other two actors discussed above, the newspaper data suggests that the CDU/CSU shifted its position on the minimum wage between 2003 and 2012. Thus, between 2003 and 2005, all recorded statements by CDU/CSU politicians are opposed to the minimum wage, conforming to the expectations under the conditions of an expert discourse strongly critical of the minimum wage. From 2006 to 2012, 30.1 percent of all coded statements by CDU/CSU politicians oppose the minimum wage, 26.9 percent take a mixed or neural position, and 42.3 percent support it. This is roughly in line with the expectations from the quantitative model. In contrast to the cases of the DGB and the SPD, the quantitative model from Chapter 6 would attribute the CDU/CDU's preference change mostly to the parallel shift in the expert discourse.

7.1.5.3.2 Qualitative Analysis

The first step in the qualitative analysis is to check whether the description of the CDU/CSU's position on the minimum wage that was derived from the quantitative data matches the parties' actual position. This is approximately so. In 2004, leading CDU/CSU politicians strongly criticized proposals from SPD and Green politicians regarding the introduction of a minimum wage. This was based on concerns regarding its impact on employment and the economy (Frankfurter Allgemeine Zeitung, 2004). In 2005, one year before a tentative move towards the minimum wage becomes visible in the quantitative data, CSU party leader Edmund Stoiber and CDU labor market expert Karl-Josef Laumann first signaled their readiness to engage in talks about the introduction of a minimum wage, should low-wage employment continue to grow (Frankfurter Allgemeine Zeitung, 2005). During this time, however, the preferred model to deal with low-wage employment among CDU/CSU politicians was the negative income tax (interview 3.3), and the two parties explicitly rejected the introduction of minimum wages in their 2005 election manifesto (Christlich Demokratische Union/Christlich-soziale Union, 2005). Between 2005 and 2009, the CDU/CSU formed a coalition government with the SPD, who repeatedly pushed for the introduction of industry-specific minimum wages during this time period (see above). The response from CDU/CSU politicians was mixed. On the one hand, the introduction of minimum wages in single industries by the means of generalizing collective agreements was—sometime grudgingly—accepted. On the other hand, a general minimum wage was rejected (Frankfurter Allgemeine Zeitung, 2007). In its 2009 election manifesto, the CDU/CSU again rejected the introduction of a general minimum wage, advocating the concept of a negative income tax instead (Christlich Demokratische Union/Christlich-soziale Union, 2009). After the election, however, when the CDU/CSU formed a coalition government with the economically conservative FDP, CDU Minister of Labor Ursula von der Leyen pushed for the introduction of minimum wages in industries such as temporary work and caregiving (Frankfurter Allgemeine Zeitung, 2010a, 2010b). Some more left-leaning CDU/CSU politicians organized in the party group *Christlich Demokratische Arbeitnehmerschaft* also pushed for the introduction of a general minimum wage, while economically more conservative politicians rejected this demand (Sattar, 2011). The dispute was settled by including a demand for a general lower limit for wages (*Allgemeine Lohnuntergrenze*) into the 2013 election manifesto, a concept stipulating the extension of industry-specific minimum wages through the generalization of collective agreements for all industries (Christlich Demokratische Union/Christlich-soziale Union, 2013).

The above discussion shows that it was not the change in the expert discourse happening after 2005 that brought the minimum wage on the CDU/CSU's agenda. Rather, the two parties' engagement with the minimum wage was driven by the SPD, as well as the general increase in low-wage employment (interviews 3.2, 3.3, 3.4).

Once the minimum wage was on the political agenda, however, an expert influence on how the CDU/CSU evaluated the minimum wage is plausible. Thus, the issue was very strongly discussed in terms of minimum wage effects within the CDU/CSU, especially regarding effects on employment and the economy. In the newspaper data set, there are 11 recorded statements about minimum wage effects on employment or the economy made by CDU/CSU politicians between 2003 and 2012, as compared to 60 statements on the desirability of a minimum wage. The share of statements relating to minimum wage effects is much higher share than for the SPD or trade unions. Also, all interviewees agreed that the central argument against the minimum wage was its potentially negative impact on employment and the economy (interviews 3.1, 3.2, 3.3, 3.4).

The way in which these effects were evaluated within the CDU/CSU changed over time. In the years around 2005, many within the CDU/CSU perceived minimum wages as a threat, in particular to employment. These concerns became rarer over time, as more CDU/CSU politicians became convinced that the introduction of a statutory minimum wage would not have a large negative impact on employment (interview 3.2, 3.3, 3.4). The interviewees' account of this change is also visible in the newspaper data set. Thus, ten statements about negative minimum wage effects on employment are recorded in the years from 2003 to 2009, but only one in the period from 2010 to 2012 (and none thereafter). Unlike questions regarding minimum wage effects on employment and the economy, the preservation of *Tarifautonomie* or the coordination with trade unions does not seem to have played a role for the CDU/CSU (interviews 3.1, 3.2, 3,3, 3.4).

Scientific research was crucial for evaluating what effects a minimum wage would have on employment and the economy. Regarding the sources of information about minimum wage effects, the accounts from CDU/CSU interviewees resemble those from SPD interviewees. Scientific studies and publications by scientific institutions were consistently ranked among the most important sources of information by the interviewees, next to experiences with branch minimum wages and other countries' experiences with the minimum wage (interviews 3.1, 3.2, 3.3, 3.4). Among the sources of scientific expertise deemed to be important by interviewees was the IAB (interviews 3.1, 3.4), whose expertise was also valued by SPD politicians. Moreover, several studies commissioned by the Federal Ministry of Labour and Social Affairs, which did not show a strong negative impact of the existing industry minimum wages, played an important role in convincing CDU/CSU politicians that the introduction of a general statutory minimum wage would not have large detrimental effects on employment and the economy (interview 3.1; Aretz *et al.*, 2011; Boockmann *et al.*, 2011; Bosch, Hieming, *et al.*, 2011; Bosch, Kalina, *et al.*, 2011; Egeln *et al.*, 2011; Möller *et al.*, 2011). The results of three of these evaluations were also published as scientific journal articles, and thus entered the sample of articles that was coded as the German expert discourse (König and Möller, 2009; Aretz, Arntz and Gregory, 2013; Boockmann *et al.*, 2013). Moreover, the *Konrad-Adenauer-Stiftung* a foundation close to the CDU, published policy papers which summarized scientific literature on minimum wage effects. The studies cited in these papers are partly articles that from the German or the international expert discourse (Funk, no date; Rindfleisch, 2011). An important role for accumulating knowledge about minimum wage effects, moreover, was the direct access to scientific literature (interview 3.4).

The conclusions that CDU/CSU politicians drew from scientific expertise are in line with the evaluation of minimum wage effects in the German expert discourse presented at the beginning of this chapter. Thus, the interviewees generally perceived experts' evaluation as being very negative in the earlier years of the minimum wage debate, and to have become more open towards minimum wages thereafter. Immediately prior to the introduction of the general statutory minimum wage in Germany, their own expectation—based on the scientific and other information they had—was that the minimum wage would have no strong negative effects on employment and the economy (interviews 3.1, 3.2, 3.3, 3.4).

Compared to this strong use of scientific expertise for policy-oriented learning, the political use of research is less visible in the case of CDU/CSU. Thus, in contrast to the DGB and the SPD, CDU and CSU did not energetically promote studies whose claims supported the CDU/CSU's policy preference on their web sites or in campaign materials.

In sum, the qualitative analysis shows that policy-oriented learning from the expert discourse played a major role in the CDU/CSU's shift from opposing to moderately supporting minimum wages. Thus, concerns regarding adverse minimum wage effects on the economy and employment were the dominant argument motivating the CDU/CSU's initial rejection of the minimum wage. These concerns became weaker over time, in parallel with the shift in the German expert discourse. The analysis suggests that the two developments are connected. Thus, scientific sources connected to the German and the international expert discourse on minimum wages played a major role in forming the CDU/CSU's assessment of what effects of a minimum wage would be. The evidence for a political use of scientific expertise is weaker than for the DGB and the SPD.

7.2 Summary and Conclusion

The results from the three case studies can now be summarized. Doing so, this section addresses the goals of the qualitative analysis that were formulated at the beginning of this chapter.

7.2.1 Validity of Data

The first goal of the qualitative analysis was to evaluate the validity of the two main data sets, gathered from scientific journal articles and newspaper articles on minimum wages. Thus, it was necessary to make sure that this data accurately describes the central concepts from the theoretical model formulated in Chapter 2.

First, regarding minimum wage policy subsystems, the main problem was to ensure that the data gathered from newspaper articles allows to recover the policy preferences of political actors in minimum-wage policy subsystems. Analyzing three organizations at two points in time, the qualitative analysis in this chapter compared these organizations' positions on the minimum wage as recovered from the newspaper data with their position as identified using a broader information base including interviews, further newspaper articles, and other documents. The qualitative analysis suggests that the quantitative data correctly describes the change in the organizations' minimum wage preferences. This is an important precondition for the validity of the analyses presented in previous chapters.

Second, the validity of the data on the expert discourse on minimum wages was tested. This meant showing that the scientific expertise used by political actors is directly or indirectly related to the scientific journal articles coded as the expert discourse on minimum wages, and not to some other body of knowledge unrelated to this research. The case studies affirm a close connection between the studies that were coded as the German and the international expert discourse, and the expertise used by the actors in the German minimum wage policy subsystem. Thus, among the most important sources of scientific expertise used were publications by publicly funded economic research institutes such as the IAB, studies and policy papers published by party think tanks, and economic research published in scientific journals. All of these sources are related to the German or the international expert discourse on minimum wages. While some of publications that the interviewees identified as important are included in the sample of articles coded as the German expert discourse, others summarize literature from the German or the international expert discourse.

7.2.2 Validity of Expert Influence on Political Actors

The second goal of the qualitative analysis in this chapter was to assess the validity of a central result of the analyses so far. Thus, Chapter 6 concluded that there is a correlation between the expert discourse and political actors' minimum wage preferences, which is based on policy-oriented learning from the expert discourse. This causal influence was expected to be strong in the case of the CDU/CSU, to be of moderate strength for the SPD, and to be nonexistent for the DGB. To test for its presence, the case studies looked at four observable implications of an expert influence on the three organizations' minimum wage preferences. The results confirm the expectations.

Thus, at the beginning of this chapter, it was *first* argued that an expert influence on political actors' minimum wage preferences requires a correlation between the evaluation of minimum wages in the expert discourse and the actor's minimum wage preference. This was true for all organizations, who started out more or less opposing the minimum wage in 2003 and ended up (moderately) supporting it by 2012. This shift happened in parallel to a change in the evaluation of minimum wages in the German expert discourse.

The *second* observable implication identified at the beginning of this chapter was that the organization's preference change was based on an argument about the effects of minimum wages. Looking at the inner-organizational debates around the minimum wage suggests that this can be affirmed for the CDU/CSU. Here, the minimum wage was initially rejected out of concerns regarding its effects on employment and the economy. When these concerns became smaller over time, the two parties started to tacitly support the introduction of minimum wages. In contrast, the most important influence on the SPD's position on the minimum wage were trade unions. The social democrats had initially been critical of the minimum wage mostly because of the DGB's unclear position. When support for the minimum wage grew among trade unions, this also led to a change in the SPD's position. Still, arguments about the effects of a minimum wage on employment and the economy had some relevance for the discussions within the SPD. Between 2003 and 2006, several influential politicians had rejected calls for the introduction of a minimum wage based on its allegedly adverse consequences. In later years, such concerns subsided. Finally, for the DGB and its member unions, arguments about the effects of minimum wages did not play a role in the preference formation on the issue. Here, the internal debate centered on an increasing proportion of low-wage workers and the principle of *Tarifautonomie.* An expert influence on the DGB's position towards the minimum wage is, therefore, implausible.

The *third* observable implication of an expert influence on political actors is that the actor used research from the expert discourse to assess the effects of minimum wages. This is true for both the CDU/CSU and the SPD, who drew heavily on scientific research from Germany and other countries to assess minimum wage effects.

Finally, the *fourth* observable implication presented above was that political actors not only use scientific sources to assess minimum wage effects, but also draw lessons from these sources which are in line with the general messages that can be drawn from the German expert discourse. This is what was observed in the case studies. In accordance with the data on the German expert discourse presented above, interviewees from SPD and CDU/CSU mostly perceived scientific research as having been critical of the minimum wage in the early years of the minimum wage debate. In the later years of the minimum wage debate, scientific research was perceived as being more favorable towards the minimum wage, predicting less adverse economic and labor market effects.

Interestingly, the case studies also showed that SPD and CDU/CSU not only used expertise from Germany, but also from other countries such as the United States and the United Kingdom. At first sight, this seems to contradict the conclusion that it is the German, and not the international, expert discourse which influences political actors in Germany. A possible explanation might be that the way domestic experts perceive the minimum wage has a filtering effect on which studies from other countries political actors believe to be relevant for the domestic context. In other words, when faced with contradictory evidence about minimum wage effects in other countries, political actors might give greatest weight to those parts of the evidence that conform to the information they receive from experts in their own country. This, however, is a question which cannot be solved based on the data presented in this chapter, and which deserves attention in further research.

Together, these findings conform to the expectations derived from the quantitative analyses presented in the previous chapter. Thus, as expected, the qualitative analysis points to a strong expert influence on the CDU/CSU, a weaker influence on the SPD, and no influence on the DGB.

Conclusion 8

Following an analysis of the literature on the use of scientific expertise in policy making and its gaps, the introductory chapter of this book has formulated two goals for the analysis presented in subsequent chapters. The first one was to test how different scope conditions mediate the role of scientific expertise in the policy process. The second one was to quantify the influence that learning from scientific expertise has on the policy preferences of different political actors. In Chapter 2, these broad goals were translated into theoretically grounded, testable hypotheses. Subsequent chapters then presented a host of empirical analyses of the role of scientific expertise in minimum wage policy making in Germany, the United Kingdom, and the United States between 1970 and 2015. This chapter sums up the results, updates the theoretical model, and discusses how the results relate to existing knowledge about the role of scientific expertise in the policy process.

8.1 Summary of Findings

8.1.1 Minimum Wage Policy Subsystems and Expert Discourse

Using newspaper data from Germany, the United Kingdom, and the United States, the empirical analyses presented in this book started with a description of the three countries' minimum wage policy subsystems. Apart from providing context for analyzing the use of expertise by actors in the three policy subsystems, this initial analysis helped to corroborate the central claims on which the comparative design of this research rests. Thus, minimum wage policy making in the three countries was assumed to be similar enough to be comparable regarding the use of scientific expertise in the policy process. Besides obvious similarities such as

F. Klein, *The Role of Scientific Expertise in Minimum Wage Policy Making*, Vergleichende Politikwissenschaft,
https://doi.org/10.1007/978-3-658-32746-0_8

high levels of democracy and of economic development in all three countries, this included the assumption that minimum wage policy subsystems and political debates about the minimum wage are similarly structured in all three countries. On the other hand, cross-national differences, most importantly different styles of using scientific expertise, were needed to provide variation on some of the context variables hypothesized to mediate the use of scientific expertise.

The analyses from Chapter 4 paint the expected picture of similarities and differences. Minimum wage policy subsystems in Germany, the United Kingdom, and the United States are similarly structured. The most important actors and organizations in all three subsystems are the major political parties and their representatives in national parliaments, parts of the executive branch of government such as ministries of labor or finance, trade unions, employer organizations, and organizations involved in policy advice, such as think tanks. In all three countries, questions about the effects of the minimum wage on poverty and inequality, employment and unemployment, and on the economy play a major role in the political debate. Using statements about these effects and about the general desirability of minimum wages, it is possible to group the organizations present in each of the three countries into coalitions supportive or skeptical of the minimum wage. These coalitions conform to a common-sense understanding of minimum wage politics: trade unions and left-wing political parties tend to support the minimum wage, while right-wing political parties and employer organizations tend to be critical.

At the same time, differences were found between the policy subsystems. Regarding the provision of scientific expertise, the US minimum wage policy subsystem is populated by many research-related actors with connections to interest groups. Government-funded or nonpartisan bodies providing policy advice play a smaller role. This conforms to expectations for a country with a pluralistic style of using scientific expertise. In contrast, in Germany and the UK, the most important actors providing policy advice are of the nonpartisan, government-funded type. Another remarkable difference between the three countries is the polarization between the two coalitions, which is much higher in the US than in the two European countries. Moreover, while the coalition structure of the US minimum-wage policy subsystem is stable throughout the period of analysis, a change can be observed in Germany and the UK, where the anti-minimum wage coalitions significantly weakened their opposition to the minimum wage over time. The higher stability of the US coalition structure could be a result of the higher age of the policy there.

Chapter 5 described another major component of the theoretical model, the expert discourse on minimum wages. It was shown that there are hundreds of studies evaluating minimum wage effects, mostly on employment, poverty or social inequality, and the economy. While most research finds that minimum wages alleviate poverty or reduce inequality, introducing or raising a minimum wage is mostly expected to reduce employment. Effects on the economy and other effects are sometimes found to be desirable, sometimes to be undesirable. A closer look revealed over-time as well as geographical variation in the scientific evaluation of the minimum wage. Thus, the overall evaluation of the minimum wage became more positive over time. Moreover, the evaluation varies between the three national expert discourses that were analyzed. Thus, research conducted by scholars working in or using data from the United States—the US expert discourse—is much more likely to find undesirable minimum wage effects than research from the UK. The German expert discourse comprises very few publications in the early years of the German minimum wage debate, which all find negative minimum wage effects. In later years, an increasing number of studies finds mostly undesirable, but sometimes desirable effects, a picture that resembles the US expert discourse.

8.1.2 Scientific Expertise in the Media Discourse

Having described minimum wage policy subsystems and the expert discourse in the three countries, the next step was to analyze how, how often and under what circumstances research-related actors appear in in the newspaper discourse on minimum wages. As argued in Chapter 2, the presence of scientific expertise in the mass media indicates that the general public can learn about research on minimum wages, and use this knowledge to evaluate the claims political actors make about the effects proposed changes in minimum wage legislation will have. Moreover, the presence of scientific expertise in the media discourse may result from or spur the political use of research by actors such as political parties or interest groups.

The analyses from Chapter 5 showed that scholars, their research, and other actors providing policy analysis play an important role in newspaper reporting on minimum wages. There are several context variables that influence the degree to which scientific expertise is present in the media discourse on minimum wages. *First*, the more scientific research on minimum wages is published in the *international* expert discourse, the more expertise finds its way into the public discourse, while the number of articles in the domestic expert discourse has no independent explanatory power. Thus, apparently, it is not primarily the results from domestic research which are important in the minimum wage policy process. Looking at which individual scholars are cited by the newspapers, however, seems to contradict this result, since most researchers cited in newspaper articles are domestic. *Second*, there are strong differences between the three countries, with the presence of scientific expertise in the public discourse on minimum wages being lower in Germany and the United Kingdom compared to the US. The dividing line conforms to the distinction between a pluralist style of using scientific expertise on the one hand, and a consensual or corporatist policy making style on the other hand. This result is in line with the theoretical expectations formulated in Chapter 2. The higher political use of scientific expertise under the conditions of a pluralist style leads to a higher presence of research in the mass media. However, a plausible alternative explanation which could not be ruled out attributes the cross-national differences to different traditions of journalism in the US compared to Germany and the UK. *Third*, there is some evidence that research-related actors are more present in the media discourse in times in which the results from new studies challenge long-held certainties about minimum wage effects.

The expertise that is presented in newspapers was found to resemble the evaluation of minimum wages in the international, but also in the respective domestic expert discourse. The distribution of statements about different minimum wage effects made by scholars and think tanks cited in newspaper articles relatively well matches the research results concerning the effects published in the expert discourse. Not only does information about the results of scientific research enter the mass media, but the information that does so well represents the available research on minimum wages. Likewise, over-time changes in the domestic as well as in the international expert discourse are visible in the public discourse. For example, if new research results show that minimum wages do not harm employment, more statements of this kind will be made in newspaper articles. While the newspapers analyzed for this book generally paint an accurate picture of existing research on minimum wages, they are not free from political bias. Center-left papers are more likely to cite research results supporting the minimum wage, center-right newspapers more often cite research pointing to adverse minimum wage effects.

8.1.3 Influence of the Expert Discourse on Policy Beliefs and Preferences

While the analyses from Chapter 5 focused on the presence of scientific expertise in newspaper articles, Chapter 6 dealt with the influence of the expert discourse on the beliefs and policy preferences of actors in minimum wage policy subsystems. In Chapter 2, such an influence was hypothesized to result from policy-oriented learning from the expert discourse.

The first step in testing for the presence of this influence was to compare political actors' evaluation of minimum wage effects on poverty, employment, and the economy with the evaluation of these effects in the expert discourse. The analysis revealed a strong agreement between the evaluation of these effects by political actors and the corresponding evaluation in the domestic expert discourse. This correlation results from the fact that political actors usually refrain from making statements incompatible with the expert discourse. For example, in the US, where most research points to adverse minimum wage effects on employment, even actors supporting a higher minimum wage rarely state that a minimum wage hike would create jobs. Rather, they tend to point to beneficial minimum wage effects on poverty, a statement compatible with the expert discourse. The strong agreement between experts and political actors does not, however, extend to the policy preference. Perhaps unsurprisingly, no matter what researchers find in terms of minimum wage effects, different political actors still take wildly different positions when it comes to supporting or opposing the minimum wage.

To get a better view on the apparently weaker relation between the expert discourse and political actors' minimum wage preferences, several regression analyses were conducted. The central result is that there is an influence of the domestic expert discourse on policy preferences, while the international expert discourse has no independent effect. The strengths of this influence was found to depend on several context variables. In particular, large differences exist between the countries analyzed. The influence of the expert discourse on political actors' minimum wage policy preferences is much stronger in Germany and the United Kingdom than in the US. Moreover, experts have less influence in election years.

The analysis also showed which actors are most likely to be influenced by changes in the expert discourse. While results suggest that political actors learn from and are influenced by the expert discourse regardless of their preexisting preference for or against the minimum wage, a slight adjustment of beliefs in favor or against the minimum wage will not radically change the position of steadfast supporters or critics. In contrast, for those actors who do not have a strong preference for or against the minimum wage in the first place, expert influence can "tip the balance", turning former critics into supporters, or vice versa. Which types of actors are most likely to have no clear preference regarding the minimum wage depends of the specific constellation of the policy subsystem. In Germany and the US, the actors most likely to be influenced by the expert discourse were those connected to the executive branch of government. In Britain, right-wing political parties were most likely to be affected by changes in the expert discourse.

The analysis not only showed that there is an influence of the expert discourse on political actors' minimum wage policy preferences, but also made it possible to quantify this influence. For some actors in Germany and the UK, this influence is substantial. Between 2003 and 2012, the German expert discourse experienced a large shift from a negative towards a more positive evaluation of minimum wage effects. In this time, the predicted probability of an actor affiliated with a center-right political party of opposing the minimum wage declined from 97 percent to 21 percent. While the influence of the expert discourse was estimated to be equally strong in the UK and in Germany, the British expert discourse does not show the same amount of over-time variation as its British counterpart. Therefore, it does not play an equally important role in causing preferences *changes*. In the US, expert influence is smaller than in the two European countries. For example, between 1985 and 2001 the evaluation of minimum wages in the US expert discourse became much more favorable. In this period, the probability of an actor affiliated with the Democratic party to support higher minimum wages rose from 78 percent to 90 percent. For an actor affiliated with the Republican party, the probability only rose from 2 percent to 6 percent.

Finally, Chapter 6 included analyses to shed light on the inverse direction of influence running from the minimum wage policy subsystem to the expert discourse on minimum wages. A clear link was found in terms of first-level agenda setting. When minimum wages are high on the political agenda, this sparks new research that becomes visible in the expert discourse a few years later. No support was found, however, for an effect on the content of scientific research. The way actors in minimum wage policy subsystems evaluate the minimum wage does not influence how scientific research evaluates minimum wage effects.

8.1.4 Plausibility Check

Finally, to make sure that the quantitative findings do not misinterpret reality due to badly operationalized variables or spurious correlations, Chapter 7 presented the results from three qualitative case studies. The case studies analyzed the use of scientific expertise by two German political parties—SPD and CDU/CSU—and the German trade union confederation DGB between 2003 and 2012.

The results show that the two main data sets used in the quantitative analyses measure the concepts they are intended to measure. The data gathered from newspaper articles provides an accurate description of how the three organizations positioned themselves towards the minimum wage, and of how this positioning changed over time. The data describing the domestic expert discourse provides a good understanding of what scientific expertise reaches and is used by political actors.

Moreover, the results from Chapter 7 suggest that the statistical correlation between the expert discourse and political actors' minimum wage preferences is based on a causal process involving policy-oriented learning from scientific expertise, as specified in the theoretical model. The case studies show that there was a substantial flow of information from the expert discourse to the actors in the German minimum wage policy subsystem. Interviewees from the three organizations that were analyzed were generally well informed about minimum-wage related research. Their perception of how science evaluated minimum wage effects matched our measure of the expert discourse. While all three organizations used expertise politically or to better understand their own preferences, policy-oriented learning from the expert discourse was found to have influenced only the CDU/CSU's and—to a lesser degree—the SPD's position towards the minimum wage. This confirmed the expectations derived from the quantitative analyses presented in Chapter 6.

Based on these findings, it is now possible to update the theoretical model on which the research presented in this book is based. This will be done by evaluating the hypotheses from Chapter 2.

8.1.5 Hypotheses about Expert Influence

Of the hypotheses formulated in Chapter 2 the most basic ones, hypotheses H1.1 through H1.4, refer to whether the international and the domestic expert discourse are used in minimum wage policy making, and in which ways. As summarized above, research from the *domestic* expert discourse both enters the media discourse about the minimum wage and influences the policy preferences of certain political actors. Moreover, the research from the *international* expert discourse enters the media discourse on minimum wages but does not influence the policy preferences of actors in minimum wage policy subsystems. There is thus support for hypotheses H1.1 through H1.3, but not for hypothesis H1.4 (see Table 8.1).

Table 8.1 Support for hypotheses H1.1 through H1.4

Hypothesis	Supported
H1.1: Scientific expertise from the domestic expert discourse is present in the media discourse on minimum wages.	+
H1.2: The domestic expert discourse influences the beliefs and preferences of actors in minimum wage policy subsystems.	+
H1.3: Scientific expertise from the international expert discourse is present in the media discourse on minimum wages.	+
H1.4: The international expert discourse influences the beliefs and preferences of actors in minimum wage policy subsystems.	–

Finding strong support for the use of scientific expertise in minimum wage policy making and a substantial influence of the domestic expert discourse over the minimum wage preferences of specific actor groups, the research presented in this book sides with those parts of the literature that give expertise an important role in the policy process. According to our results, scientific research is used not only as ammunition in the political debate around minimum wage policy, but also as an influence on the preferences of political actors. When the scientific evaluation of an issue rapidly and strongly shifts, even marked policy changes like those described in the epistemic communities literature (Adler and Haas, 1992) appear to be plausible in the light of this book's findings. Of course, this book only deals with minimum wage politics, and it is not clear how well its results travel to other issue areas. However, minimum wages are similar to many other social and economic policy issues in that they involve a mix of technical and normative questions. There is at least no a priori reason to suspect that the results from this book do not apply to other, similarly structured issues.

8.1.6 Hypotheses about the Conditions of Expert Influence

8.1.6.1 Properties of the Expert Discourse

The theoretical model proposed three hypotheses regarding how different properties of the expert discourse affect its use in the policy process. Two of them concerned the quantity of scientific research published on the minimum wage. First, Chapter 5 found that the more research on minimum wage effects is published, the more scientific expertise is discussed in newspaper articles on minimum wages. This effect, however, is so weak that it does not matter much in practice.

Moreover, a higher number of scientific articles being published does not translate into a stronger influence on political actors' policy preferences. For an expert influence on political actors' policy preferences, the decisive fact seems to be *that* there is research on the issue, not *how much* research there is.

In addition to the number of scientific studies published, the analyses from Chapter 6 tested the effect that agreement among those studies has on the persuasive power of scientific expertise. The results suggest that the degree of unanimity among the scientific articles in the expert discourse does not matter for how much it influences political actors' policy preferences (see Table 8.2).

Table 8.2 Support for hypotheses H2.1 through H2.3

Hypothesis	Supported
H2.1: The more studies of minimum wage effects are published, the more scientific expertise is part of the media discourse on minimum wages.	+/–
H2.2: The more studies of minimum wage effects are published, the higher is the influence of scientific expertise on the beliefs and preferences of political actors in minimum wage policy subsystems.	–
H2.3: The influence of scientific expertise on the beliefs and preferences of political actors in minimum wage policy subsystems is higher when unanimity in the expert discourse is high.	–

In the light of the literature, particularly the clear rejection of hypothesis H2.3 is unexpected. Hypotheses about a relation between the analytical tractability of an issue, or, relatedly, the ability of researchers to find common answers to policy-related questions and the probability of scientific expertise influencing political decisions are widespread (e.g. Jenkins-Smith, 1990, chap. 4; Meijerink, 2005). Such claims are usually based on the assumption that political actors will only believe scientific research if it is able to find clear answers. In contrast, our results point to a situation in which political actors accept disagreement among researchers and orient themselves towards what they perceive to be the "average" research result. This finding, moreover, is not an artefact of disagreement about minimum wage effects being limited to details. As Neumark and Wascher (2006, p. 120) point out in a review of the literature on minimum wage effects on employment, estimates for the elasticity of teenage employment differ strongly between different studies. The case studies from Chapter 7 offer some hints regarding how political actors deal with this diversity. Thus, several of the interviewees dismissed the more extreme claims of how the introduction of a minimum wage in Germany would affect employment, for example a study published by think tank ifo Institut, predicting up to 900,000 jobs lost (Knabe, Schöb and Thum, 2014), as implausible, given that it diverged too much from what other studies found. There might thus be a tendency to concentrate on those research results situated between the extremes.

8.1.6.2 Uncertainty

The regression analyses presented in this book include two variables supposed to capture situations in which political actors are particularly uncertain about the effects of minimum wages. The first one indicates times in which new scientific findings challenge existing knowledge about minimum wage effects. The second one marks the years preceding and following the introduction of the minimum wage. The two variables were hypothesized to be correlated with a higher presence of scientific expertise in the media discourse and a higher influence on political actors' policy preferences.

Overall, the findings provide little support for these hypotheses. There is some evidence for a higher presence of research in the media discourse in times in which new research challenges existing knowledge about minimum wage effects. Research-related actors are cited more frequently in newspapers in these time periods, even if this results narrowly misses statistical significance. In contrast, the presence of research-related actors in newspaper articles is clearly not higher in the five years preceding and following the introduction of a minimum wage. Regarding policy-oriented learning from scientific expertise, the analyses from Chapter 6 revealed that there is no stronger influence of the expert discourse on actors' policy preferences when the minimum wage is new or when new research results challenge existing knowledge. Thus, while there is some support for Hypothesis H3.3, Hypotheses H3.1, H3.2 and H3.4 are refuted (see Table 8.3).

How are these results reconcilable with the widespread claim that uncertainty absout a policy's effects is a prerequisite for research utilization? A possible answer is suggested by Cross (2012), who argues that some amount of uncertainty is needed to make political actors turn to scientific expertise for answers. Once this threshold is met, however, more uncertainty does not necessarily increase the influence of scholars and their research. In this interpretation, with regard to an issue as complex as minimum wages, political actors are always uncertain enough to care about new research.

Further investigation of this issue would be instructive. Instead of just assuming generally higher uncertainty in particular situations, such research should focus on individual actors, how uncertain they are about minimum wage effects, and how they individually use scientific expertise. With the data available for the research presented in this book, this type of fine-grained analysis was not possible.

Table 8.3 Support for hypotheses H3.1 through H3.4

Hypothesis	Supported
H3.1: More scientific expertise is present in the media discourse on minimum wages when the minimum wage is a new policy.	–
H3.2: The influence of scientific expertise on the beliefs and preferences of political actors in minimum wage policy subsystems is higher when the minimum wage is a new policy.	–
H3.3: More scientific expertise is present in the media discourse on minimum wages when new research results strongly contradict traded knowledge about minimum wage effects.	+/–
H3.4: The influence of scientific expertise on the beliefs and preferences of political actors in minimum wage policy subsystems is higher when new research results strongly contradict traded knowledge about minimum wage effects.	–

8.1.6.3 Culture, Institutions, and Coalition Structure

Regarding the environment in which minimum wage policy making takes place, the theoretical model from Chapter 2 developed hypotheses relating to the systemic as well as to the subsystem level. On the systemic level, two broadly defined styles of using scientific expertise were identified. A pluralistic style of policy making prevalent in the United States was connected to a high presence of scientific expertise in the media discourse, but less influence on political actors' policy preferences. Conversely, a corporatist or a consensual style, prevalent in the United Kingdom and Germany, was linked to less discussion of scientific expertise in the mass media, and to more influence on political actors' policy preferences.

The statistical analyses from Chapters 5 and 6 support these hypotheses. The results from Chapter 5 suggest that the presence of scientific expertise in the media discourse is highest in the United States. In contrast, the results from Chapter 6 suggest that the influence of scientific research on political actors' policy preferences is strongest in Germany and the UK.

However, there is a plausible alternative explanation for the higher presence of research-related actors in the US media discourse. Rather than being based on different styles of using scientific expertise, the difference could also be explained by different journalistic norms. Thus, while hypothesis H4.2 is fully supported, hypothesis H4.1 is cautiously supported (see Table 8.4).

On the subsystem level, hypotheses relating to the advocacy coalition structure were evaluated. Where the minimum wage policy subsystem is polarized with an adversarial coalition structure, the presence of scientific expertise in the media

Table 8.4 Support for hypotheses H4.1 and H4.2

Hypothesis	Supported
H4.1: Under the conditions of a pluralistic style of using expertise, scientific expertise is more present in the media discourse on minimum wages than under the conditions of a consensual or corporatist style.	(+)
H4.2: Under the conditions of a pluralistic style of using expertise, the influence of scientific expertise on the beliefs and preferences of political actors in minimum wage policy subsystems is weaker than under the conditions of a consensual or corporatist style.	+

discourse was expected to be high, but its influence on political actors' policy preferences to be low. In contrast, where the coalition structure in the policy subsystem is less polarized, less discussion of scientific expertise in newspaper articles was expected, along with more influence on political actors' preferences.

The analyses from Chapter 5 showed that the presence of research-related actors in the media discourse does not depend on the level of subsystem polarization, leading us to reject hypothesis H4.3. In contrast, high multicollinearity made it impossible to test how polarization mediates the influence of expert discourses on political actors' minimum wage preferences. For now, Hypothesis H4.4 cannot be evaluated (see Table 8.5).

Table 8.5 Support for hypotheses H4.3 and H4.4

Hypothesis	Supported
H4.3: Where the policy subsystem has an adversarial coalition structure, scientific expertise is more present in the media discourse on minimum wages than in collaborative policy subsystems.	–
H4.4: In adversarial policy subsystems, the influence of scientific expertise on the beliefs and preferences of political actors is weaker than in collaborative policy subsystems.	?

With regard to the existing literature, the findings regarding the mediating effect of different national styles of using scientific expertise are a novelty. While there is research exploring the use of scientific expertise under different policy-making styles, explicit tests of how often learning across coalitions takes place under different styles are nonexistent so far. The results thus offer empirical support for claims derived from a literature that has so far been explorative rather than hypothesis-testing.

8.1.6.4 Actor Properties

Finally, the analyses in this book assessed the role of pre-existing beliefs. Chapter 6 tested whether the policy preferences of actors belonging to organizations that have expressed moderate beliefs towards the minimum wage in the past are more likely to be influenced by the expert discourse. The results showed that the latent preference of all types of actors is equally likely to be influenced by scientific expertise, meaning that all actors equally learn from the expert discourse. As shown in the simulation presented in Chapter 6, such learning mostly leads actors with a moderate position towards the minimum wage to reconsider their support for the minimum wage. Still, since the underlying learning process affects all actors equally, Hypothesis H5.1 is rejected (see Table 8.6).

In the light of the literature, this result does not come as a surprise. Hypothesis H5.1 is rooted in the Advocacy Coalition Framework's conception of a belief hierarchy in which political actors have stable core and more malleable peripheral beliefs. From this perspective, new (scientific) information contradicting core beliefs is usually discarded (Jenkins-Smith, 1990, chap. 4). As Jenkins-Smith et al. (2014, p. 200) note, however, empirical studies have repeatedly documented policy-oriented learning which not only touched peripheral, but also changed core beliefs. Our analysis adds to this body of literature. Apparently, political actors learn from research results in the expert discourse, even if those results contradict their core beliefs.

Table 8.6 Support for hypothesis H5.1

Hypothesis	Supported
H5.1: The beliefs and preferences of actors without strong positive or negative prior beliefs regarding the desirability of minimum wages are more likely to be influenced by the expert discourse.	–

8.1.6.5 Reverse Influence

The final two hypotheses in the theoretical model referred to a reverse influence of minimum wage policy subsystems and the media discourse on minimum wages on the domestic expert discourse. The analyses found that more scientific research on minimum wages is published when the issue is high on the media agenda. In contrast, the content of these studies is not influenced by how political actors evaluate the minimum wage (see Table 8.7).

Table 8.7 Support for hypotheses H6.1 and H6.2

Hypothesis	Supported
H6.1: Increased political or mass media attention to the subject of minimum wages leads to an increase number of scientific studies on minimum wages.	+
H6.2: A more positive evaluation of minimum wages by political actors leads to a more positive evaluation of minimum wages in the expert discourse.	–

8.2 Conclusion: Scientific Expertise in Minimum Wage Policy Making

This book has started with an impressionistic account of the role of scientific expertise in minimum wage policy making. The following chapters have focused on the details, analyzing how scientific expertise is cited in newspaper articles, and how political actors' policy preferences are influenced by the expert discourse. This final chapter has brought together results from the analyses presented througout the book. It ends by taking a step back and giving an overall account of the role of scientific expertise in minimum wage policy making, structured into four general lessons learned from the research presented in this book.

The *first* lesson is that scientific expertise is an important part of the political discussion on minimum wages. There is a wealth of studies assessing minimum wage effects, providing ample empirical evidence on questions that are central in the minimum-wage related political debate in the three countries analyzed in this book. Do minimum wage hikes increase unemployment? Do they fight poverty? Do they hurt the economy? As the analyses presented in this book have demonstrated, this research does not stay confined to the ivory tower but is interlinked with the public debate on minimum wages. In all three countries, researchers and their studies are frequently cited in newspaper articles, suggesting that knowledge of scientific research results is widespread, both among political actors dealing with minimum wages and the public. Importantly, the newspapers analyzed in this book not only cite research on minimum wages but do so in a way that reflects the central findings from the expert discourse.

The presence of scientific research in the mass media can be interpreted as normatively desirable, improving voters' means to evaluate the claims politicians make about minimum wages. For a full normative evaluation of the role of scientific expertise in minimum wage policy making, however, the research results presented here are not sufficient. The quality newspapers analyzed in this book are read only by a minority of the electorate, and we do not know how other media outlets cover scientific research on minimum wage effects. Moreover, the research presented in this book did not analyze how readers react to the scientific information about minimum wages they get from newspaper articles.

Second, the role of scientific expertise in minimum wage policy making goes beyond simply being discussed publicly. Rarely do political actors make statements about the effects of minimum wages that are incommensurable with the central results from the expert discourse. Moreover, the expert discourse influences the policy preferences of political actors in the three countries analyzed in this book. While the strength of this influence is considerable at least in German and the United Kingdom, minimum wage policy making is by no means determined by scientific expertise. Thus, in all three countries, the most important predictor of an organization's position towards the minimum wage is not the expert discourse, but its general political alignment. Left-wing political parties and trade unions tend to support the minimum wage, right-wing political parties and employer organizations tend to be critical. The results of our analysis, therefore, suggest a middle ground between President Clinton's statement cited at the beginning of this book, which suggested that political decisions on the minimum wage are determined by research, and Waltman's (2000) claim of a purely political use of scientific expertise in US minimum wage policy making. Normatively, these results are good news for those who warn against taking science as the only standard of finding truth in politics (Lindblom and Cohen, 1979; Lindblom, 1990; Hoppe, 1999), as well as for those warning against the "death of expertise" (Nichols, 2017). Thus, even in the two European countries, the expert discourse only affects the preferences of those actors who are not dead-set to support or to reject the minimum wage. For voters, expert influence does not eliminate the possibility to choose between different policy options.

Third, while expert influence on political actors was found to be substantial, strong changes in political actors' minimum wage preferences or even changes in public policy due to scientific research should be expected to be rare events. The reason for this is that strong shifts in the scientific evaluation of minimum wages are infrequent. In the three domestic expert discourses on minimum wages analyzed in this book, a strong shift occurred once in the US (between the mid-1980s and the late 1990s), where the expert discourse was observed over a period of 45 years, once in Germany (between 2005 and 2010), where the expert discourse was observed for about 15 years, and not at all in the UK, where the expert discourse was observed for 25 years. As a result, while expert discourses do influence minimum wage policy making, their influence will usually only become visible when looking at long time horizons.

Finally, context matters in research utilization. While small-scale institutional factors such as incentives for researchers to develop research projects in cooperation with practitioners have been found important in many publications (for an overview, see Nutley, Walter and Davies, 2007), the research presented in this book points to the importance of large-scale institutional and cultural differences between countries. Styles of using scientific expertise crucially shape how scientific research appears in the public discourse and whether political actors learn from it. For scholars dealing with research utilization, this result contains the warning that results from one country might not easily travel to another country. For political actors seeking to enhance the role of expertise in policy making, it might mean that an important part of those context variables mediating how much influence scientific expertise has is beyond their control. While the research presented in this book can help the reader understand how and when scientific expertise becomes relevant in policy making, it does not offer simple recipes for changing its role in the policy process.

Bibliography

Adler, E. (1992) 'The emergence of cooperation: national epistemic communities and the international evolution of the idea of nuclear arms control', *International Organization*, 46(1), pp. 101–145.

Adler, E. and Haas, P. M. (1992) 'Conclusion: Epistemic Communities, World Order, and the Creation of a Reflective Research Program', *International Organization*, 46(1), pp. 367–390.

Almeida, J. A. S., Pais, A. A. C. C. and Formosinho, S. J. (2009) 'Science indicators and science patterns in Europe', *Journal of Informetrics*, 3(2), pp. 134–142.

Aretz, B. *et al.* (2011) 'Evaluation bestehender gesetzlicher Mindestlohnregelungen–Branche: Dachdecker'. Zentrum für europäische Wirtschaftsforschung; Institut für angewandte Sozialwissenschaften. Available at: https://www.bmas.de/SharedDocs/Downloads/DE/PDF-Meldungen/evaluation-mindestlohn-dachdecker.pdf?__blob=publicationFile (Accessed: 10 January 2017).

Aretz, B., Arntz, M. and Gregory, T. (2013) 'The Minimum Wage Affects Them All: Evidence on Employment Spillovers in the Roofing Sector', *German Economic Review*, 14(3), pp. 282–315.

Baltagi, B. (2008) *Econometric analysis of panel data*. Hoboken, N.J.: John Wiley & Sons.

Barro, R. J. (1996) 'Democracy and growth', *Journal of Economic Growth*, 1(1), pp. 1–27.

Bartsch, K. (2007) 'Gesamtwirtschaftliche Wirkung der Einführung eines gesetzlichen Mindestlohnes in Deutschland auf der Basis der Konzeption der Dienstleistungsgewerkschaft ver.di'. Available at: https://www.dgb.de/schwerpunkt/mindestlohn/hintergrund/studien-umfragen/++co++225bcd2a-e447-11e4-8771-52540023ef1a (Accessed: 3 January 2017).

Bauer, M. W. and Jensen, P. (2011) 'The mobilization of scientists for public engagement', *Public Understanding of Science*, 20(1), pp. 3–11.

Bauer, T. K. *et al.* (2009) 'Fiscal Effects of Minimum Wages: An Analysis for Germany', *German Economic Review*, 10(2), pp. 224–242.

Bauer, T. and Schmidt, C. M. (2007) 'Mindestlöhne und das Entsendegesetz', *Wirtschaftsdienst*, 87(3), pp. 160–163.

F. Klein, *The Role of Scientific Expertise in Minimum Wage Policy Making*, Vergleichende Politikwissenschaft,
https://doi.org/10.1007/978-3-658-32746-0

Becker, U. and Hendriks, C. (2008) '"As the Central Planning Bureau says". The Dutch wage restraint paradigm, its sustaining epistemic community and its relevance for comparative research', *Review of International Political Economy*, 15(5), pp. 826–850.

Biegelbauer, P. (2013) *Wie lernt die Politik? Lernen aus Erfahrung in Politik und Verwaltung*. Wiesbaden: Springer VS.

Bispinck, R. (2008) 'Aktuelle Mindestlohndebatte: Branchenlösungen oder gesetzlicher Mindestlohn?', *WSI Mitteilungen*, (3), pp. 151–158.

Bispinck, R. and Schäfer, C. (2006) 'Niedriglöhne und Mindesteinkommen: Daten und Diskussionen in Deutschland', in Schulten, T. and Bispinck, R. (eds) *Mindestlöhne in Europa*. Hamburg: VSA-Verlag, pp. 269–297.

Boockmann, B. *et al.* (2011) 'Evaluation bestehender gesetzlicher Mindestlohnregelungen. Branche: Elektrohandwerk'. Institut für Angewandte Wirtschaftsforschung. Available at: https://www.bmas.de/SharedDocs/Downloads/DE/PDF-Meldungen/evaluation-mindestlohn-elektrohandwerk.%20pdf?__blob=publicationFile (Accessed: 10 January 2017).

Boockmann, B. *et al.* (2013) 'Turning the Switch: An Evaluation of the Minimum Wage in the German Electrical Trade Using Repeated Natural Experiments', *German Economic Review*, 14(3), pp. 316–348.

Borgatta, E. F. and Bohrnstedt, G. W. (1980) 'Level of measurement once over again', *Sociological Methods & Research*, 9(2), pp. 147–160.

Bosch, G., Kalina, T., *et al.* (2011) 'Evaluation bestehender gesetzlicher Mindestlohnregelungen–Branche: Gebäudereinigung'. Institut für Arbeit und Qualifikation, Universität Duisburg-Essen. Available at: https://www.bmas.de/SharedDocs/Downloads/DE/PDF-Meldungen/evaluation-mindestlohn-gebaedereinigung.pdf?__blob=publicationFile (Accessed: 12 August 2017).

Bosch, G., Hieming, B., *et al.* (2011) 'Evaluation bestehender gesetzlicher Mindestlohnregelungen–Branche: Wäschereidienstleistungen im Objektkundengeschäft. Abschlussbericht.' Institut für Arbeit und Qualifikation, Universität Duisburg-Essen. Available at: https://www.bmas.de/SharedDocs/Downloads/DE/PDF-Meldungen/evaluation-mindestlohn-waeschereidienstleistungen.pdf?__blob=publicationFile (Accessed: 12 August 2017).

Bosch, G., Kalina, T. and Weinkopf, C. (2009) 'Warum Deutschland einen gesetzlichen Mindestlohn braucht'. Friedrich-Ebert-Stiftung. Available at: https://library.fes.de/pdf-files/wiso/06822.pdf (Accessed: 20 November 2016).

Bosch, G., Weinkopf, C. and Kalina, T. (2009) 'Mindestlöhne in Deutschland'. Friedrich-Ebert-Stiftung. Available at: https://library.fes.de/pdf-files/wiso/06866.pdf (Accessed: 20 November 2016).

Boswell, C. (2009) *The Political Uses of Expert Knowledge*. Cambridge: Cambridge University Press.

Brönstrup, C. (2006) '„Mindestlöhne vernichten keine Jobs"', *Der Tagesspiegel*, 15 March. Available at: https://www.tagesspiegel.de/wirtschaft/mindestloehne-vernichten-keine-jobs/693152.html (Accessed: 22 June 2017).

Brown, W. (2009) 'The Process of Fixing the British National Minimum Wage, 1997-2007', *British Journal of Industrial Relations*, 47(2), pp. 429–443.

Bukowski, J. (2007) 'Spanish Water Policy and the National Hydrological Plan: An Advocacy Coalition Approach to Policy Change', *South European Society and Politics*, 12(1), pp. 39–57.

Burkhauser, R. V., Couch, K. A. and Wittenburg, D. C. (2000) 'A reassessment of the new economics of the minimum wage literature with monthly data from the Current Population Survey', *Journal of Labor Economics*, 18(4), pp. 653–680.

Cairney, P. (2017) 'The Politics of Evidence-Based Policy Making', in *Oxford Research Encyclopedia of Politics*. Oxford: Oxford University Press.

Cameron, A. C. and Miller, D. L. (2015) 'A practitioner's guide to cluster-robust inference', *Journal of Human Resources*, 50(2), pp. 317–372.

Cameron, A. C. and Trivedi, P. K. (2009) *Microeconometrics using Stata*. College Station: Stata Press.

Cameron, G. T., Sallot, L. M. and Curtin, P. A. (1997) 'Public Relations and the Production of News: A Critical Review and Theoretical Framework', *Annals of the International Communication Association*, 20(1), pp. 111–155.

Caplan, N. (1979) 'The two-communities theory and knowledge utilization.', *American Behavioral Scientist*, 22(3), pp. 459–70.

Card, D. and Krueger, A. B. (1993) *Minimum Wages and Employment: A Case Study of the Fast Food Industry in New Jersey and Pennsylvania*. w4509. Cambridge, MA: National Bureau of Economic Research. Available at: https://www.nber.org/papers/w4509.pdf (Accessed: 30 May 2014).

Chaplin, D. D., Turner, M. D. and Pape, A. D. (2003) 'Minimum wages and school enrollment of teenagers: a look at the 1990's', *Economics of Education Review*, 22(1), pp. 11–21.

Christlich Demokratische Union/Christlich-soziale Union (2005) 'Deutschlands Chancen nutzen. Regierungsprogramm 2005–2009.' Available at: https://www.kas.de/upload/ACDP/CDU/Programme_Bundestag/2005-2009_Regierungsprogramm_Deutschlands-Chancen-nutzen_Wachstum-Arbeit-Sicherheit.pdf (Accessed: 12 August 2017).

Christlich Demokratische Union/Christlich-soziale Union (2009) 'Wir haben die Kraft. Gemeinsam für unser Land. Regierungsprogramm 2009–2013'. Available at: https://www.kas.de/upload/ACDP/CDU/Programme_Bundestag/2009-2013_Regierungsprogramm_Wir-haben-die-Kraft_Gemeinsam-fuer-unser-Land.pdf (Accessed: 9 January 2017).

Christlich Demokratische Union/Christlich-soziale Union (2013) 'Gemeinsam erfolgreich für Deutschland. Regierungsprogramm 2013–2017'. Available at: https://www.cdu.de/sites/default/files/media/dokumente/regierungsprogramm-2013-2017-langfassung-20130911.pdf (Accessed: 9 January 2017).

Clark, K., Kaas, L. and Madden, P. (2006) 'Minimum wage increases can lead to wage reductions by imperfectly competitive firms', *Economics Letters*, 91(2), pp. 287–292.

Clinton, W. J. (1995) 'Address Before a Joint Session of the Congress on the State of the Union'. The American Presidency Project. Available at: https://www.presidency.ucsb.edu/ws/?pid=51634 (Accessed: 16 January 2017).

Clymer, A. (1996) 'Republicans told to brace for vote on minimum wage', *The New York Times*, 18 April, p. 1.

Collier, D. (2011) 'Understanding Process Tracing', *PS: Political Science & Politics*, 44(4), pp. 823–830.

Corbett, J. B. and Durfee, J. L. (2004) 'Testing Public (Un)Certainty of Science', *Science Communication*, 26(2), pp. 129–151.

Cragg, J. G. and Uhler, R. S. (1970) 'The Demand for Automobiles', *The Canadian Journal of Economics/Revue canadienne d'Economique*, 3(3), pp. 386–406.

Creutzburg, D. (2013) 'Mindestlohn wird teurer als behauptet', *Frankfurter Allgemeine Zeitung Online*, 30 June. Available at: https://www.faz.net/aktuell/wirtschaft/wirtschaftspolitik/statistiken-widerlegen-spd-versprechen-mindestlohn-wird-teurer-als-behauptet-12266066.html (Accessed: 22 June 2017).

Cronin, B. (2008) 'On the epistemic significance of place', *Journal of the American Society for Information Science and Technology*, 59(6), pp. 1002–1006.

Cross, M. K. D. (2012) 'Rethinking epistemic communities twenty years later', *Review of International Studies*, 39(1), pp. 137–160.

Cross, M. K. D. (2013) 'The Military Dimension of European Security: An Epistemic Community Approach', *Millennium – Journal of International Studies*, 42(1), pp. 45–64.

Deutscher Gewerkschaftsbund (2008) 'Mindestlohn-Interview: Bosch: Mindestlohn bringt Milliarden für die Sozialversicherung'. Available at: https://www.dgb.de/themen/++co++deb165a6-d3d6-11e4-8456-52540023ef1a (Accessed: 7 March 2017).

Deutscher Gewerkschaftsbund (2010) 'Mindestlohn-Interview: Mindestlohn ohne Einfluss auf Beschäftigung Geringqualifizierter'. Available at: https://www.dgb.de/themen/++co++8c6a44e6-d234-11e4-9014-52540023ef1a (Accessed: 7 March 2017).

Dolowitz, D. and Marsh, D. (1996) 'Who Learns What from Whom: a Review of the Policy Transfer Literature', *Political Studies*, 44(2), pp. 343–357.

DPA (2004) 'Pläne für Mindestlohn vorerst vom Tisch', *Süddeutsche Zeitung*, 29 November, p. 6.

DPA (2006) 'Steinbrück warnt vor Mindestlohn', *Der Tagesspiegel Online*, 2 April. Available at: https://www.tagesspiegel.de/wirtschaft/steinbrueck-warnt-vor-mindestlohn/698764.html (Accessed: 5 January 2017).

Drake, W. J. and Nicolaïdis, K. (1992) 'Ideas, interests, and institutionalization: "trade in services" and the Uruguay Round', *International Organization*, 46(1), p. 37.

Dunn, W. N. (1980) 'The Two-Communities Metaphor and Models of Knowledge Use', *Knowledge*, 1(4), pp. 515–536.

Dunn, W. N. (1993) 'Policy reforms as arguments', in Fischer, F. and Forester, J. (eds) *The Argumentative turn in policy analysis and planning*, pp. 254–290.

Egeln, J. *et al.* (2011) 'Evaluation bestehender gesetzlicher Mindestlohnregelungen-Branche: Abfallwirtschaft'. Zentrum für europäische Wirtschaftsforschung; Institut für angewandte Sozialwissenschaften. Available at: ftp://ftp.zew.de/pub/zew-docs/gutachten/Abfallendbericht_inkl_Anlagen.pdf (Accessed: 10 January 2017).

Ehrentraut, O. *et al.* (2011) 'Fiskalische Effekte eines gesetzlichen Mindestlohns'. Friedrich-Ebert-Stiftung. Available at: https://library.fes.de/pdf-files/wiso/08071.pdf (Accessed: 20 November 2016).

Eilders (2006) 'News factors and news decisions. Theoretical and methodological advances in Germany', *Communications*, 31(1), pp. 5–24.

Ellguth, P. and Kohaut, S. (2005) 'Tarifbindung und betriebliche Interessenvertretung: aktuelle Ergebnisse aus dem IAB-Betriebspanel', *WSI Mitteilungen*, 58(7), pp. 398–403.

Elliott, C. and Schlaepfer, R. (2001) 'The advocacy coalition framework: application to the policy process for the development of forest certification in Sweden', *Journal of European Public Policy*, 8(4), pp. 642–661.
Everitt, B. S. *et al.* (2010) *Cluster Analysis*. Chicester: Wiley.
Farrow, S. (1991) 'Does Analysis Matter? Economics and Planning in the Department of the Interior', *The Review of Economics and Statistics*, pp. 172–176.
Feil, M. *et al.* (2010) 'Altersarmut vermeiden: Mindestlohn ist kein Allheilmittel', *IAB-Stellungnahme*, (5).
Feldmann, H. (2003) 'Labor Market Regulation and Labor Market Performance: Evidence Based on Surveys among Senior Business Executives', *Kyklos*, 56(4), pp. 509–540.
Feldmann, H. (2005) 'Labour Market Institutions and Labour Market Performance in Transition Countries', *Post-Communist Economies*, 17(1), pp. 47–82.
Fischer, F. (1993) 'Policy discourse and the Politics of Washington Think Tanks', in Fischer, F. and Forester, J. (eds) *The Argumentative Turn in Policy Analysis and Planning*. London: UCL Press, pp. 21–42.
Fischer, F. and Forester, J. (eds) (1993) *The Argumentative turn in policy analysis and planning*. Durham, N.C: Duke University Press.
Frankfurter Allgemeine Zeitung (2004) 'Clement weist Münteferings Mindestlohn-Vorstoß zurück', *Frankfurter Allgemeine Zeitung*, 24 August.
Frankfurter Allgemeine Zeitung (2005) 'FDP: Populismus der Union unglaublich', *Frankfurter Allgemeine Zeitung*, 9 April, p. 1.
Frankfurter Allgemeine Zeitung (2007) 'Die Union bleibt beim Mindestlohn hart', *Frankfurter Allgemeine Zeitung*, 30 January, p. 9.
Frankfurter Allgemeine Zeitung (2010a) 'Kommission für Mindestlohn', *Frankfurter Allgemeine Zeitung*, 1 March, p. 11.
Frankfurter Allgemeine Zeitung (2010b) 'Mindestlohn statt Freizügigkeit', *Frankfurter Allgemeine Zeitung*, 2 September, p. 13.
Frenk, J. (1992) 'Balancing relevance and excellence: Organizational responses to link research with decision making', *Social Science & Medicine*, 35(11), pp. 1397–1404.
Frenken, K., Hardeman, S. and Hoekman, J. (2009) 'Spatial scientometrics: Towards a cumulative research program', *Journal of Informetrics*, 3(3), pp. 222–232.
Funk, L. (no date) 'Mindestlohn/Mindesteinkommen/Kombilohn'. Konrad-Adenauer-Stiftung. Available at: https://www.kas.de/wf/de/71.12803/ (Accessed: 10 January 2017).
Gamson, W. and Modigliani, A. (1989) 'Media Discourse and Public Opinion on Nuclear Power: A Constructionist Approach', *American Journal of Sociology*, 95(1), pp. 1–37.
Gerring, J. (2004) 'What Is a Case Study and What Is It Good for?', *The American Political Science Review*, 98(2), pp. 341–354.
Gourevitch, P. A. (1989) 'Keynesian Politics: the Political Sources of Economic Policy Choices', in Hall, P. A. (ed.) *The Political Power of Economic Ideas: Keynesianism across Nations*. Princeton, N.J.: Princeton University Press, pp. 87–106.
Gow, D. (2002) 'TUC in Blackpool: Stakes raised as target of pounds 5-plus is set for minimum wage', *The Guardian*, 9 November, p. 11.
Granger, C. W. (1969) 'Investigating causal relations by econometric models and cross-spectral methods', *Econometrica: Journal of the Econometric Society*, pp. 424–438.
Gruszczynski, M. (2013) 'Kripp.boot'. Available at: https://github.com/MikeGruz/kripp.boot/blob/master/R/kripp.boot.R (Accessed: 23 March 2017).

Guardian (2000) 'Byers rules out increase in minimum wage', *The Guardian*, 31 January.
Haas, P. M. (1992a) 'Banning chlorofluorocarbons: epistemic community efforts to protect stratospheric ozone', *International Organization*, 46(1), p. 187.
Haas, P. M. (1992b) 'Introduction: epistemic communities and international policy coordination', *International Organization*, 46(1), pp. 1–35.
Habermas, J. (1968) *Technik und Wissenschaft als 'Ideologie.'* Frankfurt am Main: Suhrkamp.
Hall, P. A. (1989) 'Conclusion: The Politics of Keynesian Ideas.', in Hall, P. A. (ed.) *The Political Power of Economic Ideas: Keynesianism across Nations*. Princeton, N.J.: Princeton University Press, pp. 361–391.
Handelsblatt (2004) 'Clement lehnt Gesetz zu Vorstandsgehältern ab', *Handelsblatt Online*, 23 September. Available at: https://www.handelsblatt.com/politik/deutschland/mindestlohne-fuehren-zu-mehr-regulierung-clement-lehnt-gesetz-zu-vorstandsgehaeltern-ab/2405164.html (Accessed: 5 January 2017).
Hart, P. S. and Nisbet, E. C. (2012) 'Boomerang Effects in Science Communication: How Motivated Reasoning and Identity Cues Amplify Opinion Polarization About Climate Mitigation Policies', *Communication Research*, 39(6), pp. 701–723.
Havelock, R. G. *et al.* (1971) *Planning for innovation: through dissemination and utilization of knowledge*. Ann Arbor: Center for Research on Utilization of Scientific Knowledge.
Haveman, R. H. (1986) 'Social science and social policy: who uses whom?', in Heller, F. (ed.) *The Use and Abuse of Social Science*. London: SAGE, pp. 74–84.
Heclo, H. (1978) 'Issue Networks and the Executive Establishment', in King, A. (ed.) *The New American Political System*. Washington, D.C: American Enterprise Institute, pp. 87–124.
Heij, C. *et al.* (2004) *Econometric methods with applications in business and economics*. Oxford: Oxford University Press.
Heikkila, T. *et al.* (2016) 'Juxtaposing Advocacy Coalition: A Comparison of Hydraulic Fracturing Politics in Argentina, China, and the United States'. Paper presented at the Regional Conference on Public Policy, Hong Kong.
Hennemann, S., Rybski, D. and Liefner, I. (2012) 'The myth of global science collaboration', *Journal of Informetrics*, 6(2), pp. 217–225.
Hird, J. A. (2005) *Power, knowledge, and politics: policy analysis in the states*. Washington, D.C: Georgetown University Press.
Hopkins, R. F. (1992) 'Reform in the international food aid regime: the role of consensual knowledge', *International Organization*, 46(1), p. 225.
Hoppe, R. (1999) 'Policy analysis, science and politics: from "speaking truth to power" to "making sense together"', *Science and public policy*, 26(3), pp. 201–210.
Huber, P. J. (1967) 'The behavior of maximum likelihood estimates under nonstandard conditions', in *Proceedings of the fifth Berkeley symposium on mathematical statistics and probability*, pp. 221–233.
Ikenberry, G. J. (1992) 'A world economy restored: expert consensus and the Anglo-American postwar settlement', *International Organization*, 46(1), p. 289.
Jain, A. K., Murty, M. N. and Flynn, P. J. (1999) 'Data clustering: a review', *ACM computing surveys (CSUR)*, 31(3), pp. 264–323.
Jann, W. and Wegrich, K. (2007) 'Theories of the policy cycle', *Handbook of public policy analysis: Theory, politics and methods*, pp. 43–62.
Jasanoff, S. (2007) *Designs on nature science and democracy in Europe and the United States*. Princeton, N.J.: Princeton University Press.

Jenkins-Smith, H. C. (1990) *Democratic politics and policy analysis*. Pacific Grove, CA: Brooks/Cole.

Jenkins-Smith, H. C. *et al.* (2014) 'The advocacy coalition framework: Foundations, evolution, and ongoing research', *Theories of the Policy Process*. Edited by P. A. Sabatier and C. M. Weible, pp. 183–223.

Jung, A., Korinek, R.-L. and Straßheim, H. (2014) 'Embedded expertise: a conceptual framework for reconstructing knowledge orders, their transformation and local specificities', *Innovation: The European Journal of Social Science Research*, 27(4), pp. 398–419.

Kapstein, E. B. (1992) 'Between power and purpose: central bankers and the politics of regulatory convergence', *International Organization*, 46(1), p. 265.

King, G., Keohane, R. O. and Verba, S. (1994) *Designing social inquiry : scientific inference in qualitative research*. Princeton, N.J.: Princeton University Press.

King, M. (2005) 'Epistemic Communities and the Diffusion of Ideas: Central Bank Reform in the United Kingdom', *West European Politics*, 28(1), pp. 94–123.

Kleinnijenhuis, J. and Rietberg, E. M. (1995) 'Parties, media, the public and the economy: Patterns of societal agenda-setting', *European Journal of Political Research*, 28(1), pp. 95–118.

Klüver, R. (2004) 'SPD erwägt gesetzlichen Mindestlohn', *Süddeutsche Zeitung*, 23 August, p. 1.

Knabe, A. and Schöb, R. (2009) 'Minimum Wage Incidence: The Case for Germany', *FinanzArchiv: Public Finance Analysis*, 65(4), pp. 403–441.

Knabe, A. and Schöb, R. (2011) 'Minimum wages and their alternatives: A critical assessment', *German Politics*, 20(4), pp. 506–526.

Knabe, A., Schöb, R. and Thum, M. (2014) 'Der flächendeckende Mindestlohn', *Perspektiven der Wirtschaftspolitik*, 15(2). Available at: https://www.degruyter.com/view/j/pwp.2014.15.issue-2/pwp-2014-0011/pwp-2014-0011.xml (Accessed: 4 February 2017).

König, M. and Möller, J. (2007) 'Mindestlohneffekte des Entsendegesetzes', *Eine Mikrodatenanalyse für die deutsche Bauwirtschaft. IAB Discussion Paper*, (30). Available at: https://doku.iab.de/discussionpapers/2007/dp3007.pdf (Accessed: 12 August 2017).

König, M. and Möller, J. (2009) 'Impacts of minimum wages: a microdata analysis for the German construction sector', *International Journal of Manpower*. Edited by U. Blien, 30(7), pp. 716–741.

Kräkel, M. and Schöttner, A. (2010) 'Minimum wages and excessive effort supply', *Economics Letters*, 108(3), pp. 341–344.

Kramme, A. (2013) 'Mindestlöhne sind eine Frage der Gerechtigkeit'. Available at: https://www.spdfraktion.de/presse/interviews/mindestloehne-frage-gerechtigkeit (Accessed: 8 March 2017).

Krippendorff, K. (2004) *Content Analysis. An Introduction to Its Methodology*. 2nd edn. Thousand Oaks: Sage Publications.

Kronthaler, F. (2016) *Statistik angewandt: Datenanalyse ist (k)eine Kunst ; mit dem R Commander*. Berlin: Springer Spektrum.

Labour Party (1992) '1992 Labour Party Manifesto. It's time to get Britain working again'. Available at: https://labourmanifesto.com/1992/1992-labour-manifesto.shtml (Accessed: 23 February 2017).

Landry, R., Amara, N. and Lamari, M. (2001) 'Utilization of social science research knowledge in Canada', *Research Policy*, 30(2), pp. 333–349.

Larsen, J. B., Vrangbæk, K. and Traulsen, J. M. (2006) 'Advocacy coalitions and pharmacy policy in Denmark—Solid cores with fuzzy edges', *Social Science & Medicine*, 63(1), pp. 212–224.

Levin-Waldman, O. M. (1998) 'Exploring the Politics of the Minimum Wage', *Journal of Economic Issues*, 32(3), pp. 773–802.

Leviton, L. C. and Hughes, E. F. X. (1981) 'Research On the Utilization of Evaluations: A Review and Synthesis', *Evaluation Review*, 5(4), pp. 525–548.

Lieberman, E. S. (2005) 'Nested Analysis as a Mixed-Method Strategy for Comparative Research', *American Political Science Review*, 99(3), pp. 435–452.

Lindblom, C. E. (1990) *Inquiry and change*. New Haven and London: Yale University Press.

Lindblom, C. E. and Cohen, D. K. (1979) *Usable Knowledge. Social Science and Social Problem Solving*. New Haven and London: Yale University Press.

Lipton, E. (2014) 'Fight Over Minimum Wage Illustrates Web of Industry Ties', *New York Times*, 10 February, p. 1.

Liu, I. and Agresti, A. (2005) 'The analysis of ordered categorical data: An overview and a survey of recent developments', *Test*, 14(1), pp. 1–73.

Lomas, J. (2000) 'Connecting research and policy', *Canadian Journal of Policy Research*, 1(1), pp. 140–144.

Lomas, J. (2007) 'The in-between world of knowledge brokering', *BMJ*, 334(7585), pp. 129–132.

Long, J. S. and Freese, J. (2014) *Regression models for categorical dependent variables using Stata*. Third edition. College Station, Texas: Stata Press Publication, StataCorp LP.

Lustig, N. and McLeod, D. (1996) *Minimum Wages and Poverty in Developing Countries: Some Empirical Evidence*. Brookings Institution Working Papers. Washington, D.C.: Brookings Institution.

Macaskill, E. and Milne, S. (1998) 'Pounds 3.60 minimum wage row looms', *The Guardian*, 28 May.

Maguire, K. and Elliott, L. (2000) 'Labour to raise minimum wage', *The Guardian*, 15 February.

Majone, G. (1989) *Evidence, argument, and persuasion in the policy process*. New Haven: Yale University Press.

Mammen, E. (1993) 'Bootstrap and wild bootstrap for high dimensional linear models', *The Annals of Statistics*, pp. 255–285.

Mamudu, H. M., Gonzalez, M. and Glantz, S. (2011) 'The Nature, Scope, and Development of the Global Tobacco Control Epistemic Community', *American Journal of Public Health*, 101(11), pp. 2044–2054.

McCombs, M. *et al.* (1997) 'Candidate Images in Spanish Elections: Second-Level Agenda-Setting Effects', *Journalism & Mass Communication Quarterly*, 74(4), pp. 703–717.

McCombs, M. E. and Shaw, D. L. (1993) 'The Evolution of Agenda-Setting Research: Twenty-Five Years in the Marketplace of Ideas', *Journal of Communication*, 43(2), pp. 58–67.

Meijerink, S. (2005) 'Understanding policy stability and change. the interplay of advocacy coalitions and epistemic communities, windows of opportunity, and Dutch coastal flooding policy 1945–20031', *Journal of European Public Policy*, 12(6), pp. 1060–1077.

Metcalf, D. (1999) 'The British National Minimum Wage', *British Journal of Industrial Relations*, 37(2), pp. 171–201.

Meyer, M. (2010) 'The Rise of the Knowledge Broker', *Science Communication*, 32(1), pp. 118–127.

Mindestlohnkommission (2016) 'Erster Bericht zu den Auswirkungen des gesetzlichen Mindestlohns. Bericht der Mindestlohnkommission an die Bundesregierung nach § 9 Abs. 4 Mindestlohngesetz'. Berlin. Available at: https://www.mindestlohn-kommission.de/DE/Bericht/pdf/Bericht2016.pdf?__blob=publicationFile&v=5 (Accessed: 15 February 2017).

Minimum Wage Study Commission (1981) *Report of the Minimum Wage Study Commission*. Washington, D.C.

Mishel, L. R. *et al.* (2002) *The class size debate*. Washington, D.C.: Economic Policy Institute.

Möller, J. (2010) 'Standpunkt: Mindestlohn muss die Dienstleistungsfreiheit in der EU absichern', *IAB-Forum*, (2), pp. 24–27.

Möller, J. *et al.* (2011) 'Evaluation bestehender gesetzlicher Mindestlohnregelungen – Branche: Bauhauptgewerbe'. Institut für Arbeitsmarkt- und Berufsforschung; Rheinisch-Westfälisches Institut für Wirtschaftsforschung; Institut für Sozialforschung und Gesellschaftspolitik. Available at: https://www.bmas.de/SharedDocs/Downloads/DE/PDF-Meldungen/evaluation-mindestlohn-bauhauptgewerbe.pdf?__blob=publicationFile (Accessed: 10 January 2017).

Nedergaard, P. (2008) 'The reform of the 2003 Common Agricultural Policy: an advocacy coalition explanation1', *Policy Studies*, 29(2), pp. 179–195.

Neumark, D., Salas, J. M. I. and Wascher, W. (2013) *Revisiting the Minimum Wage-Employment Debate: Throwing Out the Baby with the Bathwater?* NBER Working Paper w18681. Cambridge, MA: National Bureau of Economic Research. Available at: https://www.nber.org/papers/w18681.pdf (Accessed: 19 February 2017).

Neumark, D. and Wascher, W. (1995) *The Effect of New Jersey's Minimum Wage Increase on Fast-Food Employment: A Re-Evaluation Using Payroll Records*. NBER Working Paper w5224. Cambridge, MA: National Bureau of Economic Research. Available at: https://www.nber.org/papers/w5224.pdf (Accessed: 19 February 2017).

Neumark, D. and Wascher, W. (2006) *Minimum Wages and Employment: A Review of Evidence from the New Minimum Wage Research*. NBER Working Paper w12663. Cambridge, MA: National Bureau of Economic Research. Available at: https://www.nber.org/papers/w12663.pdf (Accessed: 15 February 2017).

Neumark, D. and Wascher, W. (2007) *Does a Higher Minimum Wage Enhance the Effectiveness of The Earned Income Tax Credit?* NBER Working Paper w12915. Cambridge, MA: National Bureau of Economic Research. Available at: https://www.nber.org/papers/w12915.pdf (Accessed: 19 February 2017).

Neumark, D. and Wascher, W. L. (2006) 'Minimum Wages and Employment', *Foundations and Trends in Microeconomics*, 3(1–2), pp. 1–182.

Nichols, T. (2017) *The death of expertise: the campaign against established knowledge and why it matters*. New York, NY: Oxford University Press.

Norman, G. (2010) 'Likert scales, levels of measurement and the "laws" of statistics', *Advances in Health Sciences Education*, 15(5), pp. 625–632.

Norris, M. and Oppenheim, C. (2007) 'Comparing alternatives to the Web of Science for coverage of the social sciences' literature', *Journal of Informetrics*, 1(2), pp. 161–169.

Nowak, J. (2015) 'Union Campaigns in Germany directed against Inequality: The Minimum Wage Campaign and the Emmely Campaign', *Global Labour Journal*, 6(3), pp. 366–380.

Nutley, S. M., Walter, I. and Davies, H. T. O. (2007) *Using evidence: how research can inform public services*. Bristol, U.K: Policy Press.

Organisation for Economic Co-operation and Development (2015) 'Employment and Labour Market Statistics'. Available at: https://www.oecdilibrary.org/employment/data/oecd-employment-and-labour-market-statistics_lfs-data-en (Accessed: 5 August 2016).

Oh, C. H. (1997) 'Explaining the impact of policy information on policy-making', *Knowledge and Policy*, 10(3), pp. 25–55.

Organisation for Economic Co-operation and Development (2015) 'Minimum wages after the crisis: making them pay'. Organization for Economic Cooperation and Development. Available at: www.oecd.org/social/Focus-on-Minimum-Wages-after-the-crisis-2015.pdf (Accessed: 12 August 2017).

Papps, K. L. (2012) 'The effects of social security taxes and minimum wages on employment: Evidence from Turkey', *Industrial & Labor Relations Review*, 65(3), pp. 686–707.

Pellizzoni, L. (2011) 'The politics of facts: local environmental conflicts and expertise', *Environmental Politics*, 20(6), pp. 765–785.

Peters, H. P. (2013) 'Gap between science and media revisited: Scientists as public communicators', *Proceedings of the National Academy of Sciences*, 110(Supplement 3), pp. 14102–14109.

Peterson, M. J. (1992) 'Whalers, cetologists, environmentalists, and the international management of whaling', *International Organization*, 46(1), p. 147.

Pielke, R. A. (2007) *The honest broker: making sense of science in policy and politics*. Cambridge ; New York: Cambridge University Press.

ProQuest (2014) Ulrich's periodicals directory, 2015: international periodicals information since 1932 : including irregular serials & annuals. New Providence, N.J.: ProQuest.

Renn, O. (1995) 'Style of using scientific expertise: A comparative framework', *Science and Public Policy*, 22(3), pp. 147–156.

Rhein, T. (2003) 'Mindestlöhne sind wieder im Gespräch', *IAB Materialien*, (3), pp. 7–8.

Rich, A. (2001) 'United States', in Weaver, R. K. and Stares, P. B. (eds) *Guidance for Governance. Comparing Alternative Sources of Public Policy Advice*. Washington, D.C: Brookings Institution Press, pp. 31–70.

Rich, A. (2004) *Think tanks, public policy, and the politics of expertise*. Cambridge, UK; New York: Cambridge University Press.

Richardson, J., Gustafsson, G. and Jordan, G. (1982) 'The Concept of Policy Style', in Richardson, J., *Policy Styles in Western Europe*. London: George Allen & Unwin, pp. 1–16.

Rindfleisch, E. (2011) *Der Mindestlohn – Zwischen Teufelszeug und Heilsbringer: ein Beitrag zur Versachlichung einer aufgeheizten Debatte*. Berlin: Konrad-Adenauer-Stiftung (Analysen & Argumente, 94).

Ring, G. (2015) 'Der gesetzliche Mindestlohn von 8,50 Euro zum 1. Januar 2015 – ein Schritt hin zur Stärkung der Tarifautonomie?', in Kessel, T. et al. (eds) *Aspekte der Baubetriebslehre in Forschung und Praxis: Festschrift zum 60. Geburtstag von Univ.-Prof. Dr.-Ing. Dipl.-Kfm. Dieter Jacob*. Wiesbaden: Springer Fachmedien Wiesbaden, pp. 17–38.

Rosanvallon, P. (1989) 'The development of Keynesianism in France', in Hall, P. A. (ed.) *The Political Power of Economic Ideas: Keynesianism Across Nations*. Princeton, N.J.: Princeton University Press, pp. 171–193.

Rosigkeit, V. (2006) 'SPD will Mindestlohn durchsetzen', *Vorwärts*, 19 September.

Sabatier, P. A. (1987) 'Knowledge, Policy-Oriented Learning, and Policy Change: An Advocacy Coalition Framework', *Science Communication*, 8(4), pp. 649–692.

Sabatier, P. A. (1988) 'An advocacy coalition framework of policy change and the role of policy-oriented learning therein', *Policy sciences*, 21(2–3), pp. 129–168.

Sabatier, P. A. (1993) 'Policy Change over a Decade or More', in Sabatier, P. A. and Jenkins-Smith, H. C. (eds) *Policy Change and Learning. An Advocacy Coalition Approach*. Boulder: Westview Press, pp. 13–39.

Sachverständigenrat zur Begutachtung der Gesamtwirtschaftlichen Entwicklung (2006) *Widerstreitende Interessen-Ungenutzte Chancen. Jahresgutachten 2006/07*. Wiesbaden: Statistisches Bundesamt.

Salant, W. S. (1989) 'The spread of Keynesian doctrines and practices in the United States', in Hall, P. A. (ed.) *The Political Power of Economic Ideas: Keynesianism across Nations*. Princeton, N.J.: Princeton University Press, pp. 27–51.

Sattar, M. (2011) 'Merkels nächste Volte', *Frankfurter Allgemeine Zeitung Online*, 30 October. Available at: https://www.faz.net/aktuell/mindestlohn-merkels-naechste-volte-11511766.html (Accessed: 21 August 2017).

Schreiner, O. (2009) 'Mindestlohn-Interview: Neues aus dem Bus: Mit Ottmar Schreiner (SPD)'. Available at: https://www.dgb.de/themen/++co++4d4ad622-d473-11e4-b487-52540023ef1a (Accessed: 8 March 2017).

Schulten, T. and Bispinck, R. (2013) 'Stabileres Tarifvertragssystem durch Stärkung der Allgemeinverbindlicherklärung?', *Wirtschaftsdienst*, 93(11), pp. 758–764.

Schulten, T., Bispinck, R. and Schäfer, C. (eds) (2006) *Mindestlöhne in Europa*. Hamburg: VSA-Verlag.

Shoemaker, P. J. and Riccio, J. R. (2015) 'Gatekeeping', in *The International Encyclopedia of Political Communication*. Chicester: Wiley.

Sozialdemokratische Partei Deutschlands (2009) 'Sozial und Demokratisch. Anpacken. Für Deutschland. Das Regierungsprogramm der SPD.' Available at: https://www.spd.de/fileadmin/Dokumente/Beschluesse/Bundesparteitag/regierungsprogramm_bundesparteitag_berlin_2009.pdf (Accessed: 12 August 2017).

SPD-Bundestagsfraktion (2011) 'Haushaltskonsolidierung geht auch sozial gerecht'. Available at: https://www.spdfraktion.de/presse/pressemitteilungen/haushaltskonsolidierung-geht-sozial-gerecht (Accessed: 8 March 2017).

SPD-Bundestagsfraktion (2013) 'Warum der Mindestlohn notwendig ist'. Available at: https://www.spdfraktion.de/themen/mindestlohn-notwendig (Accessed: 8 March 2017).

Stevens, S. S. (1946) *On the theory of scales of measurement*. Indianapolis, IN: Bobbs-Merrill.

Stewart, H. (2002) 'CBI is crying wolf over minimum wage, says TUC', *The Guardian*, 21 October, p. 22.

Stone, D. (2001) 'United Kingdom', in Weaver, R. K. and Stares, P. B. (eds) *Guidance for Governance. Comparing Alternative Sources for Public Policy Advice*. Washington, D.C: Brookings Institution Press, pp. 89–123.

Straßheim, H. (2013) 'Politische Expertise im Wandel. Zur diskursiven und institutionellen Einbettung epistemischer Autorität', in Kropp, S. and Kuhlmann, S. (eds) *Wissen und Expertise in Politik und Verwaltung*. Opladen: Verlag Barbara Budrich (Der moderne Staat – Zeitschrift für Public Policy, Recht und Management, Sonderheft), pp. 65–86.

Süddeutsche Zeitung (2007) '„Mindestlohn für alle“', *Süddeutsche Zeitung*, 17 December, p. 6.

Süddeutsche Zeitung (2011) 'Turbo für den Fiskus', *Süddeutsche Zeitung Online*, 29 April. Available at: https://www.sueddeutsche.de/geld/xx-dda-studie-mindestlohn-braechte-dem-staat-milliarden-ein-1.1090865 (Accessed: 22 June 2017).

Takács, G. (2007) 'Verdi: Mindestlohn schafft 450 000 Jobs', *Der Tagesspiegel Online*, 26 May. Available at: https://www.tagesspiegel.de/wirtschaft/verdi-mindestlohn-schafft-450-000-jobs/855376.html.

Thomas, C. W. (1997) 'Public Management as interagency cooperation: testing epistemic community theory at the domestic level', *Journal of Public Administration Research and Theory*, 7(2), pp. 221–246.

Thunert, M. W. (2001) 'Germany', in Weaver, R. K. and Stares, P. B. (eds) *Guidance for Governance. Comparing Alternative Sources of Public Policy Advice.* Washington, D.C: Brookings Institution Press, pp. 157–206.

Turk, J. V. (1986) 'Public Relations' Influence on the News', *Newspaper Research Journal*, 7(4), pp. 15–27.

Velleman, P. F. and Wilkinson, L. (1993) 'Nominal, ordinal, interval, and ratio typologies are misleading', *The American Statistician*, 47(1), pp. 65–72.

Waever, O. (1998) 'The Sociology of a Not So International Discipline: American and European Developments in International Relations', *International Organization*, 52(4), pp. 687–727.

Waltman, J. L. (2000) *The politics of the minimum wage.* Urbana: University of Illinois Press.

Weaver, R. K. and Stares, P. B. (2001) 'Guidance for Governance: An Overview', in Weaver, R. K. and Stares, P. B., *Guidance for Governance. Comparing Alternative Sources of Public Policy Advice.* Washington, D.C: Brookings Institution Press, pp. 1–30.

Weible, C. M., Pattison, A. and Sabatier, P. A. (2010) 'Harnessing expert-based information for learning and the sustainable management of complex socio-ecological systems', *Environmental Science & Policy*, 13(6), pp. 522–534.

Weible, C. M. and Sabatier, P. A. (2009) 'Coalitions, Science, and Belief Change: Comparing Adversarial and Collaborative Policy Subsystems', *Policy Studies Journal*, 37(2), pp. 195–212.

Weigold, M. F. (2001) 'Communicating science: A review of the literature', *Science communication*, 23(2), pp. 164–193.

Weir, M. (1989) 'Ideas and Politics: the Acceptance of Keynesianism in Britain and the United States', in Hall, P. A. (ed.) *The Political Power of Economic Ideas: Keynesianism across Nations.* Princeton, N.J.: Princeton University Press, pp. 54–86.

Weiss, C. H. (1977) 'Research for policy's sake: The enlightenment function of social research', *Policy analysis*, 3(4), pp. 531–545.

Weiss, C. H. (1979) 'The many meanings of research utilization', *Public Administration Review*, 39(5), pp. 426–431.

Weiss, C. H. (1986) 'Research and policy-making: a limited partnership', in Heller, F. (ed.) *The Use and Abuse of Social Science.* London: SAGE, pp. 214–235.

Weyant, J. P. (1988) 'Is there policy-oriented learning in the analysis of natural gas policy issues?', *Policy Sciences*, 21(2–3), pp. 239–261.

Wintour, P. and Watt, N. (2013) 'Lib Dems push for minimum wage increase: Cable: "You can"t keep telling people you have to take a wage cut to keep your job", *The Guardian*, 16 September, p. 1.

The manufacturer's authorised representative in the EU is Springer Nature Customer Service Centre GmbH, Europaplatz 3, 69115 Heidelberg, Germany. If you have any concerns regarding our products, please contact ProductSafety@springernature.com

Printed and bound by CPI Group (UK) Ltd, Croydon, CR0 4YY

30/09/2026

02225688-0002